The House Will Come to Order

Focus on American History Series
Dolph Briscoe Center for American History
University of Texas at Austin
Edited by Don Carleton

The House Will Come to Order

How the Texas Speaker Became a Power
in State and National Politics

PATRICK L. COX AND MICHAEL PHILLIPS
FOREWORD BY DON CARLETON

University of Texas Press ⬥ *Austin*

Copyright © 2010 by the Dolph Briscoe Center for American History
All rights reserved
Printed in the United States of America
First edition, 2010

Requests for permission to reproduce material from this work should be sent to:
Permissions
University of Texas Press
P.O. Box 7819
Austin, TX 78713-7819
www.utexas.edu/utpress/about/bpermission.html

♾ The paper used in this book meets the minimum requirements of ANSI/NISO
Z39.48-1992 (R1997) (Permanence of Paper).

Library of Congress Cataloging-in-Publication Data
Cox, Patrick L.
The House will come to order : how the Texas speaker became a power in state and
national politics / Patrick L. Cox and Michael Phillips. — 1st ed.
    p.   cm. — (Focus on American history series)
Includes bibliographical references and index.
ISBN 978-0-292-72205-7 (cloth : alk. paper)
1. Texas—Legislature—House of Representatives—Speakers—History.
2. Texas—Legislature—House of Representatives—Speakers—Biography.
3. Texas—Politics and government.   4. Power (Social sciences)—Texas—History.
5. Political parties—Texas—History.   6. Political culture—Texas—History.
7. Oral history—Texas.   I. Phillips, Michael, 1960–   II. Title.
    JK4866.C69   2010
    328.764'0762—dc22   2009042964

Contents

   Photo section follows page 92.

Foreword

The Speaker of the Texas House of Representatives is one of the most influential people in the state of Texas. Yet historians and other scholars have conducted little research on those who have served as Speaker or on the evolution of the office. The Dolph Briscoe Center for American History, through its Texas House Speakers Oral History Project, is making an effort to correct this documentary oversight.

The Texas Constitution adopted in 1876 states that the House of Representatives, each time a new legislature convenes, will select one of its own members to serve as its presiding officer. Because no other direction is provided in the constitution, the functions of the Speaker's office have evolved for nearly 130 years. The modern era of the office of the Speaker dates from the end of World War II. As the state became more urban and diverse, the Speaker's role also changed. The Speaker's authority and prestige began to rival that of the governor and lieutenant governor. In addition, the personality and goals of each Speaker affected the history of the legislative body and the entire state.

In November 2003, the Briscoe Center launched a project to interview eleven former Speakers and the then-current Speaker. Patrick Cox, the Briscoe Center associate director, served as project director. He and project historian Michael Phillips conducted the research, interviewed the participants, and edited the transcriptions. They interviewed then-Speaker Tom Craddick and nine former Texas House Speakers: Reuben Senterfitt, Jim T. Lindsey, James "Jimmy" Turman, Ben Barnes, Gus Mutscher, Rayford Price, Bill Clayton, Gibson D. "Gib" Lewis, and Pete Laney. In addition, the wives of several former Speakers, including Nadine Craddick, Pat Senterfitt, Nelda Laney, and Jan Tunnell, gave interviews. Dr. David Carr, son of the late former Speaker and state attorney general Waggoner Carr, is part of this series, as is Virginia Carter, Waggoner Carr's sister. Also, former state representative Bill Bass and newspaper editor and publisher Bill Hartman provided information on the late Speaker Marion Price Daniel, Jr. Thus, the interviews cover the Speaker's office from the years 1951 to 2005. The oral histories also include detailed information about life and politics in Texas throughout the entire twentieth century.

This book would not have been possible without the endorsement and support of former House Speaker Tom Craddick and his wife, Nadine Craddick, who were enthusiastic supporters from the start. Larry Faulkner, who at the time was president of the University of Texas at Austin, provided critical financial support for the oral-history project.

The Dolph Briscoe Center for American History has been proud to sponsor and manage this project. I congratulate Patrick Cox and Michael Phillips for a job well done, and I am grateful to all of the participants for their help and cooperation. They have ensured that an important part of the story of Texas has been told and preserved.

Don Carleton
Executive Director
Dolph Briscoe Center for American History
University of Texas at Austin

Acknowledgments

We must start by thanking all those who participated in the Dolph Briscoe Center for American History's oral-history project on Texas House Speakers. We appreciate their patience, candor, hospitality, and generosity with time. All living former Speakers, their family members, as well as Austin political reporters and Capitol staffers suggested areas of research, pointed us to important interview subjects, and, in many cases, treated us to wonderful meals. Interviews with them formed the core of this book, and our knowledge of the speakership's inner workings would have been impossible without their kind help.

We also enjoyed invaluable assistance from authors Terrell and Dorothy Blodgett and David Scott, who shared with us their research on Speaker Pat Neff; former governor Dolph Briscoe, a generous patron of the University of Texas, who spoke to us about the relationship of governors to Speakers; Charlie Fern, for helping our research on her stepfather, Speaker Jimmy Turman; Diane Daniel, the former wife of Speaker Price Daniel, Jr., and Tom Daniel, the Speaker's son, for their kindness and their aid in researching the career of one of the state's most fascinating political figures. Our sincere thanks to Don Carleton, the executive director of the Briscoe Center, for organizing the project and giving us the opportunity to carry it out. We also owe a deep debt of gratitude to the Research and Collections staff members at the center, who labored hard to process the interview tapes and helped create a massive online database on Texas House Speakers at http://www.cah.utexas.edu/projects/speakers.php. Briscoe Center staff members Holly Taylor, head of publications, and Erin Purdy, associate director for communications, contributed their expertise and editorial skills to the final manuscript. The staff at the Texas State Library and Archives also provided professional and courteous service.

Patrick Cox would like to thank his inspiring mother and stepfather, Doris and Beven Varnon; his loving wife, Brenda; and his accomplished and talented daughter Lauren. Michael Phillips would like to thank Betsy Friauf for her affection, friendship, and support. Her love of language and her instinct for the well-turned phrase let the authors appear more eloquent than they really are. More importantly, she brought healing, kindness, and grace to one author's life. Phillips also thanks his good friend of many years, ace reporter John Moritz; Debbie Radabaugh, for being the most important and inspiring teacher in his life; Renee Rowell, for her gentle kindness and her timely reappearance; Dave Ferman, for making him laugh for so long; Samantha Shub, for her suggestions on the manuscript; Lynne Swihart, for being a great wingman; his kind friends Jon Weist and Angela Wilden, for being there; and his loyal buddy and unofficial therapist Mary Shomon, for creating the *White Metropolis* Web site and so much more. He would also like to express his gratitude to David Cullen, Kyle Wilkison, Keith Volanto, Melissa LaPrelle, Roger Ward, Sam Tullock, and all his other warmly supportive colleagues at Collin College; his brother-in-law David Pugh and his nephew Jeremy Pugh, for being eloquent and unbelievably strong; and Marie Pugh, for being a loving and supportive sister.

Dominic Shehan Phillips, during the length of this project, you learned to walk, talk, read, play some songs on the keyboard, cruise the Internet, operate a TV remote, play "Hungry, Hungry Hippos," use a Wii, become a "self-manager," and how to give and how to love. All we did was write a book. You are a bright, gentle, generous soul and a source of infinite strength. Finally, Phillips would like to remember Rebecca Carder, Bill Byrd, Marie Louise Phillips, Bernie Shub, Richard "Eddie" Byrd, and Danny Ray Pugh. The world is much poorer for their absence, but eternity has gained the light from these angels.

Assuming Center Stage

Both literally and metaphorically, Texas House Speakers live at the center of the state's political universe. This fact became self-evident in February 2005. That month, Republican House Speaker Tom Craddick took up the entire cover of *Texas Monthly* magazine. The black-and-white image, dominated by Craddick's lined face, his dark suit jacket lightened only by a Texas-flag lapel pin, showed few shades of gray. The high-contrast tones underscored the Speaker's fiercely held (critics would say inflexible) political convictions and his dominance over state politics.

The photograph signaled authority and control, an impression confirmed by a single word superimposed across Craddick's narrow frame: Power. "This guy has tons of it," declared *Texas Monthly.* The magazine, a mouthpiece of the Texas establishment, named Speaker Craddick as the most powerful man in the state. The article, which pointedly did not include Governor Rick Perry or Lieutenant Governor David Dewhurst on its list of most powerful Texans, confirmed a story almost 170 years in the making: the Speaker of the House has become the most important political player in Texas and one of the most important elected officials in the United States.[1]

"Although the governor of Texas is elected statewide and is typically the most well-known public official in Texas, he or she can ill afford to ignore the Speaker of the Texas House," former governor Dolph Briscoe recalled. "A wise governor builds a close and friendly working relationship with the Speaker as soon as possible after the election."[2]

The speakership had become so powerful that Craddick almost single-handedly muscled through the legislature the controversial redrawing of congressional district boundaries in 2003. The second Texas redistricting in two years, Craddick's move inspired House Democrats to flee to

Oklahoma to break a quorum. Later, Senate Democrats absconded to New Mexico for similar reasons. Redistricting that year aimed at making the already conservative Texas congressional delegation even more Republican.

Craddick accomplished that goal, but experienced mounting frustration in crafting school-finance reform. His refusal to accept a variety of new business taxes was most often cited as the reason the legislature proved unable to approve a school-finance plan through one special session of the Seventy-eighth Legislature in 2004, the regular session of the Seventy-ninth Legislature in 2005, and two special sessions later that summer. In both redistricting and school finance, Craddick was seen as the most important player, either as an initiator or a killer of proposed laws. "In the past, whenever he has really needed them, he's been able to turn the screw and come up with 78 or 80 votes," retired longtime Republican senator Bill Ratliff said of the failure of the school finance bill. "The question is, was this a failure of leadership, or maybe he didn't care whether he had the votes or not." Craddick became a hero among GOP conservatives for redistricting. Because of his power, he became the goat to some for the school-finance fiasco.[3]

Attributing such control over the lawmaking process to a Texas House Speaker would have been unthinkable until the late twentieth century. As this book demonstrates, institutional changes in the Texas House and larger social changes in the state since World War II transformed the speakership from a rotating, largely honorary position charged mainly with presiding over House debates to an office in which individual Speakers have wielded tremendous power and even control over state policy. This power extends beyond Texas and can send shockwaves across the nation. Part of the reason for the redistricting battle in 2003 was that its outcome would allow Tom DeLay of Sugar Land, Texas, the Republican majority leader of the U.S. House of Representatives, to ensure continued Republican domination of the U.S. House, which lasted until a Democratic landslide in 2006.[4]

In contrast to Craddick's high-profile tenure, most Speakers have labored in relative obscurity. Governors and lieutenant governors must run highly visible and increasingly expensive statewide campaigns to win office. The Speaker, however, comes to power after being elected only by the voters of a single legislative district and then being selected by peers in the Texas House. Twelve sections of the Texas Constitution, excluding amendments, describe the qualifications, duties, and powers of the governor, and four sections outline the office of lieutenant governor. Yet the constitution, in Article 3, Section 9, dispenses with the office of House Speaker in only twenty-four words: "The House of Representatives shall, when it first assembles, organize temporarily, and thereupon proceed to the election of a speaker from its own members."[5]

Obscured in that simple, brisk phrase is the power of House Speakers to shape the legislative agenda. In the past 160 years, House Speakers have either stymied or clinched the passage of legislative priorities offered by governors and lieutenant governors. Speakers can move bills to the front of the House calendar or send proposals into legislative oblivion. Some House Speakers have set a tone of bipartisanship, while others have ensured an atmosphere of rancor and suspicion. Yet most Texans could not identify a single one of the seventy-four men who have held the office. With so little specific guidance from the Texas Constitution, each Speaker has shaped the office in his own image.

"For almost a century, Texas got along just fine with a speaker of the house who was no more than what the founding fathers envisioned—a presiding officer elected by his peers to keep order in the legislative process," wrote Sam Kinch, a member of the Capitol press corps for almost half a century. "The speaker was generally a strong, independent-minded person who presided over a collection of similar individuals for a single two-year term and then resumed regular legislative service as a member."[6]

During the history of the Texas Republic, from 1836 to 1845, nine men rapidly rotated through the Texas House speakership.[7] The position remained so inconsequential after statehood that five men held the post during the first legislative session in 1846. None of these Speakers held the office long enough to pose for an official portrait.[8]

Speakers in the nineteenth century obviously created little personal political power during tenures that lasted two years at the most. Some Speakers appeared to have arisen from nowhere to the House leadership, only to return to obscurity after their term of public service. The one-term tradition clearly weakened the power of the office. During the first fifty-two speakerships (1846 to 1933), only two Speakers, Marion DeKalb Taylor and John Cochran, served two full stints, and both presided over the House in nonconsecutive terms. A rotating speakership that presided over a House with a high turnover kept political power diffuse, allowing the planter and business classes to remain the unfettered de facto rulers of the state from 1846 to 1933.[9]

The Texas House speakership has evolved in style and role through seven loosely defined historical periods.[10] From 1846, the speakership changed from a limited, obscure office to one that slowly accumulated power. This happened partly because its powers were so loosely defined by a series of state constitutions and because the Texas Constitution adopted in 1876 and still in effect today so sharply delineated the authority of the governor and lieutenant governor. In politics, power abhors a vacuum, so while nineteenth-century House Speakers stood last among equals, far less influential than governors and lieutenant governors, by the early twentieth century, this power relationship had changed. By the 1970s and 1980s, Speakers like Billy Clayton and Gib Lewis had turned the office into a fiefdom that came to dominate state government.

During the "Presiding Speakership," lasting roughly from 1846 to 1900, state politics was dominated by slave owners and post–Civil War planter elites. This period saw the highest and most rapid turnover of Speakers and is characterized by a collective style of House leadership.

Reconstruction marked a brief interruption in planter hegemony, and the only two Republican Speakers in nineteenth-century Texas, Ira Hobart Evans and William Henry Sinclair, presided over a House that greatly expanded the state government's support of education and business development as well as African Americans' voting rights. This false summer of activist government proved brief, Evans and Sinclair presiding over the lower chamber only from 1870 to 1873. Texas, like its southern neighbors, resisted federal attempts to bring the state into the national political mainstream. For the next one hundred years, Texas and its people ranked at the bottom of nearly every national socioeconomic index, severely underfunding universities, hospitals, and other services.

With the inglorious conclusion of the Reconstruction era, conservative Democrats returned to power, gutted public education and support for the handicapped and the insane, and excluded former slaves from the political process. Dissident Populists forced the House to be more sympathetic to the plight of impoverished farmers of the late nineteenth century and to impose some regulations on rapacious businesses that came to dominate the increasingly industrial and urban Texas economy, but Democratic Speakers and their elite peers continued to doubt whether the state government should exercise any power outside of occasionally crushing labor unions and sanctioning attacks on Mexican Americans and Indians.

The tone of government greatly changed during the "Progressive Speakership," from 1900 to 1921. Throughout the state's history, economic development has been the tail wagging the legislative dog. During the early twentieth century, the declining role of agriculture, immigration from other states, the increase in manufacturing, and growing racial, regional, religious, and ethnic diversity forced the legislature to become more active. Speakers became more ideological, winning leadership posts not just because they were well liked, but because of their positions on prohibition, the resurrected Ku Klux Klan of the teens and twenties, the regulation of railroads, and other Progressive Era controversies.

Politically, many Speakers of the time found it necessary to strongly oppose alcohol and the teaching of evolution in public schools, as well as to complete the disenfranchisement of blacks and poor whites as rich Anglos increasingly feared losing control of the state's politics and culture.

Speakers still rotated in and out of office in the Progressive period, but a more activist agenda created opportunities and power for charismatic individuals. This trend was solidified during the "Early Modern Speakership," from 1921 to 1949. Future governor Coke Stevenson greatly enhanced the power and visibility of the Speaker's office. In 1935, Stevenson became the first Speaker to serve two consecutive terms. In Stevenson's speakership race, his opponent, future Speaker Robert W. Calvert, warned that allowing a member to serve multiple terms as Speaker threatened "tyranny." A precedent had been set, however, and after World War II, speakerships lasting several terms became the norm.

By the time of Stevenson's 1935 reelection campaign, governors and ex-governors deeply involved themselves in Speakers' races. Speakers, concerned about maintaining the continuity of policies, openly arranged for the election of their successors. In this era, an increasingly visible division between conservatives and liberals arose within the Democratic Party. Conservatives themselves were divided between pragmatic business conservatives, who sought governmental support for education and health care as a sound investment that would create job growth, and traditionalists like Stevenson, who viewed nearly all taxes as oppressive and saw little benefit in expanding the governmental agencies that regulated growth, protected workers and consumers, and educated the masses. The liberal-conservative split made managing the House more difficult. The ease of overseeing the old, unchallenged conservative hegemony gave way to the more complicated task of coalition building, even as the state dealt with the Great Depression, World War II, and the rapid industrialization of Texas during the war years.

The office became a power center during the "Dynastic Speakership" era, which lasted roughly from 1949 to 1969. Speakers implemented the desegregation of Texas public schools mandated by the U.S. Supreme Court's decision in *Brown v. Board of Education* (1954), and responded to the rise of modern technologies that transformed the state's economy.

They responded to these demands while they coped with a rapidly expanding population and the subsequent rising need for governmental services in education, transportation, and health care.

The size of the state government in Austin grew exponentially in the period just after World War II, and Speakers acquired more authority as a result. It became the norm for Speakers to serve at least two terms, and powerful Speakers like Reuben Senterfitt and Byron Tunnell established leadership bloodlines that could ensure the continuity of policy beyond their tenures. Beginning with Senterfitt, Speakers used the press to advance their legislative agendas and at times worked independently of the governor and lieutenant governor. They also began to expand their administrative staffs so that they could work when the legislature was not in session. When Ben Barnes took the Speaker's oath in 1965, only the equally charismatic governor, John Connally, matched his young protégé in political skill and influence. When the plodding Preston Smith followed Connally as governor, Barnes became the first Speaker to command front and center for the Capitol press.

Business lobbyists frequently determined who became Speaker and what legislation was passed, so lobby support became an essential tool in Speakers' political arsenals. This "pay to play" system came crashing down when banker Frank Sharp faced accusations that he bribed Speaker Gus Mutscher to shepherd favorable bills through the legislature. This era, the "Speakership in Crisis" (1969–1975), resulted in the criminal conviction of Mutscher for corruption and ruined the careers of some men only remotely or not at all connected to the so-called Sharpstown scandal. The next elections swept from office men like Barnes, once touted as a future president, Speaker Rayford Price, Governor Preston Smith, and much of the House and Senate rank and file. The scandal deeply wounded the long-dominant Democratic Party, widening the gulf between the party's liberal and conservative wings, and increased the participation of Republicans, African Americans, Mexican Americans, and women in the state House.

During this chaos, Price Daniel, Jr., vaulted to the speakership in 1973 on a reform agenda. Committed to democracy, Daniel believed that lobbyist money had corrupted the House leadership and sought to return the office to the style of the earlier "Presiding Speakership." He announced at the beginning of his administration that he would serve one term only and that during his two years as Speaker, he would focus on rewriting the state constitution, which he believed hindered the state's economic development and left the public at the mercy of special interests. Unfortunately, Daniel's openness and his explicit desire to not dictate constitutional reform proved a tactical error. Harder-edged legislators and lobbyists interpreted his open, more laissez-faire approach to the speakership as weakness rather than a desire for consensus. Daniel failed to win approval of a new state constitution, and the speakership returned to the status quo ante.

Special interests again dictated each session's legislative priorities. During the era of the "Executive Speakership," from 1975 to 2009, conservatives like Billy Clayton and Gib Lewis held the speakership for four or more terms, dominating the office. They reached power by developing relationships with lobbyists while balancing the demands of a membership that began to reflect the racial and ethnic composition of the state. The money provided by lobbyists allowed conservative Democrats to hold on to the legislative leadership even though conservatives had become a minority within the Democratic Party.

Such conservative Democrats had to rely on alliances with an increasingly powerful Republican Party, but at the price of eroding the power of Democrats as a whole. Explicit racial demagoguery, a mainstay of conservative rhetoric in Texas until the early 1960s, faded and gave way to repeated pleas for limited government, regulatory relief for big businesses, and a return to traditional family values. Embracing these positions, conservative Democrats increasingly migrated to the Republican Party, which became the majority party in the 1990s and the first decade of the twenty-first century.

By 2009, it seemed that the executive speakership had crashed in flames. Just as happened under Gus Mutscher in the Sharpstown era, House members accused Republican Tom Craddick of being a dictator, and the rank and file rebelled. As Speaker, Craddick had carried more clout than his predecessors by acting not only as the chief presiding officer of the House, but also as the de facto head of the Republican Party. Craddick created a powerful political machine that played a role in electing virtually every Republican then under the Capitol dome. No Speaker has ever been more influential in his party's success, more instrumental in the makeup of his caucus, more partisan, or more powerful in advancing his policies and stymieing those of his opponents. That power proved illusory. Craddick's fall came quickly, and by 2009 dissident Republicans, angered with what they saw as his imperial leadership style, aligned with the House Democratic caucus and overthrew the GOP leader. Like Price Daniel after Sharpstown, Craddick's replacement, Joe Straus, came in as a reformer promising to curb the power of the office. As of this writing, the speakership faces an uncertain future.[11]

Much of this book is derived from research conducted by the authors from 2003 to 2005 at the University of Texas at Austin. In November 2003, the Center for American History at the University of Texas (now the Dolph Briscoe Center for American History), in cooperation with Speaker Craddick and his wife, Nadine Craddick, launched "A Speaker from Its Own Members: A Project Documenting the History of the Speakers of the Texas House of Representatives." The authors of this book interviewed ten former Speakers, the wives of several former Speakers, living and dead, and other relatives of the men profiled here.

Additional interviews were conducted with veteran members of the Capitol press corps, including Sam Kinch, Bo Byers, Dave McNeely, and John Moritz, as well as Capitol curator Alice Turley and Doug Young of the State Preservation Board, who assisted with a decade-long restoration project begun after a devastating fire engulfed part of the Capitol's east wing in 1983.

We conducted these interviews to document the subjects' memories and observations as completely as possible. To do this, we allowed the subjects to review the interview transcripts and make additions, corrections, and deletions as they saw fit. We were more interested in capturing how they saw the role of the Speaker in Texas and national politics than in trying to catch them in errors and lapses of memory. The transcripts of these interviews, also edited for false starts and other quirks of speech, therefore are not verbatim accounts. In addition, we used archival research and interviews with other subjects in order to check the details in each interview and ensure historical accuracy.

The tale that emerges from these interviews is the history of one state's politics as its citizens struggled with change and modernization in the post–World War II era. The story includes an account of the divisions within the solid veneer of Texas's traditionally ruling Democrats, an outline of the ascendance of the Republicans, a chronicle of Texas business and agriculture, an analysis of the Texas media and its role in shaping policy and perceptions of officeholders, and an examination of how race, class, and gender shaped events in the Lone Star State. To an extent rarely acknowledged, state Speakers have touched almost every aspect of Texas life. No other elective office underwent such a dramatic change during this era. This book represents a first attempt to explain why the Texas speakership is so important, not only to Texans but to all Americans.

CHAPTER I

Least Among Equals:
The Presiding Speakership

1846–1900

In the beginning, Texas House Speakers occupied a relatively obscure and simple niche in Texas government. Speakers presided over House debates, ruled on points of order, and ensured that total chaos did not reign in the chamber. Most served with little fanfare and then returned to private life.

Of course, not all Texas House Speakers suffered later oblivion, especially in the twentieth century. Several remained prominent, and numerous Speakers returned to their House seats after stepping down from the dais. Such Speakers included Thomas B. Love, a leader of prohibition forces in Texas and a key supporter of President Woodrow Wilson, and Coke Stevenson, who later served as lieutenant governor and governor. It can be taken as a sign of the increasing importance of the speakership during the latter half of the twentieth century that after William Otey Reed stepped down as Speaker in 1949 to become a mere member of the House, a similar transition did not occur until 2003, when Pete Laney resumed his place as a backbencher after being unseated by Republican Tom Craddick. After World War II, the speakership gained such institutional power and media attention that retiring Speakers were expected to seek higher office.[1]

Five Speakers (James Henderson, Hardin Runnells, Pat M. Neff, Coke R. Stevenson, and Price Daniel, Sr.) later became governor; six rose to the post of lieutenant governor (Henderson, David C. Dickson, Runnels, George C. Pendleton, Stevenson, and Ben Barnes); four became state attorney general (Thomas Smith, Robert L. Bobbitt, Daniel, and Waggoner Carr); three later served as railroad commissioner (L. L. Foster, Neff, and Byron Tunnell); two subsequently sat on the state supreme court (Robert W. Calvert and Daniel); and one served as Texas secretary of state (L. Travis Dashiell). Additionally, three former Speakers later won election to the U.S. House of Representatives: George Pendleton, Robert E. Thomason, and, most prominently of all, Sam Rayburn, who served as Speaker of the U.S. House for eighteen years between 1940 and his death in 1961.[2]

These prominent earlier Speakers differed from their successors in the late twentieth and early twenty-first centuries, however, in that before the late 1970s, the speakership was merely a valuable line on a résumé and a venue for political networking. Only with the speakership of Billy Clayton, from 1975 to 1983, did the office become a political end in itself. Speakers gained greater appointment power, exercised more authority in between legislative sessions, and drew greater attention from lobbyists and national political parties. Despite virtually no enabling power from the state constitution, the Speaker and the office maintained a political presence equal to that of the lieutenant governor and governor.

Texas Speakers have arisen from a narrow social base. From a sample of fifty-two of the men who have held the office, one historian of the Texas speakership, William Kent Brunette, drew a composite portrait of the politicians who served in that post from 1879 to 1979. All were white male Protestants, primarily from the Baptist and Methodist denominations. (In 2009, Joe Straus of San Antonio, who is Jewish, became the first non-Christian Speaker.) Most grew up in rural counties, primarily in Central Texas, although in the post–World War II era, East Texas and West Texas have been heavily represented. Speakers have tended to be better educated than the population at large; the majority of them earned law degrees.[3]

In the mid-nineteenth century, such men, marked by above-average wealth and associations with the elite planter class, embraced a highly conservative politics.[4] A party system did not develop in the Texas Republic (1836–1845). Instead, factions formed to support or oppose strong personalities such as Sam Houston or Mirabeau Lamar. After statehood, Anglo Texans largely sympathized with the Democratic Party, although no formal Democratic Party structures were set up in Texas until the 1848 presidential election. Opposition parties, such as the Whigs, the American (or Know-Nothing) Party, and the Constitutional Union Party, proved ephemeral.[5]

The lack of an effective opposition ensured uninterrupted slave-owner dominance of a loosely organized party apparatus and a weak state government in the two decades after initial statehood, in 1846. In antebellum Texas, slaveholders constituted the most grossly overrepresented constituency at the state level. The year before the Civil War began, slave owners represented 27 percent of the state population, but they held 68 percent of the state's political posts.[6] As political scientist V. O. Key noted in his landmark study *Southern Politics in State and Nation,* a one-party system is akin to a no-party system in that there is no organizational means by which political opponents can effectively mobilize. The ease with which the slave-owning minority muscled Texas into the Confederacy, therefore, does not accurately reflect the level of political conflict in the state during the antebellum and immediate postbellum periods.[7]

During the early statehood era (1845–1860), the framers of the Texas Constitution intentionally created a weak central government in order to hamper dissent and ensure the rule of economic elites. Speakers merely presided over House debates; they had no leadership function within parties and no personal legislative agendas. Such presiding officers proved a perfect fit for a conservative, pro-planter agenda.

Following the Civil War, elites recodified white supremacy in state law. In a bid to rejoin the Union, Texas adopted its third state constitution in 1866 (the second had been written in 1861, when Texas seceded and joined the Confederacy). Ex-Confederates joined with conservative pro-Unionists to write a constitution that tacitly recognized the Thirteenth Amendment, which banned slavery.[8] The new state charter, however, denied freedmen the right to vote, hold public office, testify in court, serve on juries, or attend public schools. Voters approved the constitution, and the 1866 legislature subsequently rejected the Fourteenth Amendment, which granted citizenship rights to African American men.[9]

Evans, Sinclair, and Bryan

These measures pushed the Republican majority in the United States Congress over the edge. There, so-called Radical Republicans realized that their party was likely to lose control of Congress if blacks could not act as a political opposition to the planters in the former Confederacy. Congress refused to seat the Texas delegation elected under the 1866 Constitution and passed its First Reconstruction Act in March 1867. The law placed Texas under army command and declared that officials elected in the aftermath of the Civil War were subject to removal.[10]

Responding to these events, three groups joined to form the state's Republican Party in the spring of 1867. Pre–Civil War Unionists (often smeared by their opponents as "scalawags"), who had established deep ties in Texas before secession, provided the bedrock of the party, along with recently enfranchised African American men, for whom the Democrats represented the party of slavery. A smaller group of more recent immigrants from the North (labeled "carpetbaggers"), consisting primarily of Union Army veterans, formed the third Republican support base. Attempting to appeal to poor white voters, Republicans held their first state convention in Houston on July 4, 1867, adopting a platform that called for free public schools for all children in Texas, regardless of race, and a homestead policy that would provide publicly held land to any settler, black or white.[11]

Republican efforts to gain a foothold in postbellum Texas inspired terrorism by still-rebellious Democrats.[12] Between 1865 and 1868, whites murdered about 1 percent of black males between the ages of fifteen and forty-nine, a murder rate greatly exceeding that in modern Dallas or Houston.[13] The Republican-controlled Congress, outraged by the violence against freedmen and Unionists, then required the state to hold another constitutional convention before it could rejoin the Union; the delegates had to be elected by all male citizens age twenty-one and older, regardless of race, color, or previous condition of servitude. An election boycott by ex-Confederates combined with black suffrage to create a disproportionately Unionist voting public, which approved another state constitution in 1869. The 1869 constitution explicitly outlawed slavery for the first time and provided for black citizenship and the legal equality of all persons, regardless of color.[14]

This constitution greatly increased the power of the governor and the legislature. Tasked with reconstructing the state government, the economy, and deeply embedded attitudes about race, Republicans sought to give the new regime breathing room by lengthening the terms of office of elected officials. The governor's term expanded from two to four years, and state senators' from four to six. The constitution called for annual legislative sessions. The governor now appointed the state attorney general and the secretary of state, both previously elective posts, as well as all judicial offices.[15]

Republicans controlled the state government only from 1870 to 1874, and the party's two House Speakers, Ira Hobart Evans and William Henry Sinclair, had little time to make noticeable changes in the office itself. Republicans did prove, however, what an energetic state government unshackled from the limitations imposed by a reactionary ruling clique could do. Although funding mechanisms for public education had existed since the presidency of Mirabeau B. Lamar (1838–1841), in the days of the Texas Republic, education in the state had remained in the hands of private schools through the 1860s. Until the 1870s, prospective students had to pay tuition at small local academies, a burden that made even elementary education unaffordable for many Texas families.[16]

Reconstruction-era Republicans created the first free public school system—one open to both black and white children—and passed a compulsory-education law that required attendance for children age six to eighteen. The Republican administration also passed legislation creating Texas Agricultural and Mechanical College (later Texas A&M University), the first public higher-education institution to open in the state. During Reconstruction, outside investment flowed into Texas, and railroads underwent extensive construction.[17]

Unlike the planter-friendly Democrats, who before the Civil War had placed a long succession of interchangeable, predictably conservative proslavery men in the speakership, Republicans proved too divided over policy to effectively use the office, and the party's short tenure was marked by instability and conflict. The Republicans were split between the so-called Radicals, who controlled fifty of the ninety seats in the legislature, and the Moderates. The Radicals earned their name through their insistence on full African American citizenship rights and their eagerness to ally with blacks to form a strong, biracial Republican Party in Texas. Radicals also insisted on greater caution in governmental spending to stimulate the economy. Moderates supported greater governmental involvement in the economy, hoped to accommodate the pre–Civil War Texas leadership, and resisted attempts to make blacks equal partners in the new Texas Republican organization.[18]

An ugly spat over the timing of state elections led to the overthrow of the first Republican House Speaker, moderate Ira Hobart Evans. The Republican caucus replaced him with the Radicals' favorite, William Henry Sinclair.[19] Democrats swept the elections held November 5–8, 1872, and regained control of the state House and Senate. A Republican, Edmund Davis, still held power as governor, and his party still controlled the judiciary. Democrats in the state House immediately rolled back Republican reforms, placing severe limits on the ability of local school boards to raise taxes. Aiming at a complete takeover, Democrats passed a bill calling for a one-day general election on December 2, 1873. The Democratic gubernatorial candidate, Richard Coke, overwhelmed Davis, carrying 66.7 percent of the vote in an election in which black turnout was heavily suppressed through white intimidation and violence.[20]

Speaker Guy Morrison Bryan represented one of the so-called "Redeemer" Democrats now in command of the state government. A native of Herculaneum, Missouri, Bryan came from a family that settled on a plantation south of Brazoria in 1831. As a teenager, Bryan briefly served in the Texas Revolutionary Army in 1836 before enrolling in Kenyon College, in Ohio, where he struck up a friendship with future president Rutherford B. Hayes. He served another brief stint in the military during the Mexican War in 1846 before he left his post to accompany an ailing brother back home. Bryan first served in the Texas House from 1847 to 1854, in the state Senate from 1854 to 1857, and in Congress from 1857 to 1859. At the insistence of his wife, Bryan returned with his family to Texas, where he became a rancher near Galveston.[21]

At the outbreak of the Civil War, Bryan joined the Confederate Army as an assistant to several generals and as a military liaison to Confederate president Jefferson Davis. Bryan won election to the Fourteenth Legislature and served as Speaker from 1874 to 1876.[22] Like other nineteenth-century Texas House Speakers, Bryan spoke for the planter class and served as its temporary mouthpiece. "You refer to my entrance into public life, and election to the speakership," Bryan wrote his friend on February 1, 1874. "The first [my political career] was forced upon me, and the latter [my speakership] came without the slightest electioneering on my part with unanimity on the part of the members."[23]

The planters Bryan represented saw no place for African Americans in Texas politics. "There is *no desire on the part of the South to put back the negro into slavery or its equivalent* [emphasis in the original]," wrote Bryan to Hayes, who would become president in 1877 after a particularly controversial and convoluted election. "What is desirable for both sections is, that both *intelligence* and *property* have their proper weight *in government* . . . All concur that the negroes are *citizens,* that they are entitled to *protection,* and that they *must have it.* But we want *good government,* for their sakes as well as our own. *They* do not know how to *govern* . . . it would be far better for the negroe [*sic*], that the intelligent tax paying citizen should govern."[24]

Bryan himself indirectly acknowledged the tiny part the Texas House Speaker played in the larger machinery of Texas politics. An autobiographical sketch he authored supplies a long summary of his Civil War experiences. His speakership, on the other hand, is summarized in twenty-four brisk words: "I discharged my duties as Speaker during that long session and an extra session. The following year I declined re-election to the succeeding Legislature."[25]

The Constitution of 1876

In 1875, the legislature called for a new constitutional convention, the fourth in fourteen years. Democrats made up more than 80 percent of the delegates, who drew up an extremely conservative document; it was approved by voters in 1876. The new charter dramatically reduced the power of the governor and decentralized authority in the executive branch. To this day, Texas governors lack the power to appoint a cabinet, and since offices like lieutenant governor, attorney general, and treasurer are elective posts, they can be held by the governor's political opponents. Further, the Constitution of 1876 reduced gubernatorial terms once again to two years (an amendment in the early 1970s provided for four-year terms for executive-branch offices).

Since 1876, Texas governors have lacked the power to remove most officials in state agencies. The governor can, however, veto either individual line items in appropriations bills or an entire state budget. Legislative override of a veto requires the support of two-thirds of the legislature. This is the most substantial authority given the governor under the 1876 document.

The framers of the Constitution of 1876 intentionally divided power between the governor and the lieutenant governor. In fact, since the adoption of the current constitution, the lieutenant governor (who occupies a crucial position in both the executive and legislative branches) has generally been the key player in Texas politics. The lieutenant governor presides over the state Senate. Because that body writes its own procedural rules, powerful lieutenant governors have used their influence over the formulation of Senate rules to expand the reach of their office. The lieutenant governor determines which committees bills are assigned to as well as when and whether they come up for debate before the full Senate. Because the lieutenant governor also appoints the committees, his power to assign bills essentially means he can determine the fate of proposed legislation.

The built-in weakness of the governor's office and the division of executive authority between the governor and lieutenant governor provided Speakers of the House with an opening. The Constitution of 1876 outlined few specifics regarding the Speaker's duties or powers, or limitations on that office's authority. To strong personalities, this represented not a handicap but an open door.

In addition to the historical responsibility of maintaining order on the House floor during debates and ruling on parliamentary questions, Speakers' main powers since 1876 have been granted by the House membership and embodied in the House Rules of Procedure. Adopted by a full House vote at the start of every regular session of the legislature, the House rules allow the Speaker to appoint the chairs, vice-chairs, and members of all standing committees. Like the lieutenant governor, the Speaker has the power to assign proposed bills to committees. This, combined with his power of committee appointments, gives him a great deal of influence over whether a bill comes to a vote by the full House.[26]

The Constitutional Convention of 1875 also provided that the legislature would meet only once every two years, instead of annually as in the 1869 constitution, and could incur no more than $200,000 in indebtedness.[27] As a result of the spending cap, legislators slashed funding for schools and abolished the office of state superintendent of education. By design, the 1876 document hampers the state government's ability to raise revenues and launch public projects: debt limits are strictly set, and new taxes can be imposed only by voter-approved constitutional amendments. As author John E. Bebout noted in 1971, the 1876 constitution "was deliberately written to prevent active government, by men who felt they had suffered from too much government and felt the need for relatively little government action, even in the field of education."[28]

Perhaps the most onerous provision of the state constitution is the requirement that it specifically detail the powers, duties, and limitations of the state government. This has rendered the still-operative 1876 charter, amended more than 400 times, one of the longest constitutions in the world. As of 2003, the Texas Constitution contained almost 86,000 words (as opposed to fewer than 8,000 words for the U.S. Constitution). The flaws of the Texas Constitution reach comic proportions. "The wordy document contains misnumbered sections, misspelled words, and articles left blank," one recent Texas government textbook notes. "One sentence contains 756 words. Some sections devoted to the same subject are scattered throughout the body of the Constitution rather than grouped in a single article."[29]

The new constitution required that voters approve any enactment of an income tax, a requirement that bedeviled attempts throughout the twentieth century to provide adequate funding for public schools, universities, health care, and prisons. By 2005, Texas was one of the states most dependent on sales taxes. Such taxes disproportionately affect lower-income people; by the mid-1990s, the poorest 20 percent of the Texas population spent 13.8 percent of their income on various taxes, while the richest 1 percent spent only 4.4 percent of their income in this way. (Only

Michigan and Florida more heavily taxed the poorest 20 percent of their populations, at 17.1 percent and 14 percent respectively.)[30]

"Burdened by restrictions from another century, the Legislature has been unable fully to rise to the challenge of the present age," concluded the Citizens Conference on State Legislatures, which was commissioned in 1973 to study the impact of the state constitution on the effectiveness of Texas government. "The present Legislature is a weakened body constrained by limited biennial sessions, by its inability to review vetoed bills after adjournment, or to call itself into special session," the report concluded. "These limitations . . . restrict the Legislature's power to act effectively."[31]

The Populist Interlude

The tone of government shifted temporarily with the Populist agrarian revolt of the late nineteenth century. Texas farmers relied heavily on cotton cultivation for their income. However, overproduction, aggravated by the spreading system of sharecropping and foreign competition, ravaged the state's farmers. The price of cotton plummeted from 15 to 5 cents a pound even as the federal government removed so-called "greenback" paper currency and silver-backed certificates from circulation, causing painful deflation. Farmers also faced harsh overcharges from lenders, grain-elevator operators, and railroads during lengthy depressions in the 1870s and 1890s. These hardships radicalized farmers and led to the formation of the People's, or Populist, Party in the early 1890s. The Populists adopted a bold political program in 1886 in Cleburne, Texas. The "Cleburne Demands" called for a vast expansion of the nation's money supply and, in order to cut out greedy middlemen, for Austin and Washington to provide direct credit to farmers.[32]

By the time they competed on the state ballot in 1892, Populists more seriously challenged the Democrats' hold on white voters than had the Republican Party during Reconstruction. Democrats responded to the threat by adopting some of the milder Populist demands as their own. A brief era of political reform ensued during the term of Governor James Stephen "Jim" Hogg, from 1891 to 1895. As state attorney general, Hogg had prosecuted "wildcat" insurance companies and worked with Speaker Frank P. Alexander in 1889 to pass antitrust legislation that targeted restraint of trade and price-fixing. Alexander, who served as Speaker from

1889 to 1891, provides one of the most mysterious stories in Texas political history. In spite of his three terms in the legislature, historians know virtually nothing about Alexander's life before he entered politics or his postspeakership career or the place and time of his death. As a House member, he advocated antitrust laws and proposed the creation of a railroad commission that would set freight charges. His railroad-regulation proposal suffered defeat, but a similar law passed in 1891 after Alexander left the speakership. Such Populist-leaning sentiments were not the norm for the conservative Texas House.[33]

Alexander and his successor as Speaker, Robert Teague Milner, represented the two most policy-driven presiding officers in the nineteenth century. Milner, who authored a bill mandating the teaching of Texas history in public schools, served as Speaker from 1891 to 1893. He had previously promoted agrarian causes as the editor of the *Henderson Times* in East Texas. Milner strongly supported James Hogg and served as Speaker during the governor's first term.[34]

Creation of the Texas Railroad Commission was the highlight of the Hogg-Milner partnership.[35] The commission consisted of three elected members empowered to set railroad rates based on fair valuation and to regulate the business practices that railroads used to manipulate stock values.[36] Although Hogg never embraced programs at the heart of the Populist movement, such as public ownership of the railroads or government-supplied credit for farmers, his support for the railroad commission, his advocacy of silver coinage to increase the money supply, and his tangles with the insurance industry made him popular enough to dent support for the Populists, who began to crumble during the 1896 presidential election. The biggest obstacle that Populists faced, however, came from white members' collaboration with parallel black Populist organizations, which led Texas Democrats to charge the Peoples' Party with undermining white supremacy.[37]

Democrats again used the terrorism that had proved effective in crushing the state's Republican Party in the 1860s and 1870s. On Election Day in 1896, forty Democrats in Robertson County held rifles while surrounding the courthouse to block entrance by black voters. The county judge later wrote, "I went down to the polls and took my six-shooter. I stayed there until the polls closed. Not a Negro voted."[38]

Brutal suppression and subsequent election "reforms" that severely restricted blacks' and poor whites' suffrage eliminated the only viable competition Democrats faced in Texas until the resurrection of the Republican Party in the 1960s. The voting reforms advocated by future Speakers such as Pat Neff, however, had unintended consequences. By eliminating potential rivals from the electoral process, Democrats felt free to split on issues such as prohibition.

As southern historian John Boles points out, "This opened up white politics to influence by organized pressure groups, and by disenfranchising blacks and most dispossessed whites, politics was rendered safe enough to allow spirited debate . . . [and] the emergence of a bifactional politics that pitted . . . reform forces against the forces of the status quo."[39] In Texas, this meant the political initiative would be taken by a series of progressive, reform-oriented Speakers such as Pat Neff, Thomas B. Love, and Sam Rayburn.

CHAPTER 2

Accumulating Clout:
The Progressive Speakership

1900–1921

At the beginning of the twentieth century, the Democratic Party came under the strong influence of Progressives, who believed that well-educated experts could use governmental agencies to combat social ills such as poverty and alcoholism. Despite the short-lived Progressive Party, which rose and fell between 1912 and 1924, Progressivism represented less an organized political movement than a viewpoint embraced by many middle-class idealists who believed that advances in the physical sciences could be duplicated in the social sciences. Progressivism became such a broad movement that its adherents at times included Democrats and Republicans, conservative southerners and northern liberals, and socialists.[1]

In the South, Progressives focused on the social good that could result from the elimination of drinking, via a prohibition amendment to the U.S. Constitution. They also viewed blacks and poor whites as ignorant and easily manipulated by corrupt politicians, and hoped that disenfranchising them would clean up the political process.[2] The Progressive agenda heavily influenced Texas speakerships in this era. Unlike their nineteenth-century predecessors, Speakers in this period believed that government could play a positive role in making the state economy function efficiently. They generally saw public education and public universities as sound investments in the state's economic future. Progressives also believed in policing private behavior, such as banning the sale and consumption of alcohol. To Progressives, prohibition represented not just a legitimate exercise of governmental power but an essential one. Alcohol, they believed, caused waste, domestic violence, criminality, unemployment, and a host of other problems plaguing a gradually more urban and industrial state economy. In fact, they emphasized prohibition as the road to a just and prosperous society almost to the exclusion of all others.

Texas Progressives saw African Americans as congenitally ignorant and, because of their wage dependence on whites, especially prone to political manipulation by their employers. Two Progressive Speakers, Thomas B. Love and Pat Neff, particularly worried about the ill effects of uninformed voters. The legislature tackled ballot "reform" in 1903 and 1905. Effectively, the new laws solidified Democratic, one-party rule in the state and eliminated organized opposition from Republicans, Populists, and Socialists. Among other changes, the so-called Terrell laws instituted a poll tax that severely hampered the ability of the poorest Texans, white and black, to vote.[3]

More ominously for African Americans, the 1903 election law allowed major political parties to determine who could vote in their primaries, regardless of the voting rights guaranteed by the 14th and 15th Amendments to the U.S. Constitution. The state Democratic Party established a whites-only primary system. Since the collapse of the state Republican Party in the 1870s and the Populists in the 1890s, the Democrats held a virtual monopoly on elective office. Thus, the winner of the Democratic primary almost always won the general election. The new rules meant that African Americans in Texas would have no real voice in determining who would win statewide office.[4]

Speaker Neff

Pat Neff fought persistently for ballot "reform." Born on November 26, 1871, on a farm straddling McLennan and Coryell counties in Central Texas, Neff graduated from Baylor University and earned his law degree at the University of Texas.[5] When Neff was a young man, his earnestness made him seem much older. "It cannot be said that he was like other boys," Baylor roommate Samuel P. Brooks said later. "Strange to say, though a Texan born and a rustic, to this day he has never shot a gun, baited a fish hook, used tobacco in any form, nor drank anything stronger than Brazos water. He does not know one card from another and cannot play any kind of social game."[6]

Running for the state House of Representatives for the first time in 1898, Neff supported passing an "educational qualification" or "property qualification" standard for voters. Neff spoke favorably of the poll tax, which "has proven to be a good law and seems to me should be enacted into the laws of Texas."[7] On the fourth day of his first term in the Texas House, he introduced a bill amending the state constitution to require a poll tax. Referred to the Committee on Constitutional Amendments, the bill languished there. In the same session, he cosponsored another poll tax proposal that failed to pass.[8] Neff experienced success in his second session, in 1901, when he supported poll-tax legislation that passed both the House and Senate, winning voter approval as a constitutional amendment by a 2–1 margin in 1902.[9]

The new ballot restrictions disenfranchised not just blacks but also lower-income whites. Such measures proved highly popular with middle-class and upper-income Anglos. "A majority of whites—conservative Democrats, reform-minded Hogg Democrats, and Populists alike . . . remained angry over the way both sides had appealed to and used the black vote during the recent political battles," historian Randolph Campbell wrote. "They agreed that disenfranchisement of blacks would mean fairer fights between whites. Moreover, Hogg Democrats saw disenfranchisement as a means of convincing white Populists to return to their old party and help in the fight against conservatives."[10]

In addition, both Neff and Thomas B. Love, who served as Speaker from 1907 to 1909, supported the poll tax and disenfranchisement as means to help enact prohibition. Both viewed blacks as morally lax and self-indulgent, partly blaming black voters for Texans' failure to pass a prohibition amendment. "The Negro ought not to be permitted to vote on the question of whether or not liquor shall be sold in Texas any more than the Indian should be permitted to vote on the question of whether or not liquor shall be sold in Indian country," Love said, casually implying that blacks and Indians shared a propensity for drunkenness.[11] With the elimination of the black vote, Love argued, prohibition enjoyed a better chance of becoming law.

Neff made much the same argument, but claimed that Germans, not African Americans and Mexican Americans, were the main targets of ballot restrictions. "That [the poll tax constitutional amendment] had nothing to do with the Negroes," Neff told an interviewer in the late 1940s. "The Negroes were never members of the Democratic Party. We drys put that in there to keep the wets from stealing elections from us." Neff was then asked about the provision of the election code that prohibited election officials from helping voters in any language but English. Neff denied that was aimed at Spanish-speaking Mexicans. "That was to stop the Germans down at Fredericksburg . . . A lot of them couldn't speak English . . .

so they couldn't vote . . . They were all wet voters, those Germans down at Fredericksburg."[12]

Such strongly stated positions made Neff stand out among his peers. Neff apparently spent little time socializing with his fellow House members at the Capitol. Instead, he focused on his ambitions. Neff had already formed a close relationship with Speaker Robert E. Prince, a second-term member from Corsicana. Prince tapped Neff to be "in the chair," presiding while Prince took breaks, on the second and third day of the session. This became a regular practice. Neff shared the title of speaker pro tem with two other representatives, acting as Speaker twenty-six times during the 1901 session.[13]

The Prince-Neff partnership formed a pattern that characterized the "dynastic speakership" era after World War II. Reigning Speakers essentially designated their successors by giving them highly visible leadership positions and allowing them to preside frequently over the chamber. By the end of Neff's second term, many of his peers and the Capitol press were promoting his rise to House leadership. According to one Waco newspaper, Neff was "a presiding officer of dignity and his impartiality has made him friends."[14] Not everybody was a fan, however, and some found him sanctimonious. "Even Christ made wine and went fishing," one political opponent snidely suggested, "and but for this Christ might have tied with Neff in Morals and habits but as the book stands today Mr. Neff has Christ bested two points."[15]

With no opponents in either the 1902 Democratic primary or the general election, Neff focused all of his energy on the speakership race, mounting his campaign fifteen months before the 1903 session began.[16] After sixty-two ballots, the thirty-one-year-old Neff beat L. S. Schluter of Jefferson 73–57.[17] As expected, Neff appointed Alexander Watkins Terrell chair of the Committee on Privileges, Suffrage and Elections. Terrell authored a law that established uniform election procedures and times for Democratic primary races across the state. Officially, it provided for a secret ballot, though further legislation would have to be passed in the 1950s to ensure voter privacy. The law also set the time for paying required poll taxes between October and February.[18]

The ballot reforms of 1902–1903 shaped Texas politics for the next sixty years. To vote in a meaningful election, one had to attest to being a white Democrat and, until the 1920 election, when women could exercise suffrage for the first time, one had to be male as well. The poll tax made voting rights a fiction for many poor Anglos. African Americans, the largest constituency opposed to segregation, were silenced. Viable Republican or

Populist challenges to ruling Democrats became impossible. Surprisingly, though, the shrinking of the electorate left the House a more contentious place than previously.[19]

Speaker Love

One of the brightest members of the reform coalition, Thomas B. Love, won the speakership in 1906. Love dispensed his duties while wearing a grim "bulldog expression," historian Norman Brown writes. The new Speaker struck his peers as "aggressive and tenacious and a ruthless, unforgiving political infighter. When he had a campaign under way, all of the details were at his fingertips; seldom did any escape him."[20] Love preferred to operate behind the scenes. As one opponent noted, Love could walk upon "a string of pianos and never strike a note."[21] More than Neff, he used his speakership to advance the Progressive agenda.

The Thirtieth Legislature, in session from January to May 1907, represented a Progressive apotheosis. The legislature passed bills setting a maximum fourteen-hour workday for railroad workers and an eight-hour workday for telephone operators and railroad telegraphers. It established new rules for the insurance and banking industries, instituted food safety regulations, created an office to aid farmers, banned railroads from issuing free passes to reporters or public officials in order to curry favor, and strengthened antitrust laws.[22]

Speaker Kennedy

Progressivism had reached its peak, but remained dominant through the new century's first decade. Austin Milton Kennedy, elected Speaker in 1908, proved one of the most prolific bill writers in the House. The founder and editor of the *Mexia Democrat* first won election to the Texas House in 1898, representing Mexia until 1901. Moving to the town of Mart, near Waco, he again won election to the House, serving from 1905 to 1909. He subsequently represented Waco and Kerrville in the lower chamber. Kennedy authored laws taxing gross business receipts, creating a corporate franchise tax, and authorizing home rule in cities with a population of more than 5,000.[23]

Kennedy's reform agenda stalled, however, when he rose to the top House leadership. After serving as Speaker during the regular session in early 1909, Kennedy faced a challenge to his leadership during a special session that began on March 13 of that year. A controversy arose after his election as the House's presiding officer over whether state money had been spent to buy personal items for the Speaker's apartment. Kennedy's wife had stirred the opposition by using the state's money to purchase $1,070 worth of items for the Speaker's apartment, including rugs, drapes, and a $70 brass bedstead. Kennedy was also charged with putting a stenographer on the House payroll for $120 a month ($2,400 a month in 2005 currency), even though she was still living in Kansas City and would not arrive in Austin until the sixth week of the legislative session. Although the Speaker was exonerated of wrongdoing concerning the purchase of furniture, he was pressed to resign because legislators disputed whether the stenographer had performed any work for the state and questioned the size of her compensation.[24] Kennedy surrendered the speakership on March 15, 1909, although he remained a House member until he died in office on July 19, 1914. One of Kennedy's fiercest supporters was an East Texas state representative who became one of the most powerful Texans in the twentieth century: Sam Rayburn.[25]

Speaker Rayburn

Sam Rayburn began life near the Clinch River in Tennessee on January 6, 1882. The Rayburn family moved to Texas five years later. The future Speaker's father eventually selected the Fannin County seat of Bonham as the family's permanent home. After a brief stint as a teacher, Sam Rayburn won election to the Texas House in 1906.[26] He thrived under the Terrell laws governing elections. Those laws banned the selection of Democratic candidates at state conventions, which had been "long dominated by powerful, often corrupt party bosses," as Rayburn biographers D. B. Hardeman and Donald C. Bacon put it. Instead, candidates had to run in direct primaries. "Rayburn saw this as a lucky break for him," Hardeman and Bacon continue. "In a convention he would have little chance of getting a nomination, for he knew none of the influential political leaders in the county. But in a primary—that was another story."[27]

Perhaps partly because of the contacts Rayburn made as a teacher, he was well known and well liked.[28] His typical campaign outfit, a black suit and a black wool hat, made him look older than his twenty-four years. Hardeman and Bacon describe Rayburn as looking like an apprentice undertaker. The sense of gravitas he conveyed made a strong impression in the Texas heat. Rayburn had no specific platform, winning largely on his congeniality.[29]

Rayburn's House tenure resembled Neff's to a remarkable degree. In a frank mood, he told other House members he sought responsibility because he wanted the power that came with it. In this pursuit, Rayburn, like Neff, lived a "good life, not afflicted by drink or chasing women."[30] While other, rambunctious peers climbed out of back windows of the House chamber during late sessions to enjoy Austin's nightlife, Rayburn stayed anchored to his desk.[31]

His temper became famous, and he was known for the unfortunate habit of spitting when he flew into a rage. "In dark moods," one acquaintance said, "the profanity was shattering . . . Mr. Rayburn's face blackened in a terrible scowl and his bald head turned deep red . . . That was the way he looked in a rage, and few cared to see such a mien turned upon themselves." Nevertheless, he assiduously built a network of future supporters. "He had a reputation for honesty and fair dealing," one legislator said. "You could always swear by anything Sam told you." He expected the same of others. "Once you lied to Rayburn, why, you'd worn out your credentials," an aide recalled. "You didn't get a second chance."[32]

Upon receiving a law degree from the University of Texas, Rayburn moved from Windom to Bonham and secured reelection to the House in 1908.[33] In another parallel with Neff, Rayburn found a mentor in the reigning House Speaker, A. M. Kennedy, who appointed the East Texas representative to numerous powerful committees. Rayburn chaired the Constitutional Amendments Committee and the Committee on Banks and Banking and served on the committees overseeing education and the private corporations committees. Kennedy frequently allowed Rayburn to preside over the House.[34]

Rayburn earned the respect of his colleagues for his dogged loyalty to a besieged friend, Speaker Kennedy. In March 1909, Kennedy denied the charge that he had spent state funds, without legislative approval, on his staff and to provide furniture for his official residence in the Capitol. "There is not one scintilla of evidence that Kennedy is corrupt," Rayburn declared.[35] Regardless, the House passed a motion (70–48) requesting Kennedy's resignation and the reimbursement of a disputed $120. Kennedy promptly resigned on March 15, 1909.[36]

Immediately, talk surfaced of electing Rayburn as Kennedy's replacement for the rest of the Thirty-first Legislature. A bare majority of sixty-seven members signed a petition supporting Rayburn's candidacy, and the *Galveston News* predicted Rayburn would grab the post. Such a prospect, however, infuriated Thomas Love, a former Speaker who was still serving in the legislature. Although Love and Rayburn agreed on many issues, Love was outraged by Rayburn's past association with U.S. senator Joseph Bailey, an antiprohibitionist who had been accused of accepting bribes from an illegally operating railroad company. Love also didn't care for Rayburn's defense of Speaker Kennedy, whom Love saw as corrupt. Love warned colleagues that voting for Rayburn would be political suicide. Members relented, instead electing John Wesley Marshall of Whitesboro. The House continued its reform campaign, turning its attention to a prison system suffering from financial mismanagement, lack of sanitation, unpalatable food, and sometimes-murderous violence by guards. The legislature appointed a prison auditor, limited the physical punishment of inmates, and put an end to the leasing of convicts to landowners and other employers, a system that had resulted in numerous prisoner deaths.[37]

Rayburn's bid for the speakership may have been premature, but his actions during the Thirty-first Legislature greatly increased his popularity at home, and he shattered a local tradition by winning a third term to the Texas House. In the months leading up to the 1911 regular session, Rayburn emerged as one of the two serious candidates for the speakership, along with fellow prohibitionist Clarence Gilmore of Wills Point. Remembering Rayburn's loyalty, Kennedy, a former Speaker and still an influence in the legislature, announced his support for the Bonham representative.[38]

Months of campaigning left Rayburn and Gilmore in a virtual deadlock. When the House convened, the clerk read out loud the votes, the tally reaching 65–65, but Rayburn received the next three votes and appeared to have won. Rayburn briefly lost control of himself and "gave a cotton patch yell" as his supporters cheered, but the pandemonium quickly turned to confused silence.[39] The final count was 71 to 65. Though 136 ballots had been cast, there were only 133 members of the House. Either some members had voted more than once or nonmembers had voted, but whatever the reason for the mishap, the election had to be held again. Tension thickened as each member walked to the front of the chamber to drop a vote in the ballot box. This time, Rayburn won 70–63.[40]

Rayburn later indicated the improvisational nature of the Texas speakership in that era: "I muddled through that first session as Speaker of the Texas House of Representatives, 'by God, by desperation, and by ignorance.'"[41] Under Rayburn's speakership, some important pieces of the Progressive legislative agenda, such as shorter working hours for women, child labor laws, and appropriations for a Confederate widows home and a tuberculosis sanitarium won passage.[42]

Rayburn's personality thrived on orderliness and precision, so upon election as Speaker, he requested the appointment of a special committee to determine "the duties and rights of the Speaker."[43] This became the first codification of the Speaker's power. According to biographer Alfred Steinberg, he became the most effective Speaker in several legislative sessions. "Rayburn came to the Speakership after close observation of three previous Speakers (Love, Kennedy and Marshall), who had more or less wallowed in indecision regarding the power and duties of their office," Steinberg wrote. In contrast, Rayburn "had the gavel, the right to name committee members and chairmen, and control over the House's activities, yet he never flaunted his power." Rayburn used his office to ensure the passage of bills he favored, to doom measures he opposed, to reward friends, and to punish enemies. "I saw that all my friends got the good appointments and that those that voted against me for Speaker got none," he said. "The man in politics who is not faithful to his friends isn't worthy to be the scavenger of the smallest town in Texas."

In 1912, Rayburn won election to the U.S. House of Representatives, where he served until his death, in 1961. He became House majority leader in 1937 and Speaker for the first time in 1941 (the first, and so far the only, politician from Texas to be both state and U.S. House Speaker). Despite his many accomplishments, Rayburn rated his service as Texas House Speaker as the most enjoyable period in his long political career. "That job had real power—that's what a man wants—but power's no good unless you have the guts to use it," he said.[44] Whether or not Rayburn overvalued his years as Texas House Speaker, he certainly drew on them to become one of history's most influential members of Congress. Rayburn still owns the record for the longest tenure as Speaker of the U.S. House of Representatives.[45]

The Progressive Achievement in Texas

Rayburn and other Speakers from the early twentieth century derived power from being associated with the Progressive agenda, which enjoyed broad support within the legislature. No political movement in Texas history has had a more enduring impact. Under the influence of the Progressives, a Texas legislature ostensibly averse to centralized power greatly expanded the reach and depth of the state government. Rayburn, for instance, lent his considerable influence to support a law that made textbooks more widely available to Texas schoolchildren, another establishing a state board of health, and one that created a department of agriculture.[46]

Progressives also revamped the state's primitive education system, which was still dominated by rural one-teacher, one-classroom schools. The state government had virtually abandoned Texas schoolchildren after Reconstruction. State expenditures on education ranked near the bottom nationally, and in terms of quality, one survey in 1920 rated Texas thirty-ninth of the forty-eight states. Progressives committed to spending more per pupil, and new state laws reduced administrative costs and improved efficiency. One reform package allowed one-room schoolhouses to consolidate into larger districts even as the state increased the budget for improving rural roads and as more districts provided free transportation for students. Under a 1918 reform, the state of Texas provided free textbooks to children for the first time. In 1915, Texas passed its first compulsory-attendance law since Reconstruction, requiring all children between the ages of eight and fourteen to attend school for at least a sixty-day school term. (Texas was one of the last five states in the nation to require school attendance.) During the next two years, the legislature lengthened the school year to 100 days, with certain exemptions allowed in agricultural areas. By 1929, Texas schools averaged 156 school days an academic year, the high mark in the South and only six days short of the national average.[47]

Progressives also improved teacher training. As of 1920, nearly half of Texas teachers lacked even a high school diploma. Only 5 percent held a college or university degree. To improve teacher standards, the state legislature established normal, or teacher-training, schools across the state, including North Texas Normal in Denton in 1899, Southwest Texas Normal in San Marcos the same year, and Stephen F. Austin Normal in Nacogdoches in 1917.[48]

Progressivism briefly stalled during the scandal-plagued administration of Governor Jim Ferguson (1915–1917), but resumed after Ferguson's impeachment.[49] The Progressive movement experienced such extraordinary success for such a long time in Texas because the agenda of moral regeneration that animated it tapped deeply into Texas religious culture, which in the first decades of the twentieth century was dominated by Baptists and Methodists.[50] By the 1920s, Southern Baptists constituted the largest Protestant denomination (19.9 percent of the Texas population), and Methodists the second largest (17.8 percent). The large number of adherents ensured that these two churches and their social views would be well represented in the state House. As part of this culture, Speakers in this era brought a fervent support for prohibition and moral renewal to policy debates.[51]

The era of reform in Texas politics from the 1890s to the 1920s saw the rise of eight Speakers from the Baptist or Methodist denominations.[52] Conservative Baptists and Methodists tended to view political activism as an extension of their religious beliefs. Progressive political, social, and religious movements coalesced around prohibition and a number of other social reform issues. Support for prohibition created a strong coalition for many Speaker candidates.

In addition, prohibition supporters shared in the growing Anglo sentiment of xenophobia and racism, seeing "racial minorities as impediments to honest government," as historian Lewis Gould put it. Exemplified by men like Neff, the reform movement "drew its strength from the unquestioned moralities of the white Protestant American."[53] As the *Baptist Standard* put it, the fight for prohibition was "an issue of Anglo Saxon culture" and its survival amid a black, brown, and southern and eastern European onslaught.[54]

Prohibitionists successfully promoted their cause as a necessary precursor to triumph in World War I. "To not drink became patriotic," as Texas historians Robert Calvert and Arnoldo De León noted. "People did not work well with hangovers, alcohol was needed in the war effort, and saloons corrupted U.S. servicemen." In 1918, the legislature passed a state prohibition amendment, and the Eighteenth Amendment, prohibiting the sale, manufacture, and distribution of alcohol, became part of the U.S. Constitution the following year. This, plus the ratification of the Nineteenth Amendment, guaranteeing women's suffrage, marked the Progressives' last major achievements.[55]

As Calvert and De León point out, the same impulses that propelled prohibition also inspired demands for cultural conformity when the United States entered World War I. "In an effort to unite a heterogeneous population into a public consensus for a war effort, propaganda committees extolled patriotic goals and middle-class American values," they write.[56] Texas made public criticism of the American flag, the war effort, the U.S. government, or soldiers' uniforms crimes punishable by imprisonment. The legislature required that public schools teach patriotism and, except during foreign-language courses, conduct all classes in English. One legislative committee called for removal of all books and periodicals in the state library that depicted Germany or German culture favorably, and in 1919, Governor William Hobby vetoed appropriations for the German Department at the University of Texas.

This political atmosphere gave a provincial, defensive air to Texas culture for the next three decades. In spite of its label, Texas Progressivism often represented a cultural rearguard action aimed more at preserving a supposedly golden past than at opening doors to a strikingly different future. Such efforts set the stage in the 1920s for the rise of the Ku Klux Klan, a hooded order that would soon dominate state politics.

"Calculatin' Coke": The End of Progressivism and Birth of the Early Modern Speakership

1921–1949

To understand the subtle but significant transformation that the Texas speakership underwent between the 1920s and the late 1940s requires a detailed look at the social changes the state experienced during that time. This period marked a transition from the age of King Cotton to the age of oil, which began with the January 10, 1901, discovery of the Spindletop oil field near Beaumont.[1]

Investors poured billions of dollars into Texas in a search for oil and natural gas, producing cheap fuel that forever changed American transportation and the U.S. economy. Meanwhile, Beaumont, Port Arthur, Orange, and other communities on the state's Gulf Coast became major centers for oil refining and storage; corporate giants destined to economically dominate the twentieth century, such as Texaco, Gulf Oil, Sun Oil, Magnolia Petroleum, and Exxon (now ExxonMobil), trace their origins to the Spindletop boom.[2] Spindletop accelerated the state's transformation from a southern-identified agricultural province to a western-identified technological and financial powerhouse.[3] And one that was becoming urbanized. Texas remained mostly rural at the start of the 1920s, but population growth in cities was increasing ten times faster than in the countryside. By 1919, about 33 percent of Texas's population lived in urban centers; 15 percent lived in Houston, Dallas, and San Antonio alone.[4]

Of necessity, the speakership changed as the state underwent this metamorphosis. The volatility of the oil economy pressured the state government to enact regulations to prevent wild fluctuations in energy costs from undermining economic growth.

Elites, meanwhile, feared that increased industrialization would fuel the rebirth of political radicalism, represented by the Populists and other groups that battled dominant Democrats from the 1870s to the 1890s. Governors used the Texas Rangers to crush strikes. Red-baiting joined racial demagoguery as a favored tactic of conservatives, who reasserted power in the state House following World War I. State newspapers portrayed unions as violent and dictatorial, and business groups formed "open shop associations" that refused to hire union workers.[5]

Already-bad race relations in Texas took giant steps backward as living conditions for black Texans deteriorated. In 1891, the Legislature had passed a law requiring railway segregation and streetcar segregation in 1907. Although blacks made up 20 percent of the state's population by 1900, they represented 50 percent of the state's prisoners. Many suffered virtual slavery as African American men were sentenced on trumped-up charges of vagrancy and then leased as labor to wealthy landowners. Death rates from tuberculosis, typhoid, malaria, and other diseases among leased prisoners at times reached a stupefying 50 percent.[6]

Race riots erupted across the state. In 1908 in Beaumont, whites burned two black amusement parks after the arrest of a black man for raping a white woman. Similar events broke out in Sherman, Port Arthur, Houston, and other cities.[7] Texas compiled a shameful record of lynching. From 1882 until 1930, lynch mobs murdered 492 Texans, including 143 whites and 349 blacks, the third-highest number of lynchings in the nation. In May 1916, a mob of 15,000 burned to death a black youth, Jesse Washington, while children watched. For the most part, the state's daily newspapers only sporadically condemned mob violence on their editorial pages.[8]

The Resurgent Klan and the Anti-Progressives

Few should have been surprised by this turn of events, since the Progressives had risen to power on black disenfranchisement. Progressives helped set the stage for the resurgence of the Ku Klux Klan in the 1920s. Their xenophobia, prohibitionist politics, and self-righteous moralism overlapped with the reborn Klan's political agenda. Anxiety over immigration from eastern and southern Europe as well as Mexico in the years 1880 to 1920 inspired the birth of the revitalized Klan, which preached an antiblack, anti-federal-government, anti-Semitic, anti-Catholic, and anti-immigrant gospel.[9] By the mid-1920s, the organization could boast of approximately 3 million members nationwide.[10] Progressive elites in Texas often enjoyed Klan support. Pat Neff, the former Speaker who served as governor from 1921 to 1925, won a "favorable" rating from the state Klan, partly because of his conspicuous silence on the organization and his apparent efforts to quash the Texas Rangers' investigation of Klan violence. Another former Progressive Speaker, Thomas Love, supported Klan candidate Felix D. Robertson when he ran unsuccessfully against Miriam "Ma" Ferguson in the 1924 gubernatorial race. Love rationalized his support on the grounds that the Klan supported prohibition and that Ma Ferguson's husband, Jim, expected to be the power behind the throne, had led a scandal-plagued administration before his 1917 impeachment, rendering the Fergusons morally unfit to govern.[11]

The Klan used its influence to sweep into office state representatives, state senators, mayors, county judges, sheriffs, and countless other officials. By 1923, the Klan politically controlled Dallas, which boasted the nation's largest Klan chapter, Fort Worth, and Wichita Falls. A large percentage of the state's congressional delegation either belonged to or supported the Klan, and a majority of the members of the Thirty-eighth Texas Legislature held Klan memberships. This meant prospective Speakers had little to gain by tangling with the Klan.[12]

The gathering conservative backlash of the 1920s also gained force from the right wing of the Democratic Party. Reactionary Democrats felt fury over what they saw as President Woodrow Wilson's and other Progressives' betrayal of the party's traditional Jeffersonian ideology of limited government, as when the administration greatly expanded federal regulations and bureaucracies during World War I and intervened in some cases on the side of labor unions that were battling employers for higher wages and reduced working hours. Joseph Weldon Bailey of Texas, a U.S. senator from 1901 to 1911, angrily resigned his Senate seat over the dominance of Progressives in the national Democratic Party and campaigned hard to retake control of the state party. In 1920, Bailey entered the race for governor, facing off against Neff, the Progressive former Speaker.[13]

Anti-Progressives like Bailey and Jim Ferguson opposed prohibition, women's suffrage, taxes, and U.S. participation in the League of Nations. Other than rolling back Progressive legislation, however, Democratic conservatives had no real platform. Instead, Bailey spewed crude racism everywhere he campaigned. Rather than support increased teacher pay, for instance, Bailey opposed a bill that would raise pay for federal workers because "under it . . . the negro men who clean out the cuspidors and the negro women who scrub the floors of our Federal buildings in Texas would be paid more than the white school teachers of Texas."[14] It never occurred to Bailey, apparently, that teachers' salaries could be raised as well. At another campaign stop, Bailey proclaimed he had "no prejudice against the negro, mind you. I like the negro in his place. It's all right if Massachusetts wants to permit negroes to intermarry. It's a matter of taste. No, not altogether a matter of taste either. It's partly a matter of smell."[15]

Robert Ewing Thomason, another former Texas House Speaker, represented the most genuine Progressive in the 1920 gubernatorial race. The forty-one-year-old Tennessee native and University of Texas law school graduate first won election to the state legislature from El Paso in 1916. A prohibitionist, Thomason served on the House committee investigating charges against Governor Jim Ferguson in 1917 and wrote the report condemning the governor's actions. In his legislative service, Thomason also successfully advocated for the creation of the state's first worker's compensation law and for a bill creating the state highway commission. He became a strong supporter of women's voting rights and rose to the speakership at the urging of colleagues during his second term, in 1919.[16]

"I have accepted a heavy responsibility," Thomason said upon winning the leadership post. "Liquor is bad; women should vote; only citizens should vote; capital and labor should be friends; we need mass education and a University of the first class."[17] Speakers traditionally did not engage in legislative debates or propose bills while presiding over the House. Thomason, nevertheless, said one of his proudest moments as Speaker came when he stepped down temporarily from the dais to oppose a bill authorizing the use of the Texas National Guard to suppress strikes. Such prolabor sentiment from the speakership would virtually disappear after Thomason's term. Most relevant for the 1920 gubernatorial race, however, he also advocated repeal of the poll tax, arguing that blacks and Mexican Americans were already excluded from voting in primaries by Democratic Party rules. This opened him to racist attacks by his chief gubernatorial rival, Pat Neff. Thomason saw his lead in the gubernatorial race peak in early July but disappear by the time of the primary later that month. The primary left Bailey in the lead, facing Neff in a runoff. In that election, Bailey received only 40 percent of the vote, and Neff stood assured of victory in the November governor's race.[18]

Neff, however, entered the governor's office with a slim agenda. In the end, Progressivism touched few people where they lived. So much attention was devoted to alcohol as the root of all social evils that once prohibition became the law of the land, Progressives felt they had little left to do. On matters of social justice, as historian Lewis Gould points out, the Progressive record in Texas proved particularly scanty. "While a few educators, journalists and politicians called for effective child labor, minimum wage and public health laws between 1911 and 1921, the majority of citizens remained cool to effective governmental intervention in these areas," Gould writes.[19] Minimum-wage laws for women and children remained on the books for only two years, and the suggestions of child and family advocates went largely ignored. Progressives were similarly unconcerned about the state's poisonous race relations. However, the Progressive cupboard was not entirely bare. Rising prosperity and an expanding population brought some improvement to the lives of many Texans, especially if they lived in cities, which offered more public services and job opportunities. Women, who gained the right to vote in the 1920s, now exerted more political influence and made some headway in the workplace. Nevertheless, although the foundations for change were laid, Texas remained tied to its southern traditions, both cultural and political, until the Great Depression.[20]

The Oil Boom and the Economic Bust

Two events almost simultaneously marked the birth of a more complex economy. In October 1929, the stock market crashed, to be followed soon by a banking crisis that left mass unemployment in its wake. Shortly afterward, in late 1930, Columbus Marion "Dad" Joiner discovered a major oil field near Kilgore, Texas, which soon accounted for one-third of the nation's then-known oil reserves. Independent oil producers, quickly realizing the potential of the Kilgore strike, rushed in and grabbed 80 percent of the field before major oil firms could set up claims. By 1933, the chief year of production, the East Texas field produced an amount of oil equal to the total production in the rest of the state.[21]

The Kilgore gusher affected oil prices nationally. Prices dropped from slightly more than a dollar a barrel in 1930 to, briefly, as low as two cents a barrel in 1931. Major oil producers complained that Kilgore independents had depressed the world oil market.[22] During the Populist era, the state had created the Texas Railroad Commission, and by the 1930s, the legislature had given the commission the power to prorate oil—to establish the maximum amount of oil that could be pumped from individual wells. The commission could act if excess production threatened future oil supplies or the environment. It was uncertain constitutionally whether the commission had the authority to slow oil production just to keep prices high for producers. Nevertheless, in 1931, the commission issued a proration order on Kilgore production, which was soon stalled by a court injunction. Many independents ignored the commission.[23]

East Texas business elites pressured Governor Ross Sterling, a former Humble Oil executive, to intervene, and on August 17, 1931, he issued an executive order commanding Kilgore producers to stop drilling and sent National Guard units to enforce the directive. As a result, workers and producers benefiting from the oil boom perceived Sterling as a tool of Humble, Standard Oil, and other major producers.[24]

Meanwhile, a simultaneous collapse of cotton prices, from ten cents to five cents a pound, also due partly to overproduction, had a devastating impact on the state economy. Unemployment reached 23 percent in Houston, and thousands of the unemployed tramped across the state by foot or rail in search of work.[25] Officials turned off half the streetlights in Houston to save electricity. Beaumont turned off streetlights completely, slashed the city's school budget by half, and reduced the library appropriation to almost nothing. Across the state, the Depression severely hit those most economically vulnerable: women, Mexican Americans, and African Americans. Blacks suffered under an unemployment rate nearly twice that of whites.[26]

Buffeted by the simultaneous collapse of farm-commodity and oil prices, the state tried in vain to prop up the economy. Speaker Fred Minor (who presided over the House from 1931 to 1933) assisted in passage of landmark legislation that gave the Railroad Commission the power to regulate oil production and stabilize prices. Again, conservative Democrats dramatically increased the power of the state government, but this time it was due to economic desperation rather than Progressive idealism.[27]

In 1934, the legislature passed a law requiring refiners to disclose totals of petroleum refined and the sources of that petroleum. The legislature also passed the Connally Act, named for U.S. senator Tom Connally of Texas, which made it illegal to transport "hot" oil, that is, oil pumped in excess of state-imposed limits. These laws greatly strengthened the ability of the Railroad Commission to enforce its orders, leading to a consolidation of production in the hands of major producers, who gained control of 80 percent of the East Texas oil field.[28]

This consolidation created a new class of superrich Texas oilmen, who moved their corporate offices from Tulsa, Oklahoma, which had been the center of the industry, to Dallas, which became the capital of East Texas production. Texas oil tycoons became a political factor in the state after

World War II and received national attention in the 1950s and 1960s as they began to fund far-right-wing and rabidly anticommunist political organizations and radio and television broadcasts.[29]

Conservatives regained state political power in the 1930s, a hold they have yet to relinquish.[30] This, however, was not Bailey-style "Jeffersonian" conservatism. "The greatest effect [of the Progressives] . . . was on attitudes towards the power of government," Gould asserts. "As legislation and bureaucratic action demonstrated the benefits the state could convey, the old Democratic faith in localism and obstruction perceptibly relaxed."[31]

Speaker Stevenson

The transition to a new politics did not proceed smoothly. Conservatives in the 1930s, like Speaker Coke Robert Stevenson, had no interest in expanding state government. Economic policy during his two terms as Speaker, from 1933 to 1937, seemed like a throwback to the harshest stinginess of the so-called Redeemer governments that followed Reconstruction. What was revolutionary about the Stevenson era was how the power of the speakership itself expanded, even if Stevenson primarily used that power to obstruct rather than implement reform. No Speaker had ever wielded so much influence as did the man born in a Mason County log cabin on March 20, 1888. The son of a teacher, Stevenson had a rootless childhood, but by 1905 the family had settled in Junction in Kimble County. At age sixteen, Stevenson launched his first business venture, running a freight line from Junction to Brady. He sought an accountant's job at Junction State Bank, but took the only opening available, that of janitor and errand boy. Quickly, however, he moved up to clerk, and by 1909 his boss had promoted him to cashier.[32]

Largely self-taught, Stevenson pursued a law license and won admission to the bar in 1913, successfully running for Kimble County attorney in 1914. In 1918, he won a two-year term as county judge, then stepped down to resume his private law practice. In 1921, the First National Bank board in Junction named him president, and Stevenson expanded his financial empire to include ownership of a newspaper (the *Junction Eagle*), a hotel, a movie theater, and a Ford dealership. In 1928, a group of Kimble County ranchers fanned out across the ten-county district in search of a candidate who would press the legislature to pay hunters to kill the wolves feeding on area livestock; they persuaded Stevenson to run for the state House.[33]

After winning, Stevenson's first stab at reducing the wolf population in his district backfired. The state payments for killed and trapped wolves attracted scam artists who brought in wolf carcasses from outside Kimble County to claim the bounty. Stevenson then pushed through a bill that outlawed the transportation of wolf carcasses across county lines. Early on, he demonstrated fiscal conservatism. He later reported feeling shocked when he discovered during his first term in the House that the state had no auditing system. Stevenson authored a bill creating the office of state auditor, the first step toward giving Texas a modern budget system.[34]

Stevenson's role in crafting this law showed his early grasp of House procedures. As his bill for predator control indicates, he welcomed the use of governmental power to help wealthy landowners protect their investments. Stevenson, however, was an extremely cautious spender, which became apparent when he vigorously opposed Governor Ross Sterling's plan to sell $100,000,000 (approximately $1.2 billion in today's dollars) in bonds to pay for highway construction and to compensate counties that had bond indebtedness for road construction. After the Senate authorized submitting the bond sale to voters, the House needed 100 affirmative votes to place the measure on the ballot. As many as 99 House members voted in favor of the bonds, but Stevenson's anti faction held strong through several roll calls, striking down Sterling's road program. Stevenson steered through a compromise measure in which the state highway department was provided a yearly budget from which construction funds would be drawn.[35]

Stevenson's success in opposing Governor Sterling's highway plan marked him as a star legislator and propelled him to the speakership in 1933. Stevenson's friendly relationship with Ma and Pa Ferguson also helped.[36] Stevenson emerged as leader in part because of charisma augmented by a vicious sense of humor. While hunting with a lobbyist and several legislators, a rancher who was friends with Stevenson told him of a horse on the property that was so old it should be destroyed. The rancher asked Stevenson to do the job. As the car carrying the hunters passed by the intended target, Stevenson asked the driver to stop, whereupon he got out and declared, "I think I'll kill that ol' horse." Stevenson raised his muzzle and shot the animal in the head. His unsuspecting companions stared at Stevenson until the lobbyist finally asked, "Why did you shoot that horse?" "I just always wondered what it would feel like to shoot a horse," Stevenson replied. "Now I'm wondering what it would feel like to shoot a man."[37]

Perhaps the incident was meant as a practical joke, but as a politician, Stevenson proved he could be as coldhearted as a man who would kill just to satisfy curiosity. "Throughout his political career, Stevenson had been an ultraconservative," Texas political historian Kenneth E. Hendrickson wrote. "He exhibited no liberal tendencies at all and few that could even be described as constructive; he was a reactionary, penurious, and in some cases downright cruel."[38]

Irony marked Stevenson's alliance with incoming governor Miriam Ferguson, who served a second, nonconsecutive term as the state's chief executive from 1933 to 1935. Stevenson opposed social welfare on principle, but one of Ferguson's boldest initiatives was the issuance of a $20 million bread bond to buy clothing and food for the poor, who were the worst hit by the Great Depression. Ferguson and her husband, Jim (who, many believed, ran the government behind the scenes), had opposed the Progressives in the 1910s and 1920s, but this time the pair aligned themselves with President Franklin Roosevelt and the Texas liberal faction.[39]

The 1933 legislative session proved the longest to date in Texas history, ending one week short of five months, as the legislature dealt with the deepening depression.[40] As Speaker, Stevenson cultivated an image as a long tall Texan who refused to be rushed into a decision. Charles E. Simons, writing in a March 1942 edition of *Texas Parade,* summed up the seemingly easygoing style with which the Junction businessman commanded the Texas House: "While the members were milling or shouting or debating and wrangling, Stevenson would calmly load and light his pipe and solemnly puff while he pondered the situation and watched the ebb and flow of the tide. Picking the psychological time, he would gather up the loose ends, bring them up short with a pointed observation and gentle the members into getting about the business at hand."[41] Stevenson certainly proved a commanding presence as Speaker. He "kept greater order by rapping on the speaker's podium with his pipe than most of us have done with a five-pound gavel," as Ben Barnes, Speaker from 1965 to 1969, commented in a speech in Bay City on July 16, 1966.[42]

By the end of the 1933 session, talk was already buzzing around the Capitol about a possible gubernatorial run by the Speaker. During Stevenson's debut term on the dais, one significant piece of legislation with long-lasting consequences reached the governor's desk: the creation of the Lower Colorado River Authority, which built dams to control

flooding, parks for recreation, and other public facilities that improved
the economy of Central Texas. Miriam Ferguson chose to not run again
in 1934 after serving a relatively uncontroversial two-year term. Stevenson, however, decided to bide his time. James Allred of Bowie, who had
handily defeated Robert Lee Bobbitt, a former House Speaker, in a 1930
race for state attorney general and had then captured the office for a second term two years later, emerged as a leading gubernatorial candidate.
Allred ran on a modest platform calling for creation of a public utilities
commission; placing the repeal of prohibition before voters; creating a
more modern, better-trained, and more efficient state police force; cutting
taxes; granting more power to the Board of Pardons and Paroles in order
to prevent future abuses of the clemency power by governors (as some
said had happened under the Fergusons); and regulating the activities of
lobbyists.[43]

Allred was a more genuine liberal than the Fergusons, who lacked a co-
herent ideology. Allred "focused on reform of the capitalist system without destroying the foundations for free enterprise."[44] Texas Progressives
had obsessed about cultural causes for poverty and other social ills, paying
little attention to economic policy. Economic liberals of the 1930s and
beyond, however, believed unregulated free markets undermined democracy. To men like Allred, capitalism left unrestrained by government led
to the uneven distribution of wealth, unemployment, and the abuse of
power by big business.

Allred won the Democratic nomination for governor by a 4,000-vote
margin.[45] The 1935 Speaker's race was entangled thoroughly with the gubernatorial campaign. Stevenson, who, as a member of the House, had
already displayed more power and influence than previous governors Ross
Sterling and Ma Ferguson, took the unprecedented step of asking for a
second term as Speaker. This event, longtime Capitol correspondent Sam
Kinch, Jr., argues, served as the most pivotal event in the speakership's
history. Before Stevenson, the Speaker:

> generally was a strong, independent-minded person who presided over a
> collection of similar individuals for a single 2-year term and then resumed
> regular legislative service as a member.
>
> Beginning about 1935, though, the office of speaker began evolving
> into something else, something more powerful and politically important.
> Aspiring public officials began seeking the office not as a service to their
> colleagues but as a route to upward mobility.[46]

Stevenson's opponent in the 1935 Speaker race, Robert W. Calvert, warned that tyranny would result from a multiterm speakership. By this point, however, Stevenson had emerged as leader of the state's conservatives. Several historical factors, historian George Norris Green argues, promoted a conservative hegemony in Texas by the late 1930s. Texas's experience as an independent republic, as part of the losing Confederacy, and as a western outpost at the mercy of Washington's perceived weak response to Native American resistance all laid the precedent for a troubled relationship with Washington, D.C., by the second half of the 1930s. Distrust of Washington merged with rising right-wing fears concerning President Roosevelt's domestic policies. Before Roosevelt won election to a second term, Texas conservatives united against the New Deal, now seen as dangerously prolabor and pro–African American. Even if most Texas voters remained loyal to Roosevelt, reactionaries like Stevenson and W. L. "Pappy" O'Daniel soon eclipsed Progressives like Allred and seized control of the political establishment.[47]

Tensions with Washington combined with troubled race relations to feed elite fears of a powerful federal government, particularly in the realm of civil rights. The worry of Texas conservatives that the White House might enforce black voting rights arose with Franklin Roosevelt's ascension to the White House in 1933, the same year Stevenson became Speaker. Conservatives may have collaborated with the New Deal in Roosevelt's first term, but Texas politicians like John Nance Garner and Stevenson expressed estrangement in the second half of the 1930s. Even though Garner agreed in 1936 to campaign as Roosevelt's running mate a second time, early in the new term he openly expressed regrets about his alliance and began collaborating with the right-wing opposition to the New Deal.

Stevenson entered the race for reelection tagged as a Ferguson man and therefore an opponent of governor-elect James Allred, a strong supporter of FDR. Stevenson held close ties to big industries, such as sulfur and oil. Allred's actions as state attorney general, on the other hand, indicated his willingness to rein in corporations and bring them to court if they violated state regulations. "Nowhere have [big corporations] found in [Allred] the warmth of that welcome to which they have been accustomed," reported the *Austin American* on January 8, 1935. "Not unnatural that their slogan should be 'STOP ALLRED IN THE LEGISLATURE.'"

The Fergusons openly backed Stevenson as their man. Allred, on the other hand, saw in Calvert someone who could carry his reform programs in the legislature. Perhaps no prominent political figure in twentieth-century Texas overcame more obstacles to reach the limelight than

Calvert. Calvert's family lived in poverty, and at age seven, the Tennessee native saw his father lapse into a severe illness and die. Calvert's mother, Maud, struggled to keep her family of five children together, settling in Corsicana, where she earned a living running errands for ill or elderly people.[48]

Desperately poor, Maud Calvert committed the eight-year-old Robert, his sister Maxie, and his brother Grady to the State Orphan's Asylum in Corsicana. In his memoir, *Here Comes the Judge*, he recalls the trauma of being torn from his mother: "When Superintendent W. F. Barnett [of the asylum] came in an old Model T touring car to pick up the three of us to take us to the State Home, they had to pull me out from under my bed, screaming that I did not want to go." Calvert spent the rest of his childhood in this institution and its schools.[49]

The children living at the state home paid the price for the low priority Texas politicians placed on social welfare. Calvert's sister died during the influenza pandemic of 1918. Conditions at the home bordered on the primitive. Calvert recalled, "We had a terrible infestation of rats in the building. Some of the little boys were bitten by the rats on various parts of their bodies, some on their face. One bit me through the end of one of my fingers during the night while I was sleeping; the finger became infected and the skin of the entire joint hardened and peeled off." He remembers that during a mandated quiet time on Sunday afternoons, an employee at the home would gather up leftover bread and allow the boys to have their choice of light bread, corn bread, or biscuits. "[She] made talks to us, had prayer, and invariably reminded us that we were wards of the State of Texas, and that the taxpayers of the State of Texas were good to us and blessed us with a good home. She would ask, 'Children, who gave you this fine home?' And she taught us to respond in unison, 'The taxpayers of Texas.' And then she would ask, 'And how will you repay the taxpayers of Texas?' And we were taught to respond, 'By being good citizens.'"[50]

In spite of unbelievable hardships, Calvert graduated from the high school provided at the orphanage. He remembered that life there improved after the appointment of Odie Minatra as superintendent. Minatra started two public-speaking societies at the institution's high school, and Calvert excelled at debate. After noticing Calvert's oratorical talents, Minatra dispatched the sixteen-year-old to the state Capitol to lobby for a new boys' dormitory. It was an auspicious debut for the future legislator, who persuaded the House and the Senate to appropriate $100,000 (about $962,000 today) to construct the dorm. Minatra also initiated a "big brothers" mentoring program with Corsicana-area businessmen, and through this Calvert came under the wing of Luther Johnson, who was elected to Congress in 1922, and future Texas governor Beauford Jester. The two, he said, later influenced his decision to enter the University of Texas law school. Calvert earned money for tuition by working as a water boy at a refinery and then as an elevator operator at the Capitol. He graduated, received his law license in 1931, and then opened a law practice in Hillsboro.[51]

Calvert first won election to the Texas House in 1933, from a so-called "flotorial district" that included Hill and Navarro counties on the western edge of north-central Texas.[52] His experience in the state home deeply influenced his behavior in the state House. Calvert had been "raised at the State Home on an anti-Ferguson diet by Mr. Minatra, who . . . lost the superintendency of the State Home because of his anti-Ferguson persuasion."[53]

This placed him in direct conflict with the newly elected chief executive. In spite of his dislike of the governor and her husband, Calvert supported the Speaker candidacy of Coke Stevenson. In his first term, Calvert became a leader of the anti-Ferguson forces, however, through his heated opposition to a bill that would have allowed Ferguson to replace the three incumbents on the state highway commission with five new commissioners, who would serve for about a year and a half before they faced election in 1934. "There was much talk during the gubernatorial campaign of 1934 about the Fergusons raising campaign funds by selling jobs to be delivered in the highway department once she was elected," Calvert said. "When the discussion of the bill started, the proponents had a safe margin for passage; but with all due modesty, I think this was one occasion when a speech on the floor of the House turned the tide on pending legislation."[54] Calvert attached an amendment that would have postponed reform of the highway commission until the 1934 general election. With Calvert's amendment, the bill passed the House by a 74–63 vote; in the Senate, Ferguson allies lost interest and failed to bring up the measure for consideration.[55]

This set up an intense race for Speaker in 1935, when Stevenson sought a second term. Before the Stevenson era, state newspapers had provided little analysis of upcoming Speaker contests. As in 1933, however, the 1935 race received extensive newspaper coverage. Reporters depicted the race as a test of wills between incoming Governor Allred and the departing Fergusons. In spite of his public image as a reluctant politician compelled to serve his constituents, Stevenson ran his campaign with Machiavellian zeal. Stevenson's supporters circulated a petition asking him to run.

Calvert had already signed a petition for Bert Ford, a representative from McLennan County, so he told the Stevenson people no: "The persons circulating it [the petition] said there was no possibility that Stevenson would return to the house and offer for the speakership again; they simply wanted to make this showing of confidence in the event he became a candidate for governor. I told them to change the petition to read that and we would support him for governor and I would sign; otherwise I would not."[56]

When 115 members had signed the petition, Stevenson announced that he had enough votes for a second term. Told that some members had thought the petition was a vote of confidence for a potential gubernatorial race, Stevenson denied this had ever been the intent of the petition. His move, however, forced Ford to drop his campaign. Calvert said that he and eleven other anti-Ferguson representatives decided to oppose Stevenson. Calvert entered the race with his 11 supporters against the 115 men who had signed Stevenson's petition. Allred's victory in the Democratic gubernatorial primary gave Calvert much needed momentum, and the governor-elect openly supported Calvert. By the last week of the campaign, Calvert said he was winning the race. In an attempt to prove he still enjoyed the support of the majority of House members, Stevenson asked his backers to wear red carnations. Fewer than the required 76 representatives, however, wore the flowers on their lapels. When House members cast their ballots, Stevenson won 80–68, a much closer race than anyone had anticipated. Regardless, such was the power of Stevenson that governor-elect Allred felt compelled to immediately meet with the newly reelected Speaker and declare peace before assembled reporters.[57]

By winning, Stevenson re-created the Speaker's office. The fact that Jim Ferguson and James Allred used the Speaker campaign as a proxy battle for control of the Democratic Party provided a frank acknowledgment that, in the right hands, House Speakers could hold considerable power in their own right.

Stevenson and Allred soon found themselves on a collision course. Under Ferguson, Texas voters had approved a constitutional amendment authorizing payment to the elderly and the poor. The amendment, however, did not specify a funding mechanism for the program. After rejecting a proposal for a state sales tax, which he saw as regressive, Allred suggested various business taxes and even an income tax to fund the pensions. Stevenson responded with his favorite tactic: slowly lighting his pipe, endorsing no proposals, and doing nothing while he insisted the problems would solve themselves. Allred proposed the transfer of $3 million from state highway funds to keep the pension checks flowing, but again Stevenson stymied the initiative, insisting that "gasoline taxes and other motor imposts were special taxes that . . . could be used only for . . . building and maintaining highways."[58]

Speaker Calvert

Stevenson turned his attention to running for lieutenant governor. Calvert, a hero to legislators because of his fierce opposition to the Fergusons, faced no opponent in his race for reelection in 1936, and he ran unopposed for Speaker. "In the '30s, speakers did not have legislative programs of their own," Calvert wrote. "I had no legislative program which I called the speaker's program, except that I did state to members of the house that I felt that the program advocated by Allred [who had been reelected as governor] . . . was entitled to fair consideration."[59] Calvert underestimated the role he played as Speaker when Stevenson became lieutenant governor. Together, Allred and Calvert enjoyed a relatively productive session after the reactionary Stevenson years. Calvert, who had been active in setting up the Old Age Assistance Commission in 1935 (which later became the Texas Department of Human Services), had not forgotten his youth in the state home and successfully advocated laws benefiting neglected, blind, and dependent children. By 1939, he had played a key role in passing a law extending the power of the Railroad Commission to regulate how much oil each well in the state could produce. If his predecessor proved the power of Speakers to obstruct, Calvert proved the critical role that Speakers could play in enacting legislation.[60]

The influence of Texas House Speakers grew spectacularly in the 1940s as a string of deeply divisive chief executives occupied the Governor's Mansion. When Allred departed after two terms as governor, the way was cleared for country-music performer and flour executive W. Lee "Pappy" O'Daniel. Kenneth Hendrickson characterized O'Daniel as "undoubtedly one of the most incompetent individuals ever to hold the office of governor in Texas." An Ohio native who grew up in Kansas, O'Daniel became the manager of a Fort Worth milling company. In 1925, he served as sales manager for Burrus Mills in Fort Worth, and was named director of radio advertising three years later. By 1931, O'Daniel had launched a popular radio advertising campaign for Burrus's Light Crust Flour; the ads featured the music of O'Daniel and a country-and-western band called the Light Crust Doughboys. After forming his own company, Hillbilly Flour, in 1935, O'Daniel began hosting a highly popular radio show built around flour, country music, and bits of homespun wisdom. On Palm Sunday 1938, he asked his listeners whether he should run for governor. According to O'Daniel, he received 55,000 cards, letters, and other responses, most of them urging his candidacy. O'Daniel called the Golden Rule his motto and claimed the Ten Commandments as his campaign platform. He also advocated a $30 monthly pension for all persons over the age of sixty-five, the elimination of the poll tax, and a general tax reduction. Although O'Daniel never specified how he would fund his pension plan, he won the Democratic primary without a runoff.[61]

It does not seem that O'Daniel spent any time planning how to translate his proposed old-age pension or any of his other stated goals into legislation. Once in the Governor's Mansion, O'Daniel suggested a "transaction," or value-added, tax that was advocated by the Texas Manufacturers Association but opposed by other elements in the business community. O'Daniel, however, never worked very hard to move the proposal through the House. When that idea fizzled, he supported a statewide sales tax. In the House, Marion Price Daniel, Sr., became one of the chief opponents of the sales tax. Born in Dayton, Texas, northeast of Houston, in 1910, Price Daniel would go on to occupy more top posts in Texas government than anyone else, serving as Speaker of the House, attorney general, U.S. senator, governor, and justice of the Texas Supreme Court. A graduate of Baylor University, Price Daniel set up a law practice in Liberty, where in 1938 he was first elected to the state House.[62]

In his freshman term, Price Daniel gained fame as part of the so-called Immortal 56—House members who consistently voted down sales-tax proposals to fund old-age pensions. He complained that a sales tax was regressive, hitting the poor the hardest, and pointed out that O'Daniel's plan would ban the use of any other tax to fund pensions. Vowing political vengeance after this defeat, O'Daniel campaigned personally against the Immortals. In 1940, after a difficult campaign, Price Daniel won a second term, although many of his allies, tagged as opponents of pensions, lost. The following year, U.S. senator Morris Sheppard died, and O'Daniel shocked the state by appointing the eighty-seven-year-old, utterly senile Andrew Jackson Houston, the last surviving son of Texas hero Sam Houston, as his replacement. O'Daniel made the appointment to prevent a viable candidate from running as an incumbent against O'Daniel in the special election for the Senate seat the governor scheduled for June 28, 1941. Illness kept Houston from reaching the Senate floor until June, and after appearing there three times, he also died. O'Daniel prevailed in the special election by 13,000 votes over Congressman Lyndon Johnson of Central Texas; vote fraud was widely considered to have been the decisive factor.[63]

Speaker Daniel

Price Daniel's chief antagonist departed for Washington. The Liberty lawyer ran for Speaker, prevailing over incumbent Homer Leonard of McAllen.[64] With the United States already preparing for World War II and defense spending in Washington stimulating the economy, particularly in Texas, the legislature found itself in no mood for new spending programs. It approved expenditures lower than those appropriated two years before. At the insistence of Coke Stevenson, now in the Governor's Mansion, the session (at 121 days, the shortest in modern state history) was the first in forty years to not approve a single tax bill.[65]

The 1943 session found the House under Daniel cautiously awaiting the uncertain outcome of a war and the advent of an unpredictable postwar economy. The world and the state, however, continued to change. The increased political activism of African Americans, begun in the 1930s, the growing Mexican American population, and the increasingly liberal drift of the national Democratic Party inspired a continued movement rightward for Texas Democrats. In fact, the speakership stood as an effective counterweight to the revolutionary changes that came to Texas during World War II and beyond.

Speaker Reed

In a nominating speech for the Dallas-born forty-four-year-old William O. Reed, state representative John J. Bell told the House chamber, "The office of Speaker is on par in importance with the governorship." The *Dallas Morning News* noted, "If this is not an accurate estimate, it is because Mr. Bell errs on the side of underestimation. For, if there is any commonwealth in the United States that is run by its legislative branch, it is Texas. And the Lower House, as the most productive source of legislation because of its large membership and as the controlling source of state finance, has a larger responsibility in state government than does the Upper House."[66]

In the late 1940s, the question remained, power to what end? Reed experienced a childhood almost as tough as Calvert's. Born the youngest of ten children in the poverty-stricken Trinity River bottoms, Reed reached only his first birthday before his father died. Known in his neighborhood as a street fighter, he worked as a newsboy for the *Dallas Morning News*. "In those days, that meant you could sell newspapers at any corner you liked—if you could fight off all the boys who wanted that corner," a 1946 *Morning News* feature story on Reed reported. "Young Reed's expert fists held down some good corners."[67] After dropping out of high school and working for the Dallas water department, Reed landed a job in the accounting department of the Texas and Pacific Railway Company. Hitting the law books at night, Reed earned a license and began working for the railroad company's law department, specializing in railway rates.[68]

In spite of his rough, working-class origins, Reed quickly adopted the appearance and perspective of the ruling class. "Nowadays, you won't suspect a rough-and-tumble background," the *Dallas Morning News* reported, "for Reed sports a trim moustache, [and] dresses his slender, lithe frame in sartorial perfection. His speech is quiet, dignified." Even if Reed once threw off his glasses and charged toward a House colleague who had angered him—he had to be stopped by a sergeant at arms—Reed's commitment to the ruling class went deeper than his clothing style. Unlike Calvert, another early victim of childhood poverty, Reed authored or presided over the passage of some of the most reactionary Texas legislation in the twentieth century.[69]

To his credit as a House backbencher, Reed introduced a bill making it illegal for maternity homes to sell foundlings to prospective parents. But little in the rest of his career suggested such empathy for the underprivileged and struggling. Reed's priority was a balanced budget. As a member of the legislature, Reed authored the pay-as-you-go amendment to the state constitution, which was approved by Texas voters in 1942. Up to that point, the state had no system for a unitary budget. Budgets were approved for programs and departments without regard to the state's total spending for the biennium. As the state's population expanded, so did its expenses, and the result was fiscal chaos.[70]

The state relied on deficit spending, often paying employees and even lawmakers in scrip. "The first paycheck I got would have to be discounted 20 percent to get money," Claud Gilmer, a House Speaker in the late 1940s, recalled. "There was a fellow with a little black box of money. He'd run around picking up these state warrants. Most people that were working for the state had no way to get away from this kind of guy."[71] Carson Gilmer later recalled his father receiving $8 a day in scrip as a legislator and taking the IOUs to grocery stores in Austin to buy food. The stores would accept the paper at only 60 percent of face value because the state was in such financial shambles. Gilmer had a law practice and owned shares of the telephone company, so he was not as hard hit as ordinary state employees, who had to survive on only a portion of their already meager official salaries.[72]

Economic conservatives like Gilmer, Reed, and Stevenson, who served as governor from 1941 to 1947, put together a state constitutional amendment that limited deficit spending and required the state to operate on a pay-as-you-go basis. The state could deficit-spend, but only in case of an emergency, and authorization for an unbalanced budget required the approval of four-fifths of both the House and Senate and the governor's signature. Since the state legislature was rarely in favor of tax increases, this amendment, which went into effect in 1945, meant that legislators would have to rely instead on swinging the budgetary axe.[73]

The same amendment made it illegal for the treasury to use scrip to pay bills and required the state comptroller to certify that biennial budgets were balanced. The amendment allowed the state to sell bonds to make up a deficit that had reached $34 million in 1941, the first year of World War II. Raising taxes and slashing already meager state spending on education, health care, and other services also remained as options.[74]

Governor Stevenson's glacial response to a growing deficit recalled his approach to the Speaker's office. The pay-as-you-go amendment made general sense economically, but Stevenson's choices in how to implement it required draconian budget cuts that jeopardized the poor. When Stevenson became governor, he "reduced funds for river authorities, starved schoolteachers, and abolished the Old Age Assistance Special Fund, which supported the aged, the blind, and dependent children," according to historian Robert Dallek.[75] As historian Kenneth Hendrickson put it:

> Stevenson's economic policies were crude and shortsighted, and as the state's needs for increased revenues became ever more critical, the governor ignored pleas for higher taxes. He could have supported (and perhaps even secured) a hike in the wellhead oil tax to bring Texas policy more in line with those of neighboring oil producing states, but he chose not to . . . When he left office in 1947, Stevenson was proud of the fact that the state budget was in the black. A deficit of thirty-four million dollars in 1941 had been transformed into a surplus of thirty-five million dollars, but the quality of state services had declined substantially in the process.[76]

Only two years after Stevenson left the governorship, the state was forced to deal with neglected schools, hospitals, and institutions for the mentally ill. During the conservative dominance begun in the early modern period of the speakership, pennies were pinched, but at a terrible cost to the state, leaving it unprepared for post–World War II realities. In contrast, the Great Depression, the New Deal, and World War II laid the groundwork for higher expectations of the state government by Texans in the postwar era.

CHAPTER 4

Pragmatic Conservatism:
The Dynastic Speakership, Part One

1949–1961

Reuben Senterfitt never considered himself a New Dealer. Speaker of the Texas House from 1951 to 1955, Senterfitt recalls when, during the worst of the Great Depression, agents from President Franklin Roosevelt's Agricultural Adjustment Administration went to his father's San Saba County ranch in Central Texas. Worried about collapsing prices for farm products, the AAA decided to raise prices by reducing supply. In 1933, the AAA bought and slaughtered 8.5 million pigs, destroying much of the meat in order to force prices upward. The AAA also destroyed cattle. The program proved to be one of the most controversial pursued by the administration. As Senterfitt recalled in a 2004 interview: "You know, when I was in high school, they came to my dad's place, and they had people out there shooting cattle, killing them. And it looked like to me there was a better way to get our economy back in order . . . It just struck me wrong . . . They felt [it] would help the economy get back in order because . . . we were oversupplied with livestock . . . And they thought it would . . . send the prices back up and maybe help the farmers and ranchers."[1]

Senterfitt described himself as "very conservative minded." He believed social welfare programs promote dependency. "Being conservative reminds me of my ranch out here," Senterfitt said. "You can go out there and you can start feeding your cows . . . If you don't feed them good enough, they are going to sit there and starve to death because they are going to wait on you to bring them some more feed. And I think people are a whole lot like that."[2] Nevertheless, he still acknowledges the important difference some New Deal programs made in the lives of his San Saba County neighbors. The region grew prosperous from New Deal–era flood control. Federal aid to local improvement projects, especially those that fostered commerce, found favor among many local and state officials. These projects heralded a previously unheard-of level of investment in the public sector. After World War II, the forces of change, coupled with growing prosperity, would create a profound social and political metamorphosis in Texas and the rest of the South.

As historian Sarah T. Phillips notes, for "much of its history the Hill Country [in Central Texas] remained isolated, an unforgiving landscape of poor land and even poorer farmers." After cattle overgrazed, exposing the region's thin topsoil to the wind, "heat and drought scorched the bare earth, and streams dried to a trickle. Flash floods carved gullies into the hillsides and washed away the land's illusive fertility . . . Hill Country residents lapsed into a marginal existence." Four major floods originating in the central Edwards Plateau swallowed the region's "steep slopes, canyons, and shallow, nonporous soils" in the first two and a half decades of the twentieth century.[3] In 1931, the Emery-Peck and Rockwood Development Company began developing a dam in Llano County, but the company's bankruptcy the following year stalled the project.[4]

Congressman James Paul Buchanan won federal funds to restart construction on the dam in 1934. To match the much-needed dollars from Washington and to manage the project, the Texas Legislature in 1935 authorized the creation of the Lower Colorado River Authority (LCRA). Crews completed the project, now called Buchanan Dam, in October 1937. Construction of public parks commenced along the Colorado River and the Highland Lakes above Austin. Fish and game were supplied in the new parks and surrounding public lands, making the area a profitable recreational attraction. After Buchanan died and was succeeded in Congress by Lyndon Johnson, the enthusiastic New Dealer won a continuing stream of federal funds for economic development in Central Texas.[5]

Sophisticated construction projects didn't completely eradicate the ravages of nature, as Reuben Senterfitt and his family witnessed in 1938. That year saw the worst flooding in Central Texas in more than a century as ten days of relentless storms swelled the Colorado River to forty-two feet above normal. Water covered parts of Austin for three days; downstream, homes, livestock, and the year's crops were swept away. Twelve people died in the storm, and more than 4,000 people were left homeless. The flash flood overwhelmed the Buchanan and Inks dams, the only two operating in the area, partly because operators failed to correctly manage reservoir levels and did not lower lake levels in preparation for the onslaught.[6] Senterfitt was in his early twenties at the time of the 1938 flood.

Our house was on the bank of the river. My dad and I took my younger brother and my mother out to our sister's place . . . and we stayed in the house until the water got up in the floor of the house, and we were stacking furniture on top of the dining tables and it was really a mess.

It finally got into the ceiling. We know exactly the time it hit the clock on the mantel, because that's when it stopped . . . Then . . . we took a rowboat and paddled over to a railroad . . . The whole house was submerged. We had to even put some of my mother's chickens on the back porch, and, of course, they drowned.[7]

Senterfitt admitted that San Saba County benefited richly from federal dam- and lake-building programs. "It boosted the tourist trade and business," Senterfitt said. "I had a partner, and he and I put in two subdivisions on Lake LBJ, and sold lots off them." The New Deal influenced conservatives like Senterfitt in subtle ways. Texas prospered because of Roosevelt's social spending in the 1930s, the stimulative effects of federal defense spending in the 1940s, and the money and access to homes and colleges put in the hands of former soldiers in the late 1940s and early 1950s. This expansion of federal responsibility into people's daily lives greatly altered the public's expectations of government.

Senterfitt edited the *Texas Law Review* as a student at the University of Texas law school. He first won election to the Texas House of Representatives in 1941, and from the start Senterfitt was not a Coke Stevenson–style conservative. In his freshman term, he authored the bill that created the M. D. Anderson Hospital in Houston, which became Texas's premiere cancer research center. Cancer research, Senterfitt determined, "needed to be state supported." He later sponsored the Veterans' Land Bill for returning World War II soldiers and helped lead the fight for the Gilmer-Aikin education reforms, which will be explored in greater detail later.[8] All these programs meant higher taxes and a bigger government, but also delivered significant services to Texas taxpayers. From a political standpoint, these programs proved popular with the public and boosted Senterfitt's standing as a pragmatic elected official.

Like earlier Progressives, many conservative leaders in Texas during the mid-twentieth century, such as Senterfitt, recognized that the state and federal governments had a positive role to play in creating a vibrant business environment. Unlike Stevenson and O'Daniel, conservatives such as Senterfitt acknowledged that social services can enlarge the class of active consumers, whose spending drives the American economy. In any case, by the late 1940s and early 1950s, state government had reached a crisis point. The part-time, amateur ethic that had pervaded both elected and appointed offices since the beginning of statehood no longer proved adequate to the task of managing a booming, complex economy. State government expanded, and as it grew, Speakers gained more control of the political process. Speakers began running for reelection and then extending their influence past their legislative careers by mentoring legislators handpicked as their successors.

By the late 1940s, it was obvious to many that the legislature had not kept up with Texas's dramatic economic changes. Whereas oil production was a major engine of the Texas economy in the first half of the twentieth century, manufacturing would eclipse it after World War II. The war brought about the birth of the petrochemical industry along the Texas Gulf Coast, the development of steel mills in Houston and Daingerfield, tin smelting in Texas City, and wood pulping in East Texas. Meanwhile, shipyards in Port Arthur, Beaumont, Galveston, and Corpus Christi cranked out vessels for the naval fleet, and plants in Garland, Grand Prairie, and Fort Worth manufactured aircraft. Banking and financial services expanded in Dallas, Houston, San Antonio, and the other major metropolitan areas. Between 1945 and 1974, the number of farms dropped by more than half. The 1950 census showed that for the first time in the state's 114-year history, most Texans (60 percent) lived in towns or cities populated by 2,500 or more residents. Houston's population had more than doubled since 1940, and three Texas cities (Houston, Dallas, and San Antonio) were nearing the half-million mark. By 1947, the state had 7,128 manufacturing plants, which added almost $2 billion in value to the materials they converted into finished products.[9]

Texas became a magnet for immigration, drawing workers from across the United States and from Mexico. By 1947, Mexican Americans for the first time became the second-largest population group, ahead of African Americans and behind Anglos. More than a million new Texans came from outside the South. Texas's demographic and industrial growth strained the state's primitive infrastructure, including its transportation networks, schools, universities, and health care systems. And the legislature found itself unprepared for the new Texas realities. "The Depression and the war caused kind of a lull in the development of your state government history," Senterfitt said. "When I [first] went to the legislature [in 1941], it was . . . just trying to scrape by and . . . save as much as you can."[10]

The benefits of economic growth were spread unequally through the state's population. The gap between rich and poor expanded in the 1950s and the 1960s. By 1970, the Texas Office of Economic Opportunity reported that 2 million Texans had less than $3 a day to meet physical needs, giving the state a poverty rate of 18 percent, the twelfth highest in the nation. Thirty-nine percent of African Americans lived in poverty, as well as 36 percent of Mexican Americans and 10 percent of Anglos. An astounding 47 percent of the residents in heavily Hispanic South Texas lived in poverty.[11] In spite of the traditional pattern of limited public services, a consensus developed in the Texas House beginning in the late 1940s that the state government would have to grow along with the economy. Much of the pressure came from constituents. As the authors of *Texas: The Lone Star State* put it: "Farmers protested that they were not sharing fairly in the general abundance and called for greater freedom in their farming practices or for more controls, as their interest and points of view varied . . . There were pleas, fervent and often repeated, for better care of children; the advocates for the needy aged were not satisfied with the level of aid accorded them, and those with disabilities had their champions."[12]

The need for fundamental reform reached a crisis point, almost overwhelming the legislature in 1949, a year that saw the longest session in state history (lasting from January 11 to July 6). In almost seven months of debate and negotiation, the legislature modernized prisons, improved oversight of mental health–care facilities through the creation of the Board for Texas State Hospitals and Special Schools, and provided more care for disabled children. Most importantly, the legislature revamped a public education system that had changed little since the turn of the century. By the late 1940s, Texas schools still moved to agricultural rhythms. The state required only a high school education for its teachers, who toiled in often-dilapidated schools that shut down when it was time to plant crops or gather the harvest. "We had the worst educational system . . . that you could possibly have," said Senterfitt.[13]

Speaker Gilmer

After the legislature deadlocked in 1947 over a minimum-salary law for Texas public school teachers, the House and Senate named a committee to study how to improve the efficiency and funding of the public schools. The committee's recommendations, largely drawn up by state senator A. M. Aikin of Paris and state representative Claud Gilmer of Rocksprings, came before the Fifty-first Legislature in 1949.

Born in Rocksprings in 1901, Gilmer taught and worked as a high school principal in his hometown before winning election as county judge of Edwards County in 1924. He received his law license in 1929, and ran to fill Coke Stevenson's vacated House seat when the latter successfully ran for lieutenant governor in 1938. Gilmer served as House Speaker during the first postwar session of the legislature, from 1945 to 1947. As Speaker, he earned notice as an orderly mechanic of the legislative process. Gilmer ran the House with a firm hand. Quick to rap the gavel, he still proved fair in giving members time to address the House.[14]

Gilmer's fame came as a House member in the 1947–1948 session. It was during this term that Gilmer authored the pay-as-you-go amendment to the state constitution and began the restructuring of state education. The Gilmer-Aikin laws replaced the elected superintendent of public instruction and the appointed nine-person State Board of Education with a twenty-one-member elected board that had the power to appoint a state commissioner. The laws reduced administrative costs by consolidating 6,409 Texas school districts into 1,539 by 1960. The era of the one-room schoolhouse had ended. Under the reforms, the school year was extended to nine months and all students were guaranteed 175 instruction days. The legislature allocated state money to equalize funding across districts, raised teacher salaries, and provided incentives for additional teacher training. Under the new laws, teachers with a bachelor's degree would be paid a minimum of $3,204 a year (about $25,000 a year in today's dollars), with a bonus of $72 per year (about $571 in today's dollars) for each year of teaching experience.[15]

The education community, accustomed to much-needed reforms being rejected, remained wary of the highly conservative members of the Gilmer-Aikin committee.[16] Teacher opposition receded when the committee asked the state's leading teacher association to help write the legislation. Reformers, however, faced persistent opposition from State Superintendent L. A. Woods. Gilmer later said that he pushed for replacing the nine-term Woods with an appointed commissioner because Woods had turned the office into a private fiefdom, dispensing public school money as a gift to his allies and shutting out his opponents. The legislature had only recently created the position of state auditor, meaning that Woods's use of tax dollars had been going unexamined.[17] Senterfitt said that Woods was a formidable opponent: "L. A. Woods had all the county superintendents in Texas behind him because he was . . . just a complete political machine. Whoever patted him on the back always got the money."[18]

Gilmer had not run for reelection, so when the Fifty-first Legislature convened, he would no longer be chair of the House Appropriations Committee. In another complication, proreform forces faced an uncertain ally in the incoming Speaker, Durwood Manford. Nevertheless, Gilmer's close work with Manford during the education-reform battle established an important precedent for later Speakers who would extend their influence beyond their tenure as presiding officer by carefully mentoring their successors.

Speaker Manford

The scion of a wealthy ranching family from Smiley, in Gonzales County, Manford earned a law degree from the University of Texas and first won election to the Texas House in 1940 at the age of twenty-three. In 1943, Manford authored one of the most reactionary antiunion laws in the country. The Manford Bill, which was passed by an 86–37 vote in the House and a 16–7 vote in the Senate, required labor organizers to register with the state and carry identification cards. The law banned unions from making political contributions and required them to file extensive financial and organizational records. Even the archconservative governor Coke Stevenson blanched, choosing to let the Manford bill become law without his signature.[19]

Manford quickly became known as an obsessive backer of rural road construction, almost to the exclusion of everything else. Gilmer later recalled, however, that the apparent disadvantage of a Manford speakership could be turned to the reformers' advantage. "One thing helped me pass it (the education reforms): Durwood Manford . . . was a real good friend of mine," Gilmer said. "In fact, I had advised him a little . . . Durwood wanted to run for speaker, and having been there as long as I had been, if you're going to learn anything, you do it as a result of experience. So I advised him on how to go about it and so forth. He was elected, and he was speaker when these bills came up. He wasn't enthusiastic about them at all, but I was able to get him to cooperate."[20]

Gilmer's relationship with Manford set the pattern for the dynastic speakership era, when Speakers carefully prepared allies to take the reins. Gilmer observed that Manford was "tight-fisted" and mistrusted the Gilmer-Aikin proposals as "a new far-out thing." But at Gilmer's urging, Manford backed the bills in a crowded session.[21]

For much of his speakership (1949–1951), one could question whether Manford's lukewarm support represented a blessing or a curse. No Claud Gilmer, Manford led a session that became known for its painfully slow pace and for several near rebellions among House members. For the previous fourteen years, Speakers had sewn up the office before the legislative session's opening day. Manford had to fight for the speakership after the opening gavel in a bitter race against Joe Kilgore of McAllen. Kilgore conceded the race when the vote reached a 73–20 margin in favor of Manford, but rancor permeated the whole session. It began January 11, 1949, but the House wasted three weeks because Manford did not finish appointing committee chairs until February 1.[22]

Many members grumbled about the committee selections, and union-backed members particularly protested against the antiworker bias of the House's new Labor Committee.[23] Manford announced his committee assignments on a Tuesday. Members expected to introduce bills the next day; instead, Manford insisted that they be filed with the chief clerk immediately so that they could be assigned to appropriate committees the following day. The House was instructed to stand at ease while this process took place over the next hour and a half. Bored members spent the downtime on such pressing business as debating a resolution, put forward by Lamar Zively of Temple, requesting that Texans arm themselves with baseball bats in order to keep groundhogs from emerging aboveground, and taking roll-call votes of legislators who had graduated from Texas A&M, the University of Texas, Baylor, the Metropolitan Business College, etc. The *Austin American* reported that the wasted day cost the taxpayers $1,500 in House members' salaries. On February 17, it took the House two hours to approve a motion to adjourn for the weekend.[24] "Durwood was a dear fellow," recalled former House representative Jim Lindsey, who would become Speaker himself in the mid-1950s. "[But] he would procrastinate. He would sit back sometimes and he'd just wear the lieutenant governor out and so on."[25]

A bill allowing rural telephone cooperatives to receive federal aid resulted in a continuous twenty-three-hour, six-minute debate, at that time the second longest in House history. During the debate, which began on Friday, February 25, 1950, Manford ordered the chamber doors locked, and posted state highway patrolmen to prevent members from escaping. Some left the House by climbing out of windows during the night and "catwalking along the 2-foot wide granite ledge twenty feet above the ground, trying to find an open window in some other part of the Capitol."[26] Knowing this, Mrs. Durwood Manford did not become alarmed when she awoke during the night and saw a House member walking along the ledge outside the Speaker's second-floor apartment. Manford issued arrest warrants for errant members, ordering them back to the House chamber so a quorum could be maintained. As the debate dragged on through Friday night, the lockdown forced Representative Jim Sparks to spend his wedding anniversary in the chamber. Lawmakers did not break the logjam until just after 1 p.m. on Saturday. Members predicted that the House would be unable to work through the legislative calendar and would need a special session to finish its job.[27] As the session passed the 120-day mark, the state constitution required that members' daily pay be slashed from $10 to $5, yet still the session dragged on.[28]

Animosity probably intensified during the session because of ugliness surrounding the Gilmer-Aikin proposals. "It was a completely new program, a revolutionary thing," Gilmer said. "It was going to cost a whole lot of money . . . If you don't see a personal need for it that had been manifest in your district, what are you going to do? You're going to be against it."[29] During a hearing on the bills held February 8, 1949, Gilmer-Aikin opponents resorted to racial demagoguery. Yoakum school superintendent George P. Barron expressed anger that the teacher-pay-raise provisions might result in some African American educators being paid as much or more than their white peers: "I'm one of those old degreeless boys who has been working like the devil for 30 years and trying to run a public school system, with very little time to go to school—I'll get the sum of $4,500.00 while my Negro vocational teacher, whom I employed for $2,200 will draw down $5,376.00. A lot of inequities are there that you should look into."[30]

Barron's ironic claim of inequity aside, black educators at the time worked in segregated schools and received poor training from the few, always underfunded, state-supported teacher schools open to blacks in Texas. Black and white teachers experienced a wide wage disparity: the average white teacher earned $1,900 a year, whereas the average African American teacher made $1,200 annually ($15,000 and $9,500 in 2005 dollars, respectively). George Nokes, a comanager of the Gilmer-Aikin bills, would later acknowledge the historic significance this bill had for the African American community in Texas.

The Gilmer-Aikin bill was five years before *Brown v. the Board of Education* [a 1954 Supreme Court decision that ruled public school segregation violated the U.S. Constitution] and was easily ten years before there was even any significant desegregation of Texas schools. It was the first time that the state law required that black teachers in the then still segregated schools be paid on the same salary schedule. While Gilmer-Aikin was a significant increase in the pay for white teachers, it was a doubling in some cases of salaries for black teachers, and it greatly impacted the ability to attract more qualified teachers in the Negro schools. Of the relatively small number of black voters in the state [in the 1940s] a heavily disproportionate share of them were teachers. And they were all very careful to not make that a major issue. This pay change helped build grassroots support for Gilmer-Aikin, but it was way below most folks' radar screen at the time.[31]

Gilmer-Aikin opponents gave up on winning in the Senate and focused their lobbying efforts on the House. Woods, the state superintendent, took out newspaper ads, wrote letters to county superintendents, and appeared on half-hour radio roundtable discussions featuring fellow anti-reform leaders. Woods cautioned rural parents that their school districts would be closed and consolidated with larger districts.[32] Joe T. Steadham, chair of the Texas Joint Railway Legislative Board, darkly suggested that Gilmer-Aikin stood as

> one of the first approaches of Fascism . . . And if you will take time to go to the library and read how Hitler long before managed to take over the educational system of Germany, in order that his Fascist ideas would hold first place in the teaching of school children . . . you will observe the similarity of Senate Bill 115.
> . . . I can also see the Wall Street group who control the natural resources of our State, in a scheme to save a hundred million dollars a year in taxes, and pass this burden on to the local rural communities.[33]

The three Senate education bills, labeled emergency measures by Governor Beauford Jester, moved to the top of the chamber's agenda and passed by heavy margins. Manford, meanwhile, to make good on his promises to support Gilmer-Aikin, appointed a reform-friendly House Education Committee. In a break with tradition, Manford reappointed Gilmer-Aikin promoter Rae Files Still to another term as Education Committee chair. After an all-night hearing on the Senate bills on March 16, 1949, the House committee voted 17–2 to favorably report the bills, with minor amendments attached, to the full House.[34]

Opponents relied on delaying tactics to stall Gilmer-Aikin, including a walkout of opponents led by Representative Sam Hanna of Dallas, a tactic intended to prevent a quorum from being reached.[35] When a head count showed the House fell seven votes short of a quorum, Manford ordered the House locked down again while state troopers gathered another twenty-two members. With more than enough members present to provide a quorum, the walkout backfired. The state constitution requires a reading of the bills on the House floor on three separate days, and it takes a four-fifths vote to suspend that rule. Because of the walkout, the House members in attendance were disproportionately in favor of the three Gilmer-Aikin bills. The House voted to suspend the rules, and then passed the first of the education bills by an 85–30 margin. With the opposition demoralized, the House passed the other two parts of the Gilmer-Aikin reform package by April 28, 1949. After both houses of the legislature passed the conference-committee versions of the bills, Governor Jester signed the three parts of the Gilmer-Aikin laws on June 1 and June 8, 1949.[36]

The dramatic change in the fortunes of Texas public education set a precedent for many other southern states, which in the 1950s began devoting more resources to improving their public schools. As an example, with the passage of the Gilmer-Aikin law, per-pupil annual expenditures in Texas rose to $208.88, a few cents above the national average.[37]

Passage of Gilmer-Aikin marked the high point of the Fifty-first Legislature, which also created more agencies—including the newly elective State Board of Education, the Youth Development Council for the administration of juvenile facilities, and the Sabine River Authority—than any of its predecessors. Additionally, the legislature created a new medical branch for the University of Texas and boards to govern Lamar College and North Texas State College. Combined, when various federal grants are added in, the legislature that year appropriated $1 billion in spending for the biennium, the first time the state reached that landmark. However, the legislature declined to raise enough revenues to pay for the increased expenses, leaving the state $58 million in the red. The situation worsened when the Texas Railroad Commission mandated cuts in oil production, which resulted in a further $22 million state-budget shortfall. Governor Jester vetoed the second year of funding for state hospitals and special schools in order to balance the budget.[38]

Caring for the Most Vulnerable

Jester died suddenly from a heart attack while riding in a passenger train on July 11, 1949.[39] It fell to Lieutenant Governor Allan Shivers to call a special session to address funding for state hospitals and special schools. The highly conservative Shivers still recognized the need to improve conditions at the state hospitals, famously saying that Texas was "first in oil, forty-eighth in mental hospitals; first in cotton, worst in tuberculosis; first in raising goats, last in caring for state wards."[40]

The results of Coke Stevenson's earlier draconian fiscal policies were clearest at the state's mental institutions. In 1941, the state housed 1,000 mental patients in jails because of a lack of hospital space. "The State Board of Control set about to clean up this shameful condition with the tools at hand," the *Austin American-Statesman* reported. "The mentally ill were removed from jails and stacked in double-deck beds. When there were not enough of these to go around, porches, basements and halls were utilized. When that emergency space ran out, pallets and mattresses were spread on the floor."[41]

Eight years later, by the time of Manford's speakership, in the state's six mental institutions and one whites-only epileptic hospital, the *American* said, one could find a "doctor at Austin treating 400 patients daily, the ward attendant at San Antonio putting patients to sleep on floors when beds are lacking, or the cook at Terrell feeding a patient for 3 cents a day." One doctor complained to the *American* that Texas's mental health care system had "degenerated into . . . penitentiaries and an old folks home." At the hospital in Big Spring, doctors crammed patients into "teeming cages." Patients were kept under "lock and key because there are not enough guards." Facilities simply warehoused the mentally ill to keep them off the streets.[42] At the epileptic ward in San Antonio, the fifty-six patients slept on "straw mattresses soaked in human filth," walked on "a bare cement floor sticky with saliva," and viewed the world through barred windows.[43]

Because of limited space in the Austin State Hospital, patients were forced to watch their peers undergo electroshock therapy, sometimes before they received such treatment themselves, and to see the violent contortions such patients undergo.[44] Such treatments were grueling to patients and doctors alike. Experienced psychiatrists and attendants became ill watching the seizures electroshock patients underwent, *American* reporter J. P. Porter noted. "It is possible that the mental stress occasioned by witnessing the shock can be so harmful that it will outweigh any beneficial results of therapy."[45]

A nineteen-year veteran supervisor at one ward suggested that "the jails might not be so bad [for the inmates]. At least the patients would get a bed, two decent meals a day, and individual attention. Patients are lucky here if they get one of the three."[46] Allan Shivers tapped Claud Gilmer to head the new State Board of Hospitals and Special Schools, and Gilmer put together a package of "temporary" taxes that quietly became permanent revenue streams to pay for upgrading the primitive mental-health-care system. The state raised business taxes and hiked cigarette taxes by 1 percent. Shivers made an emotional appeal for the legislation.[47]

"I have seen epileptics eating in bathrooms for lack of dining space," the new governor said. "I saw 77 aged and mentally ill women locked up in a condemned building. I saw 400 mentally defective children and 800 seniles housed in prisoner-of-war shacks, constructed mostly of plywood and tarpaper. I saw dilapidated non-fireproof buildings without fire escapes, with hundreds of mentally ill persons locked in them."[48] It took just twenty days of the thirty-day special session for the legislature to impose a 10 percent increase in business taxes in addition to the added levy on cigarettes. The Gilmer-Aikin laws and the new state commission for mental health marked Texas's first serious effort since Reconstruction to take responsibility for attending to the needs of its most vulnerable citizens.[49]

The reform efforts of 1949 shared a common fatal flaw. The state House refused to tax wealth and instead depended on revenues from sales and other regressive taxes that hit lower-income people hardest. The 1949 legislature did not come close to providing adequate funding for education or for mental health care. Jimmy Turman, a native of the East Texas town of Gober and a future House Speaker, first won a seat in the Texas House in 1954. Named to the Appropriations Committee, Turman traveled with other members of the subcommittee assigned to oversee Texas's eleemosynary institutions, including mental health hospitals. In a March 23, 2004, interview, Turman recalled the horror he felt at the conditions he saw in 1955: "I went to the State School in Austin there on Guadalupe [Street] . . . They had 200 men in one room. They were hosing them off. They were mental patients, they'd lost their capacities, and there they were in cages . . . People . . . working there . . . were paid . . . around $1,900 a year [for] their basic salary [about $12,700 to $13,400, in today's dollars] . . . I couldn't help them any other way, except . . . better salaries for those."[50]

Governor Shivers

Whatever the shortcomings of the Fifty-first Legislature, there emerged three stars who would set the tone at the statehouse in the 1950s. Governor Shivers quickly displayed a mastery of realpolitik shared by so many conservatives of the 1950s. He cultivated establishment support for increased expenditures on education, old-age pensions, and other progressive programs, but he avoided taxing energy companies' exploding profits. At the same time, he shifted the tax burden to consumers, particularly through cigarette taxes. It was not until after the Supreme Court's decision in *Brown v. Board of Education* (1954) that Shivers joined other southern governors and legislators in what became known as the "massive resistance" movement to the integration of public schools. His decision to support segregation also led to his alienation from other social and economic reforms during his later years as governor. Furthermore, Shivers seized the segregation issue to counter rising criticism of corruption within his administration, lack of action against the prolonged drought gripping the state, and his decision to run for an unprecedented third term as governor in his own right.[51]

If Allan Shivers emerged from that decade as the erratic center of gravity in Texas politics, Speaker Senterfitt and his successor, Jim Lindsey, arose as the steady polestars, translating the charismatic governor's ideas into less showy reality. "Senterfitt . . . owed most of his political success to Shivers [and] tended to defer to the governor," Ricky F. Dobbs argues in his recent biography of Shivers. But the relationship was more complex, and Senterfitt played a critical leadership role. Senterfitt and Shivers almost always agreed on issues, but the Speaker from San Saba was more than willing to take the initiative if the volatile Shivers was in an impractical or distracted mood. By 1954, this had become more frequent as scandals rocked Shivers's administration.[52]

Jim Lindsey also kept busy during the 1949–1951 session. Born on a Bowie County farm near Boston, the county seat, Lindsey served in the U.S. Army Air Corps during World War II before enrolling in Baylor University, where he graduated with a law degree in 1950. Before earning his diploma, however, Lindsey was elected to the legislature in 1948. Preston Smith, a House member who later served as governor, took Lindsey under his wing and introduced him to Senterfitt, who was already Manford's heir apparent. While Senterfitt apprenticed under Manford, Lindsey apprenticed under Senterfitt. As Lindsey later recalled, "I remember sitting there one day at my desk, when Preston [Smith] . . . came over to me and he sat down. He said, 'Jim, I think someday you may get to be speaker. I want you to go over and meet with Reuben Senterfitt, who's going to be our next speaker.' . . . So I did that, and I signed up with Reuben that day . . . early on . . . and began . . . [to] cut my teeth on the Gilmer-Aikin bill, by . . . not handling it on microphone but on [the] floor . . . desk to desk."[53]

Not headline grabbers by nature, neither Senterfitt nor Lindsey fought to share the limelight with Shivers. Senterfitt had little of Shivers's charisma, but had a wry, self-deprecating sense of humor. Once, Manford joked that Senterfitt could not serve as his successor because the state constitution required that the post be filled by "qualified" members. Senterfitt drawled back, "Oh, that's all changed. You set the precedent that a Speaker doesn't have to be qualified."[54] Though not flashy, Senterfitt nevertheless changed the speakership more than any of his more colorful predecessors. Before Senterfitt, Speakers generally made news only when they won the post and when House members threw a big party to say good-bye at the end of their single term. Beginning with Senterfitt, the press began to notice the House Speaker as a figure who directly shaped policy. Reporters asked Senterfitt about his views on the budget and on what the state's priorities should be. A symbiotic relationship evolved as Speakers, starting with Senterfitt, began to actively use the media as a tool for advancing their legislative priorities.[55]

Speaker Senterfitt

Senterfitt and Lindsey were left to clean up much unfinished business, even after the productive previous session (1949–1951). Senterfitt ran unopposed for Speaker at the start of the 1951–1953 session. He immediately signaled a shift from the slow and indecisive leadership of Manford, announcing his committee assignments the afternoon he won the speakership, a pace the *Dallas Morning News* termed a speed "record."[56]

Controversy arose over Senterfitt's alleged stacking of the Appropriations Committee with rural representatives, hinting at one of the most divisive issues he faced. In 1921, the legislature established the maximum size of the House at 150 members. The legislature, however, failed to redistrict state House and Senate districts in 1931 or 1941. The state had grown increasingly urban, provoking a political crisis. The state constitution at that time limited urban areas with 700,000 people to a maximum of seven House representatives. Another representative could be added only when the city gained an additional 100,000 residents. Rural districts, meanwhile, were grossly overrepresented in the late 1940s. Based on the Texas Constitution, there was one representative in the state House for every 45,000 constituents in nonurban areas. East Texas was the most overrepresented part of the state. There, six House members represented Red River, Titus, Morris, Camp, Upshur, Henderson, and Van Zandt counties, a ratio of one House member for every 24,166 people, as opposed to the 1 to 100,000 ratio in places like Dallas and Houston. The situation was even worse in heavily Mexican American South Texas, where Senator Rogers Kelley of Edinburg served as the lone voice in the upper house for eighteen counties with a population of almost 800,000.[57]

Texas voters signaled impatience with unfair representation in the legislature by approving a constitutional amendment in 1950 that created the Texas Legislative Redistricting Board (LRB). Under the provision, if the legislature failed to redistrict in its first regular session following the release of the decennial federal census, then the LRB would meet and file redistricting plans with the Texas secretary of state. The LRB consists of five members: the lieutenant governor, the Speaker of the House, the attorney general, the comptroller of public accounts, and the commissioner of the General Land Office. If the LRB failed to agree on a redistricting map, then the Texas Supreme Court would be empowered to force board action. Members of the Fifty-second Legislature, loath to hand their political futures to the LRB or the courts, moved quickly to resolve the redistricting crisis.[58]

In 1951, Senterfitt appointed a House redistricting committee dominated by rural members. The newly drawn state House districts still provided only one House representative for every 87,000 voters in Dallas, while representatives in rural areas represented between 30,000 and 70,000 voters. The legislature also left a number of legislative seats to be elected at-large. Under this system, a county with two or more House seats could set up multidistrict "superdistricts" to elect representatives at-large. Voters in such districts could thus cast ballots in more than one House race. This forced candidates in superdistricts to campaign countywide. This system, not ruled unconstitutional until the 1960s, gave an advantage to wealthier candidates and continued to dilute already-suppressed minority voting strength.[59]

As always, state finances emerged as the most contentious issue. Here, Senterfitt established the House Speaker as an equal player with the governor and lieutenant governor. Ironically, it was up to conservative Senterfitt to argue that tax increases would be needed to balance the budget. Senterfitt felt that getting state finances straightened out would be impossible unless a unified budget was adopted. Although Coke Stevenson had drafted legislation in the 1930s to establish the office of state auditor, in the late 1940s the state budget process remained in chaos. Budgets for large departments were drawn up independently, and no one had a complete picture of the total appropriations until the individual spending bills were added up. That meant the state then had to work backward to balance the books. In 1951, without any support from Shivers or Lieutenant Governor

Ben Ramsey, Senterfitt successfully pushed for a unified budget bill.[60] As he later recalled: "I went to Governor Shivers and I went to Ben Ramsey, the lieutenant governor, . . . and told them . . . that I was going to try to establish a . . . budget system for Texas. And I got my [appropriations] chairman [Henry Rampy of Winters], and we had a press conference to come up with a new precedent, and the governor and lieutenant governor finally joined me."[61]

It would have previously been unthinkable for a Speaker to publicly take the lead in the budget process as Senterfitt did in 1951. The state, Senterfitt told the Capitol press, faced a $107 million shortfall. "The probable deficit is one of the most urgent problems facing the Texas Legislature," Senterfitt said at a press appearance that February. "In one way or another, solving the deficit problem will affect directly every citizen in Texas. He will be asked to do without some state services, or to pay more taxes, or to do some of both."[62] Senterfitt made it clear that he felt both approaches would be necessary.

In the past, Speakers rose to the leadership post almost solely on collegiality. Most avoided writing bills or stepping out in front on controversial issues. This tradition changed under Senterfitt when he named the man he groomed as his successor, Jim Lindsey, chair of the critical Revenue and Taxation Committee. This meant that Lindsey had to present a contentious set of tax proposals before the House. Lindsey discovered how hard it could be to enjoy political power and have a private life as well.

> The Revenue and Taxation Committee . . . was obviously going to be *the* committee for that session, because, unfortunately, being conservative [means that] you don't like to vote for taxes . . . But we . . . had to have the money . . . because we were on a pay-as-you-go [basis]. . . .
>
> The day my oldest daughter was born was the day . . . it had to be passed in the House. So I stayed there, and [my wife] Moja was in the hospital in Texarkana . . . And I got the bill passed about 2:30, I think. And went down to catch the train and rode—and I did my pacing on the train, on the way home. Got home, got to Texarkana, and my daughter had had a very difficult time with . . . being born . . . Moja was strong . . . And, so [my baby] made it. Her little head was all pressed out of shape. But that was . . . the day we passed the tax bill that session.[63]

Lindsey began handling many of the Speaker's duties during Senterfitt's second term. Senterfitt reluctantly accepted the post again after being drafted by men like Lindsey.[64] The San Saba representative drew no opponents, but he was already thinking about the 1956 gubernatorial campaign. Lindsey, who served as vice chair of the Legislative Audit Committee, the Legislative Budget Board, and the Texas Legislative Council during his career in the House, gathered much on-the-job training during the 1953–1955 term: "I began having meetings in his [Senterfitt's] office. I would send him to the theater or something with his family, and I would take everybody that was . . . on our team . . . into the office and sit there and we'd talk, and we spent four nights . . . and four days. I slept about ten minutes a day those four days . . . So persistence—hard work's the only way I've got anyplace."[65]

Speaker Lindsey

Lindsey wielded considerable power when he became Speaker, though he did so with a staff of only two secretaries and a volunteer parliamentarian. During the 1955–1957 term, Lindsey presided over the first overhaul of the Texas business-corporation laws since the 1870s as well as a revision of the Texas probate code. As in Senterfitt's term, while Governor Shivers felt free to grandstand on issues like the state budget, Lindsey had to ground policy in cold reality.[66]

In 1956, Shivers predicted that the Suez crisis—in which Egyptian president Gamal Abdel Nasser nationalized the Suez Canal Company, which had been controlled jointly by the British and the French, and thereby provoked a brief military response that threatened to, but ultimately didn't, lead to war—would reduce the supply of oil from Arab nations and increase purchases of Texas oil. Shivers suggested there would be no need for additional taxes and predicted a budget surplus for the upcoming biennium. Noting that projected spending for the 1956–1958 period was already $26 million above anticipated revenues, Lindsey sharply disagreed with Shivers, telling the press that it was "unfair to the men and women who will be serving in the 55th legislature to create the impression that the British, French, Russians, Egyptians and Israelis can solve all the financial problems of the state next year. On the contrary, the Legislature's job will be one of the most difficult and unsettled to face any session since the end of World War II."[67]

Rayford Price, who first won election to the state House in 1961 and became Speaker eleven years later, suggested that Texas at midcentury depended too heavily on oil. "Oil had carried the state for many years, but the economy was changing, and you needed to draw from your tax base," Price said in a 2004 interview.[68] As oil and agriculture declined in importance, however, and the state's chief resources became financial and intellectual capital, the political establishment failed to make the transition, leaving institutions like public schools, colleges, and hospitals perpetually shortchanged.

Significantly for the speakership, in 1955 Shivers won a third term in his own right as governor, but scandals involving the state's insurance industry and the veterans' land program quickly overwhelmed his administration.[69] Shivers became not just a lame duck, but also a severely wounded one, during his last two years in office. His decline meant an increase in power for Lindsey. No Texas governor had enjoyed the power held by Shivers until these scandals tarnished his golden touch. Even with the influential Shivers as governor, however, Speakers Senterfitt and Lindsey dramatically increased the power and prestige of their office in relation to the executive. They placed their stamp on the budget process, creating the unified budget system and, as Shivers grew more distracted in his last term, taking the reins on the contentious issue of taxes. While Shivers showboated and publicly dreamed about unanticipated tax windfalls from the volatile world oil market, Senterfitt and Lindsey were left with the pedestrian but more important duty of identifying where to cut the budget and how to increase state revenues.

Speaker Carr

Waggoner Carr of Lubbock ended the Manford-Senterfitt-Lindsey dynasty in 1957. Carr, born in Hunt County in East Texas and, like Lindsey, a veteran of the Army Air Corps during World War II, unsuccessfully opposed Lindsey's 1955–1957 speakership bid.[70] Carr, however, won in 1957 and 1959 in two extremely close races. Known as an entertaining and riveting speaker, Carr campaigned energetically throughout his career, zooming from one speaking engagement to another in a private airplane. In a 2004 interview, Carr's son David recalled campaigning with his father: "By the time I was born, he was [a politician] . . . So really [the] beginning of my life was when he was campaigning. My first memory . . . is having my diapers changed in the back of a Supercub, flying in a sandstorm in Lubbock, somewhere in West Texas, laughing while my mother was trying to change my diapers."[71]

Like Billy Clayton, a West Texan who later occupied the speakership,

Waggoner Carr made a priority of creating a state water plan to aid his parched home region. The extended drought of the 1950s threatened the state's growth. Under Carr's stewardship, the legislature passed a constitutional amendment, later approved by voters, creating the state's first Water Development Board, a body authorized to issue $200 million in bonds to support local water projects.[72]

The creation of this board represented the last major legislative project of the 1950s to expand state government and modernize the economy, and it required another political effort, this time by Carr, to lift Texas communities from their traditional parochialism. As Carr said in a December 1955 speech in Denton, during his speakership campaign against Lindsey: "The way it now stands, one section of Texas does not want to be taxed to help another part of the state in securing water. Past Legislatures cannot be blamed too much for not passing legislation of this nature. We have got to put the entire state before any particular area."[73] Carr followed this by reminding his Denton audience of the likely need for more taxes in order to improve universities and public schools, to maintain prisons, and to create an effective parole system.

In addition to the water board, the legislature under Carr created a tourism bureau and the Texas Youth Council and set aside money to finance a new state library and archives building.[74] Like the Speakers who followed him, Carr saw his political influence expand with the growth of the state government. For the 1959–1961 session, Carr fought a pitched battle against Joe Burkett, Jr., of Kerrville, winning a second term as Speaker by a tight 79–71 margin. In a sign of the times, Burkett did not warn his peers, as Robert Calvert had in an earlier day, that a second-term speakership represented tyranny.[75]

The Fruits of Pragmatic Conservatism

From 1949 to 1961, the state of Texas greatly expanded its responsibility for public education, provided for war veterans, supported cancer research, and improved care for the mentally ill, the elderly, and the disabled. An earlier era of reformers had sought to reform the moral behavior of the populace, believing that social improvement would follow. Conservative reformers from Senterfitt to Carr, however, set about creating a modern state, with its complex web of tax incentives, social services, and business regulations.

Conservative reformers recoiled when it came to one long-standing issue: ending racial segregation. By the 1950s and 1960s, many Anglo politicians believed that their political survival rested on public defenses of segregation. Many others, however, sensed that Jim Crow laws both faced certain judicial extinction and damaged the state economically. Some Texas politicians took the path of Carr, who viewed the issue as divisive and unproductive, and tried to shunt discussion of segregation to the sidelines. At the opening of the 1957 session, Speaker Carr told a newspaper, "There's a determination [among House members] to keep this from blocking other needed legislation. I find a good bit of determination to see that segregation does not wreck the session."[76] Carr persuaded members of the rabidly prosegregation East Texas delegation to allow the House to hammer out the state budget before they grandstanded with bills aimed at countering federal courts' desegregation decisions.[77]

Texas's African American and Mexican American leadership, however, would not leave that accommodation in place, and in the process, they would not only remake Texas society, but also change the face of the Texas legislature and the identity of the state's political parties forever.

CHAPTER 5

Liberals, Conservatives, and the Dilemma of Race: The Dynastic Speakership, Part Two

1961–1969

Although many people today think of Texas as a western state, Texas has remained closely aligned with the South throughout its history, especially when attitudes concerning race are considered. For African Americans living under the heavy yoke of segregation, life was full of uncertainties and held little economic promise. The right to vote remained an unfulfilled dream. The Democratic Party represented the only viable political party, and it barred African Americans from being able to cast a meaningful vote until the U.S. Supreme Court ruled in *Smith v. Allwright* (1944) that the Democrats' white primary violated the Constitution.[1]

Even after this victory, African Americans faced years of struggle to gain full access to the ballot box. They saw desegregated, high-quality public schools in Texas as a necessary step toward full citizenship. The 1876 state constitution stated that children of the two races "shall always be taught in separate public free schools." The segregated schools attended by black and brown Texans in the 1950s and 1960s suffered from inadequate funding, poorly trained staffs, and the demands of powerful agricultural interests that expected young African Americans, Mexican Americans, and their families to sacrifice education for underpaid service in the field during planting and harvesting. By 1944–1945, as historian Alwyn Barr notes, 81 percent of black schools still had only one or two teachers (compared to 68 percent of white schools). Only 32 percent of African American schools met state standards for equipment, the quality of instruction, and the qualification of teachers. As late as the 1930s, the state spent one-third less per pupil in black schools than in white schools.[2]

No Texas law required segregated schools for Mexican American and immigrant children, but separate and unequal schooling for Hispanics evolved as a social custom, particularly in Central Texas, the Gulf Coast, and the Lower Rio Grande Valley (Hispanic pupils generally were not segregated in West Texas or the Panhandle). Approximately 90 percent of South Texas schools discriminated against Hispanics. As a general rule, segregation against students of Mexican descent persisted only for grades 1–8, perhaps because poverty meant that most Hispanics in Texas dropped out before ninth grade. As with African Americans, Anglos consigned Mexican Americans to small, dilapidated school buildings, out-of-date textbooks, and white teachers who did not speak Spanish or respect Mexican American culture. Hispanic students found they were often nudged toward vocational programs or were classified as mentally slow because of their language gap.[3]

African Americans and Mexican Americans pursued separate paths to dismantle school segregation, but both gained an increasingly sympathetic hearing in the federal courts. The post–World War II era marked a particularly fruitful time for groups such as the NAACP, LULAC (the League of United Latin American Citizens, formed in Texas in 1929), and the newly formed American GI Forum (organized in Texas in 1948 to help Mexican American veterans receive federal benefits).[4]

A wave of successful civil rights suits filed against Texas schools began with *Delgado v. Bastrop ISD* (1948), a U.S. Supreme Court decision that banned school boards from segregating Mexican American students from Anglo children. The court followed this up with a landmark decision in *Sweatt v. Painter* (1950), which desegregated the University of Texas law school. This case laid the groundwork for the more famous ruling in *Brown v. Board of Education* (1954), which overturned *Plessy v. Ferguson* (1896), the decision that had upheld the constitutionality of "separate but equal" facilities. *Brown* declared public school segregation illegal. Finally, in *Hernandez v. Driscoll CISD* (1957), the court determined that one Texas district's practice of retaining Mexican American children in grades one and two for four years represented a form of discrimination.[5]

Response to these court decisions varied by region and demographics. By 1956, sixty-six school districts had implemented at least token desegregation, including those in cities such as Austin, San Angelo, San Antonio, El Paso, and Corpus Christi. Generally, places like West Texas, which had few African American and Mexican American students, desegregated first. East Texas and North Texas, including Dallas and Houston, strongly resisted implementing *Brown.* Even in districts that ostensibly complied with *Brown,* however, the impact was minimal, since such districts allowed white students to transfer out of integrated campuses.[6]

Some politicians exploited the racial tensions generated by desegregation. Allan Shivers urged resistance to the Supreme Court's *Brown* ruling. The governor encouraged whites who were violently blocking a federal court order that mandated desegregation of schools in Mansfield, in north-central Texas. There, enraged white mobs surrounded the city's high school on August 30 and 31, 1956, to prevent the enrollment of three African American students. Whites hanged three black-faced dummies in effigy, which dangled in front of the Mansfield High campus for days. Rather than maintain order and respect for the law, Shivers praised the Mansfield horde and violated court orders by dispatching Texas Rangers to prevent desegregation.[7]

After Mansfield, Shivers succeeded in placing three inflammatory referenda concerning segregation on the Democratic primary ballot. Democratic voters were asked whether they favored repeal of compulsory-school-attendance laws "when white and Negro children are mixed in public schools"; whether they supported strengthening the state law barring intermarriage between whites and blacks; and whether they backed the use of "interposition" to "halt illegal federal encroachment" on states' rights. All three measures were approved by large majorities.[8]

Other politicians, including some who would rise to the speakership, tried to avoid dealing with segregation, seeing it as a no-win problem, and promised instead to work behind the scenes to improve race relations. For instance, Jim Lindsey publicly stood for segregation and paid deference to states' rights in his speeches, but helped provide financial support to black churches in his native East Texas after they had been bombed. As he recalled:

There were two churches on successive Sundays blown up . . . One of the banks set up a fund to collect money for rebuilding the church. And the pastor came to me and said, "Well, what should I do about this?" and I said, "Let them take up all the money they can take up. But when you get ready to build the church and you want a black person to build it, they're not going to go with you. So come on back and bring me the money, and we'll take care of it." . . . So we supervised the construction . . . and got it rebuilt . . . We never lost a dollar financing black churches.[9]

Lindsey later said that well-intentioned whites in East Texas could not picture a world in which whites and blacks could live without segregation: "I know we were trying to have this theory of separate but equal, and we were trying, in our way, to improve the separate . . . and *make* it equal. That was our thrust at that time . . ."[10] Other East Texas politicians, like

Rayford Price of Frankston in Anderson County, said that segregation seemed less a part of the natural order as he got older. As Price recalled:

> Actually, in 1960, when I first ran for the Legislature it [segregation] was a very hot issue, at that time . . . It seemed weird . . . at first, but it was just the way it was. And then as I got older, I was active in the MYF, the Methodist Youth Fellowship . . . A group of us tried to integrate at least the Methodist Church, at that time. We even went to the bishop about it. I mean, we came to the conclusion that that was really not the way to treat people. But I've also got to say that when I ran for office, it was such a hot issue that anybody running for office in East Texas was going to be for preserving segregation at that time.[11]

Rayford Price struggled to reconcile Christianity with segregation. "It didn't go with what I thought Christianity was all about," he said. But he campaigned for segregation and states' rights when he first ran for the legislature. "Well, I'm disappointed in myself," Price now admits. "Yet, I know that if I'd done anything else, I wouldn't have gotten elected anyhow."[12] He reports that other East Texans in the Legislature felt a similar conflict between personal beliefs and political expediency. "I've talked about it with a good friend of mine, Bob Johnson, who I served with in the House and who was later my law partner," Price said. "We both ran on preserving segregation . . . We both regretted it, but we had no choice if we were to be elected at that time."[13] Another Speaker from East Texas, Jimmy Turman, who presided over the House from 1961 to 1963, agrees. "About the time I was running, it was political suicide . . . if you voted for desegregation," Turman said.[14]

Speaker Turman

Born the son of a tenant farmer in 1927 in the small East Texas town of Gober, James A. "Jimmy" Turman became principal and teacher at the Wolfe City Elementary–Junior High School at the age of nineteen, and a junior high principal in Paris at twenty-four. Turman did this while earning a master's degree at East Texas State Teachers College. Turman's career as an educator was interrupted by a stint in the navy during the Korean War. Returning home, he won election as a state representative in 1954. While a state representative, he enrolled in the graduate program in education at the University of Texas, earning his doctorate in educational administration and psychology in 1957. In 1961, he would become the first Texas House Speaker to hold a doctoral degree.[15]

Turman said in 2004 that it was impossible as a child to avoid the issue of race in his Hunt County home in East Texas. "In Hunt County when I was a kid . . . in Greenville . . . there [were] a lot of black people living there," Turman said. "And they had a big sign that went from a corner of the courthouse lot to an opposite corner of the street—a big sign that you drive under when you're going around the courthouse. There's neon, and it said, 'THE BLACKEST LAND AND THE WHITEST PEOPLE.'"[16]

Turman voted for segregation bills, but even then his public statements revealed a reticence on the issue. Asked by the *Dallas Morning News* about his record on segregation, Turman expressed no enthusiasm for Jim Crow. "In a conscientious attempt to reflect the thinking of the people in my district, I voted for the bills designed to continue separate but equal facilities in our public schools." Turman implied that he would change his position if there were a change of consensus in his community.[17]

Turman shared his moderate politics with his predecessor, Waggoner Carr. The two carefully negotiated the delicate middle ground between the Democratic Party's warring conservative and liberal factions. Turman, like Carr, considered himself a fiscal conservative, but Turman also said that his Baptist religious background, his experience growing up with dirt-poor farmers, and his shocking experience touring Texas mental health facilities inspired his support for social spending. "I had been called a liberal," Turman said. "I considered myself a conservative, but I was concerned about social issues, programs, people. I had a lot of old-age pensioners at that time in my district, and poor people, and I was concerned about the needs of those people . . . that could be provided by government. So I called myself a conservative with a heart."[18]

Liberals actively sought moderate allies in order to wrest control of the Democratic Party from the reigning Shivercrats, supporters of Democratic governor Allan Shivers who backed the Republican Party nationally and who increasingly supported the most reactionary policies within the state of Texas, particularly on racial matters. "Jimmy Turman is what we in Texas call an East Texas Liberal . . . Coming from a town of 150 with four churches, last year he sponsored the bill to outlaw nudists, who certainly would not be welcome at Sunday school in Gober," one of the state's leading liberals, *Texas Observer* editor Ronnie Dugger, wrote. "On taxes, he is a liberal person, and on state spending he is a humanitarian."[19]

In this era of Texas politics, liberalism was associated with support for civil rights, a highly unpopular stand among East Texas Anglos, so Turman, Carr, and their allies struggled with an identity that avoided use of the "*l* word." As Turman described his viewpoints in a newspaper interview, "I believe in less federal control in everything—farming, education, and so forth. In other words, I am a conservative states' righter. I'm a liberal in the areas of humanitarian needs, like education and welfare. But everything else, on a matter of any other item in state government, I'm just as conservative as the next man about spending a dollar."[20]

As a House member, Turman quickly aligned himself with Carr and persuaded the West Texan to run for a second term as Speaker.[21] Turman also received crucial support from Governor Price Daniel. After his one term as House Speaker (1943–1945), he had beaten Pat Neff, Jr., in the Democratic primary for attorney general in 1946 and served the first of three terms in that office.[22]

While attorney general, Daniel gained prominence for his efforts on behalf of the state in the Tidelands dispute, in which he argued in the federal courts that Texas, not the U.S. government, had control over the oil that lay just off the state's coastline. Daniel's position won him huge support from the oil and gas industry in his 1952 Senate campaign. In the Senate, Daniel cosponsored a joint resolution that restored tidelands to Texas, a measure signed by President Eisenhower. Daniel made the decision to enter the governor's race once he knew that Shivers would not run for another term. He declared that he would "rather be governor of Texas than President of the United States." Daniel won the 1956 Democratic primary against liberal favorite Ralph Yarborough before cruising to victory in the general election. Although basically a conservative and a voice for oil companies, Daniel rejected the shrill racist positions that Shivers used in his later career. Publicly committed to segregation, Daniel turned out to be fairly progressive as governor, supporting the passage of laws that regulated lobbyists, created a water planning board, and increased teachers' salaries.[23]

Riding a wave of popularity, Daniel won a second term in 1958 and worked closely with legislative moderates like Carr and Turman. As noted earlier, Carr prevailed in the 1959 Speaker's race by a slim, eight-vote margin, a sign of how evenly divided the Texas House was in the early 1960s. Turman served as one of Carr's lieutenants, and in return, when Turman expressed interest in the speakership for the 1961 session, Carr gave him a helping hand. By this point, lobbyists were playing a critical role in Speakers' races. Carr gave Turman a list of important contacts. "And he wrote down eight names on a piece of paper and told me to 'go see these people, and explain to them why you want to run, and get okayed with them,'" Turman said. "'You really need the blessing of these people.'"[24] Turman met with the chief oil and gas, railroad, insurance, banking, and liquor lobbyists, along with the head of the Texas Medical Association. Carr and other advisers coached Turman in approaching each of these lobbyists, and sometimes served as intermediaries. Turman, who represented a dry county, was concerned about the stance of the liquor lobby toward his candidacy. Turman's team dispatched Representative Bill Pieratt of Giddings ("the wettest district in the state," as Turman put it) to meet with Homer Leonard, who had served as House Speaker from 1941 to 1943 and who was then the chief liquor lobbyist. According to Turman, "Bill . . . [says to] Homer Leonard, 'Jimmy's not going to hurt you.'"[25]

With the rapid growth in the state's economy since World War II, lobbyists grew in power. Rayford Price, then a state representative from Palestine in East Texas, said that lobbyists always played a huge role in the legislative process. In the 1950s and 1960s, he said, lobbyists served as exclusive hired guns for large special interests, such as the Texas Manufacturers Association. In debating complex legislation sought by interest groups, Price explained, House members found themselves at a disadvantage. Price said he had only one secretary and a part-time staffer to assist him with research and all his other duties. Lobbyists, therefore, freely offered research to back their proposals, but the information was obviously slanted to advance their interests. Price and other former Speakers said that opposing groups also presented research and that the credibility of lobbyists depended on the accuracy of their presentations. "Usually there would be more than one side to an issue, and you'd be getting facts from several sources," Price said. "And I'd go to the library and see if what they told me was true." Some legislators, however, worked less diligently on pending legislation and just did the lobbyists' bidding.[26]

Wining and dining by lobbyists was very much part of the legislative process then, Price recalled, and for most House members, information and a good meal was all that was exchanged. For less ethical House members, Price said, lobbyists provided "girls and sex and liquor and, I guess, money in some cases. But I think that was very rare then and maybe more rare now."[27]

Turman said that in spite of lobbyists pressuring Speaker candidates, he was able to maintain his independence.[28] Still, during his Speaker's race, Turman made a political enemy who later haunted him. He said that Bill Heatly of Paducah, the powerful Appropriations Committee chair, pressured Turman to promise him the chairmanship of the Revenue and Tax Committee in return for Heatly's support in the Speaker's race. Turman said he refused.

> Man, he could've been so much help! But, I couldn't promise . . . He had already told me how much stock he owned and how big he was and [how] he knows everybody in West Texas and [how] he's in bed with all the rich people and they can all help me and, man, I didn't have any money . . . Anyway, he left and he got angry, and he turned against me that night, and worked his head off to defeat me for speaker.
>
> And he started . . . getting lobbies to call on [my supporters]. Bill Bass of Texarkana, freshman member, . . . did a little ranching . . . out of the Texarkana area, down in DeKalb [County] . . . He wanted to borrow $500 to help put some hay up or do something or another. I guess it was an FHA, farmers home loan thing . . . Anyway, he could not get his loan renewed. "It's because you're supporting Turman for speaker," [bankers said] . . . And they would not give him a loan, and he called and asked me, "What am I going to do about this?" . . . I said, "Well now, I haven't got any money to help you." But he said, "Well, I'm told that I cannot vote for Turman or I won't get my loan." But he had the audacity to buck the system.[29]

For the next two years, Heatly opposed Turman and Governor Daniel's tax proposals, and later joined five other legislators in accusing Turman of financial improprieties when the Speaker entered the lieutenant governor's race in 1962. In spite of Heatly, Turman grabbed the speakership by a narrow margin, winning 83 to 66 over conservative Wade Spillman of McAllen. By coincidence, Turman's swearing-in took place on the fiftieth anniversary of the inauguration of Sam Rayburn, the last Fannin County man to serve as Texas House Speaker.[30]

Rayford Price voted for Turman but said that the Speaker made a major tactical error with his committee appointments. "Jim made the mistake of putting his opposition on committees that never heard a bill. They had nothing to do except to cause trouble for him," Price said.[31]

As Turman ascended to the speakership, the power of the office had become apparent not just to Capitol insiders. The University of Texas student newspaper, the *Daily Texan,* noted the "immense power" held by U.S. House Speaker Sam Rayburn and declared that Turman "will have comparable power on the state level." The article detailed the Speaker's power to appoint committee members and chairs as well as members of the Texas Legislative Council, to control the flow of legislative debate, to appoint minor employees, and to interpret House rules. By 1961, the Speaker was expected to wield powers comparable to the governor's and the lieutenant governor's. Since Senterfitt, they were also expected to have their own agendas. Turman gave wide-ranging press interviews in which he expressed his views on taxes and spending priorities.[32]

Facing a busy session, Turman sought to avoid debates on segregation. Like many other East Texas politicians who leaned toward racial liberalism, Turman preferred working behind the scenes, allowing desegregation to take place as quietly as possible. Nevertheless, Byron Tunnell of Tyler, who would serve as the next Speaker, introduced three new segregation bills. Turman, aware that the federal courts were dismantling such laws and that many members lacked any enthusiasm for Jim Crow, saw the bills as a needless sideshow. As he remembered:

> There was just no need to get the House roused up over another issue, because I had enough issues of my own. I had this House divided between liberals and conservatives. I had it divided between city boys and rural boys . . . I had it divided between the big . . . electric utility companies and the sixty-six—or whatever they were—electric cooperatives. They were fighting each other bitterly. I had it between the railroads and the truckers . . . I had the wets and the drys.[33]

With such a fractured House, Turman was afraid to bring up segregation. Instead, he buried Tunnell's proposals.

> I . . . referred these three bills to the State Affairs Committee, which is commonly called the "Speaker's Committee" . . . and then I had my chairman refer it to a subcommittee. We jokingly say it's the "deep-freeze committee" because it's not going to ever come out.
>
> And Byron Tunnell was upset with me about that . . . I told him I just couldn't see the Legislature involved in this kind of thing anymore because . . . [integration] was the law of the land . . . We had enough problems in my session . . . to not get involved and bogged down in something like that, and I was not going to give a run on those bills. And so he said, "Okay. All right."
>
> The next day he gets up and says, "Mr. Speaker, will the gentleman yield?" "The speaker yields to the gentleman." "Mr. Speaker, I request to

speak on personal privilege." Okay, so he does. So I leave the chair. I go to the speaker's office. And Byron gets up and gives me hell because I will not side with him on those bills.[34]

Turman and Tunnell may not have known it, but the reliably Southern and prosegregationist Texas they had known was disappearing before their eyes, and Tunnell's efforts represented a near last stand for de jure segregation in Texas. By 1960, the number of residents who had been born outside of Texas represented 11.7 percent of the total population.[35] By 1994, however, that percentage grew to 35 percent. Although most Texas newcomers in the past came from southern states, the largest proportion of immigrants in the late twentieth century arrived from the Midwest.[36] This immigration deeply transformed Texas society. "In 1861 everyone considered Texas a part of the South; a century later its regional identification was debatable," historian John Boles noted.[37]

In the coming years, Texans legalized liquor by the drink and repealed blue laws, which banned Sunday sales of certain retail items. These changes marked the crumbling of traditional southern Protestant culture in Texas.[38] Racism persisted, but its legal expression became less visible and thus more vexing to change. These social changes accompanied further economic transformation, which left the legislature struggling to catch up. Texas still lagged behind much of the nation in school performance and education spending. Everyone expected Turman, as an educator, to emphasize education as Speaker. Unsurprisingly, during his term the House passed a bill that established senior and graduate studies at what became the University of Houston. Turman also made pay raises for schoolteachers and state employees his top priority, arguing that tax increases should fund the effort. "Since almost 92 percent of state expenditures are used to finance schools, highways, and welfare functions, it will be extremely difficult to make any substantial reductions in the state's budget without seriously impairing one or the other of these governmental services," Turman admitted at the time.[39]

Turman had few options for finding money for the pay raises. He deemed corporate and personal income taxes not politically feasible. His ally, Governor Price Daniel, opposed raising the sales tax.[40] Turman proposed a penny tax on each bottle of beer and soda sold. In addition, he supported Daniel's plan for a gas severance tax (a tax assessed on companies that extract gas in Texas and sell it out of state) and a corporate franchise tax. But a growing number of legislators supported a bill creating the state's first-ever general sales tax. Turman killed the sales tax in the regular session by casting a no vote, creating a tie in the House. Both Turman and Daniel saw a sales tax, backed by extremely conservative business groups like the oil and gas industry and the Texas Manufacturing Association, as regressive. A special session passed the tax, however, and Daniel let the bill become law without his signature, a devastating defeat for both the governor and Turman.[41] Rayford Price saw the sales tax as a practical necessity. "Oil had carried the state for many years, but the economy was changing, and we needed to draw from a new tax base," Price said. "The sales tax, I think, was the correct place to go at that time."[42]

The tax battle wounded Turman when he ran for lieutenant governor in 1962. Turman's race against Preston Smith, who would serve as governor from 1969 to 1973, turned nasty quickly. Six of Turman's conservative opponents in the House, including Bill Heatly, wrote an open letter in which they charged that the Speaker had paid a babysitter with state funds. The *Houston Post* and other newspapers across the state picked up the story. In 2004, Turman said that the House staffer in question, who was listed as a clerk, had worked under Jim Lindsey and Waggoner Carr and was a nurse whose services were available to everyone at the Capitol. She worked as a babysitter voluntarily and without pay, he said. "So everything's just the same—except I get tagged later for using taxpayer money for a babysitter," Turman said. His reputation smeared, Turman lost to the much more conservative Smith.[43]

Liberals faced several disadvantages in Texas, including the poll tax, which suppressed voting by blacks and working-class whites; a runoff primary system, which favored better-financed candidates; and the financial power of wealthy elites, who overwhelmingly donated their campaign contributions to conservatives favoring their interests.[44] Not surprisingly, therefore, the highly conservative Byron Tunnell, born in 1925 in Tyler, followed Turman as Speaker. "He is definitely East Texas," his wife, Jan, recalled of his conservative roots. Tunnell, who died of cancer in 2000, enjoyed an unremarkable childhood in which his father "worked at anything he could find to feed the family," according to Jan Tunnell. "He sold used cars, worked in a munitions plant."[45]

Speaker Tunnell

Tunnell served in the U.S. Navy Air Corps as a tail gunner on a P-51 in 1943 during World War II.[46] He received his law degree from Baylor University in 1952. Returning to Tyler, he rose to the position of Smith

County assistant district attorney, earning a reputation as a formidable trial lawyer and eventually arguing a case before the U.S. Supreme Court. He eventually opened a private practice with future lieutenant governor Bob Bullock. The friendship would last a lifetime, and Tunnell delivered a eulogy when Bullock died in June 1999. Jan Tunnell said that the relationship inspired his interest in politics: "They called each other 'brother.' They hung a shingle together for a while, but I guess Byron started thinking about how he had some ideas on how Texas should be run, and ran for office . . . One of his ideas was that he wanted to see Texas as a solvent state."[47]

Both Tunnell and Bullock first won election to the Texas House in 1956. As noted before, Tunnell built a record as a fiscal and social conservative, which included support for segregation. Widely liked for his dry sense of humor, Tunnell steamrolled his way to the speakership. While Carr's two races for Speaker and Turman's one campaign had been extremely close, Tunnell locked up the speakership with 94 pledges of support six months before the opening day of the legislature in 1963.[48]

Tunnell's political views were to the right of many House members. In an interview with *Texas Parade* magazine in January 1965, conducted when he appeared headed for a second term as Speaker, Tunnell vented anger at recent U.S. Supreme Court decisions that mandated "one man, one vote" as the basis for political representation, even in local elections. By the early 1960s, Texas still allowed a number of legislative seats to be elected at large. Under this system, a county with two or more House seats could set up superdistricts to elect representatives at large. Voters in such districts could thus cast ballots in more than one House race, and candidates were required to campaign countywide. This system diluted the representation of minority voters. Two U.S. Supreme Court decisions affecting Texas, *Baker v. Carr* (1962) and *Reynolds v. Sims* (1964), banned this tactic as violating the principle of "one man, one vote." The Court ruled that members of both chambers of the state legislature had to be elected from districts with approximately the same number of voters, which inevitably increased urban and minority representation in the Texas Legislature. Tunnell characterized these decisions as invasions of state sovereignty. "I'm still fighting for a constitutional amendment that would allow the states to determine the composition of at least one House of the Legislature on a basis other than population," he said.[49] Tunnell did not specify what that basis would be.

In spite of his conservatism, Tunnell made friends with liberals, thanks to his humor and evenhandedness as Speaker. He managed the House efficiently and fairly, making him one of the most well-regarded former Speakers among his small circle of peers. "Byron Tunnell, I thought, maybe was one of the better speakers that we've ever had, from that group [of legislators in the 1950s and early 1960s]," Rayford Price said.[50] Tunnell's successor as Speaker, Ben Barnes, agreed. "Byron was very careful to tell everyone the truth," Barnes noted. "Byron was very plainspoken, and he was candid, and not very many people left his office not knowing where he stood on an issue."[51] Even Carl Parker of Port Arthur, then a liberal House member and later a state senator, described Tunnell at the time of the former Speaker's death as "the most capable speaker that I served under . . . Now, I didn't like his policies. We differed on politics. But he ran an efficient House."[52]

Tunnell served a quiet term as Speaker. Creation of the Texas Parks and Wildlife Department represents one of the most significant pieces of legislation passed under his guidance. Tunnell also promoted another law, complementing legislation steered through Congress by Senator Ralph Yarborough, that set aside part of the Texas coastline to become the federally protected Padre Island National Seashore. The federal-seashore designation did not occur without opposition from area congressmen, who argued that the bill would handicap economic development. Passage of the national seashore bill by Congress and the enabling bills passed in the legislature merit attention because of the close cooperation it suggests between a segregationist, archconservative House Speaker and the state's most powerful liberal in creating an important and enduring conservation site. Perhaps because of Tunnell's leadership style, or because of the plan's popularity with the general public, ideological opposites were able to cooperate in forging policy even during an intense battle for control of the state Democratic Party between liberals and conservatives.[53]

The Return of the Republicans

The Fifty-eighth Legislature's makeup hinted that those ideological battles would no longer be contained entirely within the Democratic Party. The 1963 session included ten Republican House members, the largest slate from the GOP since the days of Reconstruction. Since the late nineteenth century, the Republican Party had lacked a political base. Voter restrictions such as the Terrell election laws virtually eliminated voting by African Americans, who had reliably supported Republicans since the end of the Civil War. White Republicans fought to eliminate the so-called black-and-tan faction of the party and to make the state GOP "lily white," a feat they had largely accomplished by the 1920s. Even segregated, however, the state Republican Party carried the historical baggage of being the party of emancipation and Reconstruction, stubborn facts that dampened white support in Texas. Between 1896 and 1950, Texans sent exactly three members of the party to Congress, all to the House of Representatives. No more than one Republican served in the state Senate, and no more than two in the state House, during any single legislative session in that fifty-four-year period.[54]

The 1950s marked a key transition for Texas Republicans, their rise led by the still nominally Democratic governor Allan Shivers. Shivers openly campaigned for Republican presidential nominee Dwight Eisenhower in 1952 and 1956, and for Republican vice president Richard Nixon against Democratic Massachusetts senator John Kennedy in 1960. In 1952, Eisenhower carried 53.2 percent of the popular vote in Texas, the first Republican to carry the state in a presidential race since Herbert Hoover beat the antiprohibition Catholic Al Smith in 1928.[55]

Postwar growth produced an economically diverse urban middle class that increasingly voted for Republican candidates in the 1950s and 1960s. Urban residents represented almost 60 percent of Texas voters by 1950, and increasingly, cities like Dallas and Houston and regions like the Panhandle and the area west of a line extending from Harris County to Midland County grew friendlier to the GOP. Democrats could no longer dismiss Republicans as serious candidates after 1961, when Republican John Tower won a special election to fill the Senate seat of Lyndon Johnson, who had just been elected vice president. The following year, GOP gubernatorial candidate Jack Cox carried almost 46 percent of the vote against Democrat John B. Connally.[56]

The GOP suffered a setback during Barry Goldwater's disastrous presidential campaign against Lyndon Johnson in 1964. Johnson held a huge advantage in Texas, and the ultraright Goldwater did not help his own cause when he dismissed the hydrogen bomb as just another weapon that commanders should be free to use in Vietnam, called for the abolition of the income tax, and declared in his speech at the Republican National Convention that "Extremism in the defense of liberty is no vice! Moderation in the pursuit of justice is no virtue!"[57] Texas Republicans suffered badly in the electoral debacle that followed. Nine of the ten Republicans in the state House lost their bids for reelection. By 1968, however, the Texas congressional delegation for the first time since the nineteenth century counted among its members three Republicans, including future president George H. W. Bush of Houston, Robert Price of Pampa, and Jim Collins of Grand Prairie.[58] In a 1962 interview, Tunnell correctly noted that the increased power of the Republican Party in Texas indicated "a trend of thinking [toward conservatism]. There is no question about a movement to the right in Texas."[59]

Speaker Barnes

This rightward drift makes the rise of Ben Barnes, a moderate but often progressive representative from De Leon, even more surprising. Born in 1938 in Gorman, Ben Frank Barnes grew up in a poor, Depression-era West Texas rural community.[60] Barnes first learned a love of politics while attending the University of Texas and working for the state health department. As Barnes remembered:

> I was working about five blocks from the Dome on 5th Street at the State Health Department, and I got to be supervisor after about six months of all the part-time employees . . .
>
> One of my responsibilities . . . was cosigning the checks that . . . went into this [bank] account. They called it the employees' flower fund. It was meant to pay for flowers for people when their granddads died or to pay for Thanksgiving parties or Christmas parties. And I had to cosign the checks, and an assistant to the Health Department commissioner brought me some checks to sign. And that was back when Texas just had private clubs, and a lot of the checks were to the Tower Liquor Store and the Tower Hotel and the Tower Club. And I said, "What are these for?" And he said, "It is none of your business. If you like the job, sign it."
>
> Well it made me very angry . . . There was a former state representative that worked at the Health Department named Bert Hall, who is now deceased. I went to see Bert Hall, and I said, "What should I do?" and he said, "I advise you to go up the Legislature and see your state representative and tell him what happened at the Health Department." And I did.[61]

Barnes said that his state representative, Ben Sudderth, introduced him to Bill Heatly and to Truett Latimer of Abilene, who launched a House investigation of the Health Department. "The commissioner of health, his secretary, and his assistant made [a deal], but they had to resign," Barnes said. "He had to leave Texas, he and his assistant. He had to give up his right to practice medicine in Texas . . . And they never came back here to visit. And they had to reimburse . . . thousands of dollars . . . seven, eight, maybe nine thousand dollars that they had taken out of this fund over a period of time." Before he testified before the legislative committee investigating the matter, Barnes said, he had rarely made it to the seat of state power. "I fell in love with the Capitol," Barnes said. "I saw what those men were doing, and women, and so my state representative was not going to run for reelection and I did."[62]

Barnes graduated from the University of Texas law school before he decided to enter the 1960 Democratic primary for Comanche County's state House seat against a heavily favored opponent. Barnes recalled:

[His name was] Ike Hickman, and Eisenhower was just leaving office, and he had all these "I like Ike" buttons, [*laughs*] so you know it was the stupidest thing that a young man could do, because nobody knew me and so it was crazy . . . We had a big rally for the Veterans of Foreign Wars and the Farm Bureau. And Hickman . . . drew to speak, and he got to speak first and told about being a prisoner of war and spending two and a half years in a German concentration camp and how he loved his country and how he nearly died for it, how he had gone through all the abuses in prison, and now he wanted to come back and serve more time. I seriously contemplated standing up and saying, "I'm going to resign and go back to law school."

I just got some kind of almost divine intervention because it just popped in my head about what I was doing in World War II. I just said, "Well, I was two years old when Pearl Harbor was attacked, but I remember my brother and I did what we could do as young boys." I said, "I had a red wagon, and I would take that red wagon and try to fill it up every Saturday with scrap iron and put it in the back of the car and take it to the scrap-iron dealer, and that was the way I tried to serve." And I saw a bunch of women in the audience just kind of nodding their head about that red wagon. I said that I would go ahead and run another day.

. . . He took me very lightly . . . I had worked for the extension service, measuring peanut allotments. And I took the soil conservation map and I took a red pencil, and every time I went to a house, I put an X on it. And when I got through, I had these three counties' soil conservation maps where I literally knocked on every door in all three of those counties, and he didn't get out and work like that. He couldn't miss. I ended up beating him two to one, surprisingly, and I felt very good. I got 90 percent of the vote in my home county.[63]

A member of the House at age twenty-three, Barnes emerged as a leader in the opposition to Turman and Daniel's tax plans. Backing Tunnell in the next session, Barnes quickly achieved high visibility, chairing the important House Rules Committee and serving as vice chair of the Banks and Banking Committee. He also served unofficially as the chief liaison between Speaker Tunnell and Governor Connally.[64]

Barnes supported Tunnell's bid for a second term, which the Speaker locked up just before the 1965 session opened. Connally, however, saw Tunnell as standing in the way of his own legislative agenda, and so appointed Tunnell to fill a vacancy on the Texas Railroad Commission. Barnes, who had cultivated support from both liberals and conservatives in the House, coasted to victory in the election to replace his mentor. Connally achieved a twofer, shunting aside an opponent of some of his key legislative proposals and replacing him with one of his closest allies in the House. At age twenty-six, Barnes became the youngest Speaker since Ira Hobart Evans in 1870–1871.

Close to Tunnell, Connally, and President Lyndon Johnson, Barnes entered the speakership with stronger political connections than any of his predecessors. As authors Sam Kinch, Jr., and Ben Procter noted in the early 1970s:

Ben Barnes is totally and completely a political animal . . . From 1960 on, all of his adult life, politics occupied almost every waking moment—and his dreams as well. Nearly all of his close friends have been politicians or interested in the art of government; his social life has been the campaign trail, the receptions, the dinner meetings, the fund-raising activities and speaking engagements ad infinitum; his work has been the affairs of state and tending to constituents' needs; and even his relaxation has served only as a short breather before the next public demand.[65]

Barnes said that he was obsessive about his political priorities because he saw that, in spite of the hype surrounding his political future (including a prediction from Lyndon Johnson that Barnes would one day be president), his window of political opportunity could close rapidly.[66] He said he told his leadership team, "We are not going to come down this trail but one time. Let's get out there. Let's not just sit over here and react. Let's go act. The Senate gets all the credit for what good legislation passes. The House has always kind of been a second place to the governor and the Senate. So let's change it. Let's get out there and be proactive. Let's make some changes."[67]

Barnes showed such single-minded devotion during his speakership because he knew that the importance of the office had grown. "All of a sudden the speaker's office kind of had a statewide base," Barnes said. "[Before,] a speaker just had to worry about his own district and worry about the members. But when I started, I was probably taking more positions on more issues before they got to the Legislature . . . I got the Sigma Delta Chi Friend of Journalism Award because I invited in the press . . . I invited them to the speaker's office every Monday morning to let them ask me questions and tell them what I wanted to get done that week. And they couldn't believe that when that practice got started. Speakers normally played their cards very close to their vest." By inviting in the press, Barnes not only gained a reputation for openness and accessibility that won him friends among reporters, but also enhanced his ability to spin the current legislative controversies to his advantage.[68]

Barnes, who three decades after leaving public office still talks like someone who could deliver a stump speech at a moment's notice, acted like a man in a hurry during his two terms as Speaker. In the early 1960s, Texas ranked thirty-third among the states in per capita income, forty-fourth in adult literacy, and dead last in per capita expenditures on child welfare. Barnes's close friend, navy veteran John Connally, who had served as Lyndon Johnson's campaign manager during his Senate campaign against Coke Stevenson in 1948, beat Price Daniel, Sr., and three other candidates in the 1962 governor's race. Connally made improvement of the state's universities a top priority during his first term. He appointed the Governor's Committee on Education Beyond the High School, and this board recommended $100 million in state expenditures to upgrade university faculty salaries, improve libraries, support research, and expand graduate programs. Connally proposed raising almost $33 million in new taxes in order to begin work on the committee's recommendations, but was forced by conservative House members like Preston Smith and Speaker Tunnell to slash $13 million from that total. Anticipating a second term, Connally vetoed another $12.5 million of expenditures in the state budget, funds that he intended to apply to higher education spending in the 1965 session.[69]

By appointing Tunnell to the Railroad Commission, the ever-practical Connally removed a legislative stumbling block to his education program.

Receiving advance word from Connally of Tunnell's appointment, Barnes established a campaign command center at the Commodore Perry Hotel. With his allies stationed at fifteen telephones, he secured support pledges for his speakership from a majority of House members within thirty-six hours.[70] Many in the legislature began to resent his seemingly effortless success, perhaps not knowing how hard he worked. "I got up every morning at 4:30 and went to bed at 11:30 or 12:00 at night," he said, describing his political campaigns, but the same tirelessness characterized his speakership.[71]

In 1965, Connally enjoyed a much friendlier House under the leadership of his ally Barnes. The new Speaker also made Texas universities a top legislative concern, and under his stewardship the state created the Texas Higher Education Coordinating Board.[72] During Barnes's two terms as Speaker and then two terms as lieutenant governor, the state tripled its higher education budget.[73]

Not considered liberal by 1960s standards, the Connally-Barnes team nevertheless passed an extraordinary number of bills boosting education and improving social services. In addition to creating the coordinating board, the pair hiked university and college faculty salaries, improved and expanded the state's community colleges, added the University of Houston to the state system, and turned Angelo State College and Pan American College into four-year schools.[74]

Barnes, however, believed that his biggest accomplishment was to persuade a parsimonious legislature that spending on education, mental health programs, and assistance to the disabled represented an investment that would pay off in the future. "Someone said, 'What is the most important thing that you did while you were in office?'" Barnes said. "I'll tell you what was the most important thing I did. I was able to work to get a majority of the House and a majority of the Senate to vote for a tax bill every single session I was in the Legislature when I was lieutenant governor [or] speaker . . . I served twelve years, and I passed eight tax bills, and that takes a lot of courage."[75]

When Barnes ran for lieutenant governor in 1968, he won 2 million votes, the first Texas politician to reach that threshold. Yet regardless of his great political skills, Barnes proved no more adept at negotiating the tricky racial politics of 1960s Texas than his political peers. In the summer of 1966, a march of mostly Mexican American farm workers began in South Texas. Not represented by a union, these farmworkers toiled in the Rio Grande Valley under harsh conditions, including long hours and low wages, and in the summer they called a strike against eight major local growers. The Political Association of Spanish-Speaking Organizations (PASSO), a group formed by activists who participated in Henry B. González's 1958 gubernatorial race and the Viva Kennedy clubs that formed in Texas during the 1960 presidential race, provided leadership for the march. Protestors faced harassment by Texas Rangers and Starr County law enforcement when the wildcat strike began. PASSO then organized a march to the Capitol to heighten the visibility of the farmworkers' plight and to enlist political support.

Connally, Barnes, and Attorney General Waggoner Carr met the marchers in New Braunfels. Connally told the strikers he would not call a special session to address the issue of farm labor nor speak in Austin at a Labor Day rally called to support the strike. In spite of this rebuff, members of Mexican American groups like LULAC and the American GI Forum joined PASSO and the farmers for the remainder of the 290-mile, 65-day march. Thousands finally rallied in Austin. Some historians believe that Carr's Senate campaign against incumbent Republican John Tower may have been hurt by Mexican American anger at his perceived lack of support for the strikers. "The sixty-five day march . . . catalyzed a militancy [among Mexican Americans] that would last until the mid-1970s," historians Robert Calvert and Arnoldo De León note.[76] Carr lost to Tower and would not again gain statewide office.

Even politically talented men like Barnes and Connally still largely operated in a whites-only world. This left the state's Democratic Party leadership ill prepared to deal with the changing political realities of the late 1960s and early 1970s. By the latter half of the 1960s, liberal, politically active African Americans, Mexican Americans, and women in Texas had lost patience with piecemeal reforms and expected full participation in state government. Anglo racial conservatives, disturbed by what they saw as Democratic acquiescence to minority agitators, drifted toward the Republican Party, leaving conservatives' control of the Democratic Party more tenuous. The old Dixiecrat Party in Texas would implode during the early-1970s scandal known as Sharpstown, and the Texas House Speaker, Gus Mutscher, would stand at the center of the wreckage.

Speaker Reuben Senterfitt, 1951–1955.
Texas House Speakers Collection, Dolph
Briscoe Center for American History.
Courtesy of the House Speakers Office
and the Legislative Library (hereafter
credited as Texas House Speakers
Collection).

Speaker Jim T. Lindsey, 1955–1957.
Texas House Speakers Collection.

Speaker Waggoner Carr, 1957–1961. Texas
House Speakers Collection.

Speaker James A. "Jimmy" Turman, 1961–
1963. Texas House Speakers Collection.

Speaker Byron Tunnell, 1963–1965. Texas House
Speakers Collection.

Speaker Ben Barnes, 1965–1969. Texas House
Speakers Collection.

Speaker Gus F. Mutscher, 1969–1972. Texas House
Speakers Collection.

Rayford Price at the Speaker's podium, April
1972. Prints and Photographs 1973/15-1. Photo by
Bill Malone for Archives Current Events Program,
Texas State Library and Archives Commission.

Speaker Marion Price Daniel, Jr., 1973–1975.
Texas House Speakers Collection.

Speaker Bill Clayton, 1975–1983. Texas
House Speakers Collection.

Speaker Gibson D. "Gib" Lewis, 1983–1993.
Texas House Speakers Collection.

Speaker James E. "Pete" Laney, 1993–2003. Texas House Speakers Collection.

Speaker Tom Craddick, 2003–2009. Texas House Speakers Collection.

House Speaker Byron Tunnell (*center*) with Lieutenant Governor Preston Smith (*right*) and Dorsey Hardeman in the House chamber, ca. 1965. Russell Lee photograph, Russell Lee Collection 3Y167, Dolph Briscoe Center for American History.

Speaker Gus Mutscher (*right*) and Lieutenant Governor Ben Barnes at the Speaker's podium during the 1971 session. 1990/187-62-HF 131 NI 1067 C-1 frame 6-A, Texas State Library and Archives Commission.

Price Daniel, Sr., a former governor and House Speaker, swearing in his son Price Daniel, Jr., for the 1973 session. 1990/187-63-HF 006 NI 0007 F-4 frame 19-A, Texas State Library and Archives Commission.

Representative Mickey Leland, of Houston (*left*), discussing legislation with Speaker Billy Clayton in the 1975 legislative session. 1990/187-64-HF 099 NI 0282 A-1 frame 6, Texas State Library and Archives Commission.

Speaker Gib Lewis surrounded by Capitol reporters during the 1983 legislative session. 1990/187-68-HF 257 NI 0929 B-3 frame 9-A, Texas State Library and Archives Commission.

Governor Ann Richards and Speaker Gib Lewis discussing pending legislation during the 1991 legislative session. 2007/070-72-HF 120 NI 0258 A-6 frame 37, Texas State Library and Archives Commission.

Representatives Libby Linebarger and Paul Sadler presenting school-finance legislation as Speaker Pete Laney presides, 1993 legislative session. 2007/070-73-HF 286 NI 465 C-3 frame 18, Texas State Library and Archives Commission.

Lauren Cox, daughter of author Patrick Cox, swinging the gavel as Speaker Pete Laney looks on during the 1993 session. Children are often invited to act as honorary pages in the House of Representatives and even to preside during the sessions. 2007/070-73-HF 297 NI 476 D-6 frame 21, Texas State Library and Archives Commission.

CHAPTER 6

The Old Order Is Dead, Long Live the Old Order: Sharpstown, the Price Daniel Revolution, and the Speakership in Crisis

1969–1975

One day, the Democrats threw a party and a wake broke out. On January 18, 1971, the night before elaborate inaugural ceremonies were to take place in Austin, a Democratic Victory Dinner featured local wit Richard "Cactus" Pryor and Las Vegas lounge act Wayne Newton. Six inaugural balls showcased country performers such as Faron Young, Ray Price, Buck Owens (from the popular syndicated television show *Hee Haw*), and Jeannie C. Riley, who had had a recent hit with the song "Harper Valley PTA." Even as hillbilly bands hooted and hollered, however, the first notes of a dirge were sounding.[1]

As Sam Kinch, Jr., and Ben Procter write in their account of the Sharpstown scandal, *Texas under a Cloud: Story of the Texas Stock Fraud Scandal,* while Lieutenant Governor Ben Barnes strolled to his seat at the victory dinner, his administrative assistant, Robert Spellings, passed on the rumor that just reelected Governor Preston Smith and House Speaker Gus Mutscher would be indicted the next day by a Houston grand jury investigating two bills pertaining to Frank Sharp, the owner of the Sharpstown State Bank and the National Bankers Life Insurance Company. Upon hearing the news, Barnes said later, "I had a hard time concentrating . . . on dinner and the festivities because I knew I was going to be a candidate for higher office in 1972."[2] As news spread of an emerging political scandal, the mood of the crowd at the January 19 inauguration ceremonies grew "smolderingly angry and hostile." At the intersection of Sixth Street and Congress Avenue, a "shouting, cursing, and threatening" crowd disrupted the inaugural parade by spitting and throwing fruit and bottles at the Texas A&M marching band and other performers.[3]

In 1971–1972, federal accusations and then a series of state charges were leveled against nearly two dozen active and former state officials.

Texas voters witnessed an unprecedented turnover in political offices from the political fallout that became known simply as Sharpstown. Preston Smith, labeled an unindicted coconspirator in a bribery case, would lose his bid for reelection. Gus Mutscher, the incumbent Speaker of the House of Representatives, and two associates were indicted and convicted. And Ben Barnes, the lieutenant governor whom many saw as a possible successor to Lyndon Johnson in the White House, badly lost his gubernatorial bid. Half of the members of the Texas Legislature chose not to run again or were voted out of office. Meanwhile, using the scandal as a springboard, liberal Democrats and outsider Republicans formed a common front by advocating reform, and thereby gained a stronger foothold in the legislature.[4]

The scandal centered, initially, on charges that Houston businessman Frank Sharp had sold cheap stock in one of his companies to legislators, financed the stock purchases through his bank, and then manipulated the stock price so that the officials could sell their stock for large profits—all in return for passing legislation benefiting Sharp and his bank. Attorneys for the Securities and Exchange Commission (SEC), late on the afternoon of January 18, 1971, filed a lawsuit in federal court in Dallas, alleging stock fraud against former Speaker and state attorney general Waggoner Carr, former state insurance commissioner John Osorio, Frank Sharp, and a number of other defendants.[5]

Even more damningly, the court papers filed by the lawyers for the SEC alleged that Governor Smith, state Democratic chairman and state banking board member Elmer Baum, House Speaker Gus Mutscher, Jr., Rep. Tommy Shannon of Fort Worth, Rush McGinty (an aide to Mutscher), and other major political figures not included in the SEC's suit had been bribed. The SEC argued that Sharp had conspired to pay off lawmakers to pass a bill allowing Sharp's bank to be insured by a state-chartered corporation rather than the more inquisitive, stricter Federal Deposit Insurance Corporation.[6]

Sharp, the SEC said, made loans in excess of $600,000 from the Sharpstown State Bank to state officials. Those officials, in turn, used the money to buy stock in Sharp's National Bankers Life, which would later be flipped for huge profits after Sharp artificially inflated the value of the stock. The SEC alleged that Governor Smith arranged to have Sharp's bank bills considered at a special legislative session in September 1969, and that Mutscher and Shannon rushed the bills through the legislature. Smith vetoed the bills after receiving advice from the state's top bank lawyers, but waited until he and Baum had cashed in on the stock-purchase deal. Authorities later estimated Mutscher made $105,000 (more than $540,000 in today's dollars) in the initial stock purchase, which he promptly lost when he sold his stock too late and the Sharpstown bank went belly up. Smith and Democratic chair Baum, an osteopath, were believed to have made $62,500 apiece (more than $322,000 today). Bill Heatly of Paducah, the House Appropriations Committee chair, made almost $49,000 (now more than $252,000); McGinty made about $45,000 (now about $230,000); and Shannon cashed in with close to $37,000 (more than $190,000 today).[7]

Speaker Mutscher

Because of their high political profiles, Barnes and Mutscher became the unwitting stars of the ensuing political drama. Born in 1932, Mutscher grew up in the tiny German community of William Penn in Washington County as "a farm boy in what could only be described as poverty-stricken circumstances," authors Kinch and Procter note.[8] Throughout his youth, Mutscher worked a variety of part-time jobs, including driving a Coca-Cola truck, serving as an electrician's helper, and clerking at J. C. Penney, but he came into his own when he attended Blinn Junior College on a baseball scholarship. A star third baseman who would spend some time as a semiprofessional, Mutscher won election as class president and class favorite before transferring to the University of Texas, where he received a degree in personnel management.[9]

Mutscher landed a position as a field representative in the sales and marketing department of Borden's Dairy. Working in Houston, he quickly acquired a reputation as a tireless and successful salesman. In 1959, the Harris County Chamber of Commerce and the Houston Merchants Association named him the outstanding young businessman of the year.[10]

Mutscher ran for the state House in 1960 almost on impulse, defeating incumbent Sanford Schmidt of Shelby in an upset.[11] Mutscher supported Jimmy Turman in his speakership race against Wade Spillman. Mutscher said he got some heat from that in conservative Washington County, since Turman was seen as a liberal, but he was rewarded for picking the winner and for his subsequent loyalty to the Speakers who followed, Byron Tunnell and Ben Barnes. Mutscher won appointment as vice chair of the Appropriations Committee and chair of both the Committee on Claims and Accounts and the Legislative Redistricting Committee, and served on the Legislative Budget Board and the Texas Legislative Council. Not known as a flamboyant or headline-seeking legislator, Mutscher rose, like his nineteenth-century predecessors, by supporting the leadership team and performing the hard work on key committees.[12]

In the mid-1960s, the U.S. Supreme Court ruled that the "one man, one vote" rule applied to state legislatures and that Texas had unconstitutionally drawn election districts to the disadvantage of African Americans. In 1965, Mutscher earned general praise for his evenhandedness on the always controversial Legislative Redistricting Committee, an assignment that usually turns into political quicksand but won the Brenham representative the goodwill of many members. If he was fair to most members, however, he didn't shy away from using the chair to play hardball politics. Anticipating that Ben Barnes would move up to lieutenant governor the next session, Mutscher drew new political boundaries to eliminate his chief rival for the speakership. The district of Gene Fondren of Taylor, in the words of a newspaper, had been "Mutscherized," that is, combined in a flotorial district with Bell County, which had a population four times that of Fondren's home county of Williamson.[13] Fondren wound up campaigning for reelection in a district that would force three incumbents to run for two seats. Fighting for his political life, Fondren dropped out of the Speaker race.[14]

Mutscher won the speakership in 1969 without opposition, and the office grew as a power center. "Mutscher had converted the $400-a-month speakership into a full-time, year-round job and the House staff into a large and politically effective unit," Kinch and Procter write. "By December 1971, when the House was not in session and, with few exceptions, not even functioning as a legislative body, Mutscher had 103 employees on the payroll. The total cost to the taxpayer for this operation was nearly four times as much as it had been seven years earlier before Barnes became speaker."[15]

During his speakership, the legislature passed a minimum-wage law, increased support for higher education, and added to appropriations for mental health. The Texas Legislature also lowered the voting age to eighteen. One regressive scheme proposed by Barnes and Mutscher, taxing groceries, fizzled because of a widespread "housewives' revolt."[16]

Aside from that controversy, Mutscher confronted heated opposition for his support of liberalized liquor laws. Although Prohibition had ended in 1933, a complex web of state laws covering the sale and distribution of alcohol maintained a de facto prohibition in many parts of Texas. A nonbinding referendum in 1969 indicated widespread support for repealing the state constitution's ban on open saloons, which would in effect allow restaurants and bars to sell mixed drinks, a practice otherwise known as "liquor by the drink." This shift in attitudes stemmed from the increased urbanization of Texas culture and the decline in Baptist dominance of state politics. In 1969, at Mutscher's urging, the legislature submitted to the voters a constitutional amendment legalizing the sale of mixed drinks. The measure won narrow approval in November 1970 because of heavy support in cities. The constitutional ban lifted, Mutscher persuaded the legislature to authorize the sale of alcohol in restaurants in 1971. Local-option elections in May of that year resulted in the public sale of mixed drinks in Texas for the first time since 1919.[17] Getting a two-thirds vote in the House necessary to submit a "wet" amendment to the voters proved difficult, however, because of the heavy representation of pro-dry rural districts in the House, according to Mutscher.

> When we took the vote, we had to have 100 votes, and I looked down at the board and it was an even 100. And . . . I said, "The gavel is coming down aye." [Then I said] . . . "Get the sergeant [at arms] here to lock the doors" . . . because I know from experience that a verification [of the vote] would have never stood up if you [didn't] . . . I'm not being critical of my colleagues, but some of them [are] going to have a sick mother or a sick child or [some other excuse to not vote again] . . . And I sure didn't want to go through that fight a second time.[18]

Some saw Mutscher's approach to alcohol legislation as evidence of both the influence of special interests on the Speaker and his heavy-handed method of leadership. Mutscher's position on conference committees deepened some members' resentments. Under old House rules, House conference committees (impaneled to meet with Senate negotiators to resolve differences between the House and Senate versions of pending legislation) substantially rewrote laws. Rank-and-file House members could then only vote the entire, often substantially altered, conference bills up or down. In 1967, Speaker Barnes initiated new rules ending House negotiators' ability to rewrite laws beyond reconciling provisions in conflict with the Senate versions. As lieutenant governor, Barnes instituted a similar rule limiting the power of Senate conference committees.[19]

Mutscher, however, insisted on giving conferees a free hand in rewriting legislation. Bills written by conference committees often came up for a vote at the end of a session, giving members little time to read or debate proposed changes. This process greatly strengthened the ability of Mutscher-picked House conferees to change legislation with no possibility of dissent and, critics charged, to load up legislation with favors to political contributors.[20] This was the case with the 1969 tax bill, according to former representative Bill Bass of Ben Wheeler in Van Zandt County. In a 2004 interview, Bass recalled that the tax bill that year gave expensive breaks to telephone vendors who had supported the Speaker in past campaigns.[21] As Bass recalls:

> The conference committee could rewrite the whole bill . . . The favored creatures . . . who were on the conference committee were doing what the lieutenant governor and the speaker decided.
>
> . . . They went off and rewrote the tax bill, tax breaks for telephone companies, whoever was favored . . . And when the bill came back from conference, we would vote on it in hours, two or three at the most, maybe forty-five minutes, but I remember that in 1971 we moved to postpone consideration for twenty-four hours . . .
>
> . . . And sure enough, when the voting board was lighting up, it looked like it might get postponed. Here came Jumbo Atwell, the chairman of the tax committee in that era, steaming toward us, fire in his eye. He was also a member of the Dallas delegation, elected at large. He had been drinking of course. Zan Holmes, one of the two black members, also from Dallas, said, "Jumbo, we just wanted a chance to read the bill." Jumbo replied, "You goddamn nigger, you don't need to read the goddamn bill." [*laughs*] It's sad, but that attitude wasn't entirely gone. Zan just smiled and shrugged his shoulders, but he persisted in his vote, and we postponed for 24 hours.[22]

In 1969, Mutscher made frequent headlines for his controversial positions on alcohol, revenues, and the reform of House procedures.[23] By April 1969, however, Mutscher received pleasant press attention when he announced his engagement to Donna Axum of Lubbock, a speech instructor at Texas Tech University with a master's degree in speech and drama, and also the winner of the 1964 Miss America pageant. Rayford Price, who in the 1969 session ruffled Mutscher's feathers when he launched an abortive run for the speakership upon rumors that Mutscher would retire from the House to become a beer lobbyist, nevertheless served as one of the ushers at the wedding.[24]

Forgiveness would be short-lived, however, as Mutscher did not reappoint Price chair of the key House State Affairs Committee during the 1971 session, prompting the Palestine representative to again openly campaign for the speakership.[25] "If Mutscher does run [for a third term in 1973,] I will campaign on the issue that we don't need a third-term speaker," Price told the *Houston Chronicle*.[26]

By this time, a broad revolt led by an odd coalition of liberal Democrats and conservative, marginalized Republicans undermined Mutscher's grip on power. The dissenters, soon to be called the "Dirty Thirty," bitterly complained about what they saw as Mutscher's dictatorial management style and the undemocratic way that bills were presented for votes in the House.[27]

Interestingly, ethics scandals involving Congress immediately preceded Sharpstown. House Speaker John McCormack, the successor to Sam Rayburn, resigned under pressure in May 1970. One of the incidents leading to McCormack's decision involved two assistants who received sentences for influence peddling. In December 1971, a jury convicted Texas congressman John Dowdy of accepting a bribe. These scandals, combined with the ongoing Vietnam War and high inflation, led many people to hold federal and state elected officials in low esteem. The well-publicized scandals would lead to a reform movement and a change in leadership in Congress. And the national events certainly left an impact on Texas.[28]

Dissent in the Texas Legislature only deepened after the SEC lawsuit concerning Sharpstown. The Dirty Thirty revolt began in early March 1971 when a traditional resolution honoring Governor Preston Smith's birthday came before the House for a vote, but two liberal members upset about the governor's spending priorities and Mutscher's leadership style, Neil Caldwell of Alvin and Frances "Sissy" Farenthold of Corpus Christi, asked that their names be taken off the resolution. On March 10, Farenthold called for a joint House-Senate investigation of Sharpstown. Five days later, Farenthold took the floor again to ask that her motion be immediately considered. Mutscher said no, prompting Lane Denton, a Waco freshman, to appeal the chair's ruling. Thrown for a loop, Mutscher left the chamber, turning the gavel over to DeWitt Hale. The House voted on the motion, which was rejected 118–30. A Mutscher supporter was heard to grumble about "those thirty dirty bastards," giving birth to a nickname proudly embraced by the House dissenters.[29]

Mutscher tried to silence critics by having close political ally Delwin Jones draw new legislative districts that would be unwinnable for members of the Dirty Thirty. One of his targets was Republican Tom Craddick, first elected from Midland in 1968 (the year Mutscher became Speaker). Delwin Jones's 1971 election map left Craddick no longer living in his district. "They split my district down the street I lived on in Midland,"

Craddick said. Craddick's hometown of Midland had been united in one district, but after Mutscher rammed his redistricting bill through the legislature "part of it ran from our side of the street, on Stanolind [Avenue], all the way over to Abilene."[30] Neighbors across the street lived in another district. In a landmark case, Craddick's lawyers argued that it was illegal to split county lines as the Mutscher bill had. The Texas Supreme Court agreed with Craddick and ruled that the redistricting plan was unconstitutional.[31] A federal court in Austin overturned a second attempt at Mutscher-mandering, in a case pursued by the Legislative Redistricting Board. The three-judge panel labeled the new Mutscher maps an unconstitutional attempt to dilute the voting strength of African Americans, Mexican Americans, and Republicans.[32]

The Speaker was losing his redistricting battles even as his personal legal troubles mounted. On September 23, 1971, a Travis County grand jury indicted Mutscher, Shannon, and McGinty on criminal charges, making the Speaker the highest-ranking state official to be charged with a felony since former Texas land commissioner Bascom Giles was indicted during the Veterans' Land Board scandals of 1954. The once seemingly omnipotent Speaker became politically radioactive, and House members were afraid to accept even interim committee assignments from him for fear they would be tagged "Mutscher men."[33]

A court ordered that the Mutscher, Shannon, and McGinty bribery trial be moved to Abilene because of the extensive coverage the Austin press gave Sharpstown. A jury took only 140 minutes on March 15, 1972, to find the so-called Abilene Three guilty. Leaving the courtroom to confer with attorneys, family, and friends, Mutscher muttered, "Unbelievable," but remained stoic for about fifteen minutes. Then he and his wife broke down in tears. The following day, Judge J. Neil Daniel handed down a sentence of five years' probation, though the conviction was a death sentence for Mutscher's political career.[34] "They destroyed my family and destroyed my politics . . . and my livelihood," Mutscher stated years later.[35]

On March 21, 1972, Gus Mutscher told his staff he would step down as Speaker, the first to resign the office midterm since A. M. Kennedy in 1909. Mutscher's formal resignation came the day before a special session opened on March 28. James L. Slider served as interim Speaker just long enough for him to preside over the election of Rayford Price as Mutscher's permanent replacement. Mutscher, however, remained a member of the House.[36]

Decades after the event, Mutscher remained deeply affected by the Sharpstown episode. Mutscher challenged the motives of Frank Sharp and his initial offer to prosecutors, to testify in exchange for a reprieve from prosecution. Mutscher blames Sharpstown on the Nixon administration's desire to embarrass Democratic political leaders in Lyndon Johnson's home state. "The politics of it was really obvious because they broke the announcement the night when we were having a Democratic victory dinner to hurt and embarrass all of us," Mutscher said. "It was so political ... It started ... with [U.S. Attorney General John] Mitchell and [President Richard] Nixon trying to save [Texas Republican senator] John Tower." Mutscher believed that Ben Barnes planned to challenge Tower for his Senate seat in 1972.[37] Barnes confirmed Mutscher's suspicions. "If I had not been on Nixon's enemies list, I don't think Gus Mutscher or Preston Smith would have ever been called into the Sharpstown thing," Barnes stated.[38] Given the excesses of the Nixon administration during this time, politics most certainly played a role in the timing and the focus of the federal investigation. Furthermore, Nixon's "Southern strategy" focused on making inroads into the former Democratic strongholds of the South, and destroying the Texas Democratic Party would certainly have boosted this effort.[39]

Waggoner Carr, in a 1977 book, argues that Senator Tower worried about Nixon's appointment of popular former Democratic governor John Connally as treasury secretary in 1971. Tower had been the conduit through which Texans seeking White House favors reached Nixon, and Tower worried that Connally would eclipse his influence. According to Carr, Tower worried that Barnes's connection to Nixon's treasury secretary might prove to be a political asset if he challenged the incumbent in the 1972 Senate race.[40]

Carr also noted that former Texas attorney general Will Wilson, who beat Carr in a race for that office in 1960, had been appointed chief of the criminal division of the U.S. Justice Department, which was headed by Attorney General Mitchell. "I felt that Wilson had held a grudge against me since I ran against him for attorney general in 1960," Carr wrote. "He did not appreciate some of the things I had said and done during the campaign; he grew very hostile."[41] As a Democrat, Wilson had lost races for governor and U.S. senator, so in 1966 he switched to the Republican Party. Tower helped secure Wilson a job in the Department of Justice. Wilson returned the favor by helping Tower's reelection bid in 1972. Wilson himself would have to resign from the Department of Justice when the extent of his legal work for Frank Sharp became public.

Carr eventually faced both a civil suit by the SEC and a criminal case. His connection to Sharpstown proved tenuous. He served as defendant

John Osorio's law partner, and he owned 100 shares of stock in National Bankers Life, which he had purchased before Frank Sharp owned the company. Carr and Osorio participated in a discussion with Ben Barnes during which the pair advocated for the bill allowing Sharp's bank to be insured by a state agency. Carr insisted that he believed the bill, which became so controversial, represented good legislation.[42]

Mutscher, who won election as a county judge in Washington County following his departure from the legislature, echoes Carr's argument. Mutscher said he backed the bill at the heart of the scandal because it was a good idea for his rural constituents, whose bank accounts were largely served by small-town, independent financial institutions during this time. Mutscher added that he obviously had no unethical motives because he did nothing to conceal his relationship with Sharp.

> I never thought I was involved with a wrongdoing, because when I worked the situation with Sharp on buying some of that National Bank stock, I signed my name right there in the open, just like if you had a paper now and entered into a contract . . . I told Sharp . . . this does not entitle you to call me about anything in Austin . . . I was for that bill anyway. I did not know that he had dived in or made contributions to pay for the Senate and for the governor and so forth.[43]

Barnes agrees that Sharpstown was a Nixon-hatched conspiracy. "I didn't even know who Frank Sharp was," Barnes said. "[President Lyndon] Johnson had stood up before 3,000 people . . . and said I was going to be the next president of the United States from Texas. I had all this national honor and recognition, and these guys around the South were talking about Barnes doing this and that."[44] Barnes said the federal government tried to manipulate former state insurance commissioner John Osorio, named in the original SEC suit with Waggoner Carr, to implicate him in the scandal: "The government offered John Osorio total immunity if he just testified that I was involved in Sharpstown. John Mitchell met with me after he got out of prison and expressed his sorrow. But there is no doubt in my mind [this was a conspiracy] . . . I was still winning the governor's race without a runoff until Gus Mutscher was tried in Abilene and Gus Mutscher was found guilty in Abilene."[45]

David Carr, whose father died of cancer in 2004, said the Sharpstown case embittered Waggoner Carr and disillusioned the former Speaker about politics. Waggoner Carr went broke and had to defend himself in two criminal trials. In March 1973, a Dallas jury, after three hours of deliberation, found Carr not guilty of twelve counts of fraud, mail fraud, filing false papers with the SEC, and conspiracy. In April 1974, another Dallas jury found Carr not guilty of other Sharpstown-related charges.[46]

David Carr said the public never knew how difficult the Sharpstown case was on his family. "All my dental classmates wouldn't talk to me during that time," he said.

> When my dad finally got through this last acquittal and the word was coming out of Watergate what was going on, my whole class stood up and applauded me when I walked in from the last trial, so it had turned completely around. My dad said that he got down to about two or three friends and that was about all he had . . . Went bankrupt, too . . . Dad, as a result, could have lost his law license, could have served a total of sixty-four years in prison. At fifty years of age, he would have spent the rest of his life in prison. This guy had been the chief law enforcement officer in Texas, you know. And he's facing this kind of charge . . . He never would talk about politics after that.[47]

Surprisingly, even a former member of the Dirty Thirty, Bill Bass, now entertains some doubts about Mutscher's guilt. "Sometimes I get the feeling he may have been taken in by Frank Sharp," Bass said. "Mutscher lost money on the deal . . . When they were tried in Abilene, you could have predicted that anyone in '73, almost anyone, after Watergate would have gotten convicted."[48] Even if the Nixon administration's interest in Sharpstown stemmed from selfish political motives, however, Frank Sharp's connection with Mutscher, Preston Smith, and others revealed the too-cozy relationship between lobbyists and officeholders and how Texas campaign financing could make the difference between political contributions and bribes difficult to distinguish.

At first glance, the Sharpstown era appeared to be a watershed event in Texas politics. The legislature initiated several reforms and passed open-meetings and open-records laws. However, in the long run, no major changes in governmental structure occurred as a result of Sharpstown. The impetus toward reform did not extend to changing the legislature's budgetary priorities regarding social services and education. Business interests still dominated lawmakers' decision making. Yet 1973 marked a changing of the guard as Texas Democrats of the John Connally–Lyndon Johnson–Ralph Yarborough era made way for younger lawmakers, who increasingly came from the ranks of African Americans, Mexican Americans, women, and Republicans. A change in the relationship between the media and elected officials marked one of the longer-lasting impacts of the era of Vietnam, Sharpstown, and Watergate, opening the field to more aggressive and skeptical reporters like Sam Kinch, Jr., Dave McNeely, Molly Ivins, and Kaye Northcott.[49]

Speaker Price

Sharpstown also ushered in an era of instability in Texas's political leadership. The speakership of Mutscher's successor, Rayford Price, proved breathtakingly brief. Born in Jacksonville in Cherokee County, Price grew up in the nearby town of Frankston in Anderson County. His father, Quanah Quantrill Price, was owner and publisher of the *Frankston Citizen*. Quanah Price's position in the community meant that while growing up, Rayford saw many local politicians, who would drop by the newspaper office or the Price home to discuss issues. Interested in the broader world, Price attended the University of Texas at Austin, where he received his law degree in 1963.[50] Price won his first election to the Texas House of Representatives before finishing law school. He had entertained no plans to run before receiving a call from the incumbent. According to Price:

> The incumbent member was Jerry Sadler . . . and at that time he was running for land commissioner. And I was in school down here in my freshman year in law school and got a call about five o'clock in the morning . . . Jerry was a snuff dipper, and I think he was dipping snuff at five o'clock in the morning. At least he sounded like it. He said, "Hi. Your dad said you might be interested in running for the Legislature." And I said, "Well, Mr. Sadler, I don't know." He said, "Well, if you are, there's nothing but an old woman running, and you ought to run" and hung up.
>
> I went back to sleep and woke up at the normal time and said, "My God, did I dream that?" So I called my dad. I had no idea of running for the Legislature, because I was concentrating on law school. My dad said, "Yes, Jerry's not running." So I went home, checked around, and sure enough, there was a lady running, who was a very nice retired schoolteacher. And so . . . I filed, and it turned out there were three more by then, five of us in the race when it all was said and done . . . I think my dad got me elected.[51]

Price represented Palestine as a Democrat from 1961 to 1973. Price's voting record reflected his conservative politics. Shortly before he won election as Speaker, an AFL-CIO scorecard graded him as casting seventeen antilabor and two prolabor votes. A business lobby poll, however, scored him at twenty "good" votes and seven "bad" votes during the recent legislative session. During his drive for the speakership, Price received support from the Texas Manufacturers Association and the Texas Chemical Council, two of the most conservative business lobbies. Price held a leadership position every term he served, including chair of the Committee on Contingent Expenses during his freshman term. He was later named chair of the Committee on Constitutional Amendments and then head of the Committee on State Affairs in his next-to-last term.[52]

Price said that when he ran for Speaker, he wanted to stop the abuses of the committee system he had seen under Mutscher. The race turned out to be particularly difficult for Price, who said he faced off against an odd alignment of conservatives and liberals. Hostility had broken out between Price and Mutscher, who remained a House member and still had allies in the chamber. Meanwhile, Price Daniel, Jr., son of the former Speaker and governor, had arisen as a favorite choice of the liberals in the Dirty Thirty coalition.[53] "So it was a 'Stop Rayford' campaign because everybody thought that if I won that, well, then there'd be no problem for me to be reelected [as Speaker] in 1973," Price remembered.[54]

Price won the speakership over DeWitt Hale of Corpus Christi by a narrow 77–65 margin, but quickly impressed critics with his commitment to reform and his fairness in dealing with his opponents. In the three special sessions he presided over as Speaker, Price said he made a point of democratizing the House: "The backroom dealings that had been going on, I wanted to get rid of. I didn't have any policy issues that I wanted to push. I wanted to clean up the legislative process and procedures . . . We adopted new rules. We reorganized the committees, and put in a limited seniority system where the speaker didn't have total control over the process."[55]

Price would find 1972 the most crowded year of his life. As author Charles Deaton wrote, virtually every challenger running in the May Democratic primaries "tried to tie Mutscher around the neck of the incumbent. In many of the races, it was quite effective."[56] Sharpstown loomed large in a primary season that featured more contested races than any legislative campaign since World War II. In Fort Worth, Betty Andujar defeated Mike Moncrief in a Senate campaign in which her ads asked, "Why fire the ventriloquist [Mutscher] and keep the dummy [Moncrief?]"

Jim Nugent of Kerrville, Delwin Jones (author of the former Speaker's infamous redistricting plan), and Tommy Shannon (who was found guilty along with the Speaker in the Abilene trial) numbered among the key Mutscher allies defeated in May.[57]

Price faced one of the fiercest contests of the year. Redistricting placed him in a largely new district where most of his constituents didn't know him. Meanwhile, redistricting had placed incumbent Fred Head of Henderson in Rusk County in the same district as fellow Dirty Thirty member Bob Grant. Rather than run against his political ally, Head, with encouragement of the rest of the Dirty Thirty, moved to his native Troup and decided to challenge Price.[58] From November to March, the Speaker's race tied up Price, giving Head a five-month head start. "It was a weird election, because I was speaker," Price said. "I was running in a district where two-thirds of it I'd never run in before, and a lot of people actually thought I was Mutscher because I was speaker. Being speaker turned out not to be necessarily an asset to me at that time, because all they'd heard about was the speaker being indicted and convicted."[59]

A University of Houston law school student, Bill Green of Palestine, also entered the race and finished third, carrying about 23 percent of the vote. That proved enough to force a runoff. Price finished in second place with 32 percent. Head enjoyed a substantial lead, winning 45 percent. Having ground to make up, Price turned up the heat in the runoff. If Head tried to caricature Price as the second coming of Mutscher, Price tried to paint Head as part of a radical hippie Left bent on taking over state government. Political consultant Danny Parrish of Fort Worth launched a telephone and handbill campaign that posed the question, "What Does the Dirty Thirty Really Stand For?" According to the Price handbill, the House dissidents advocated:

Legalization of marijuana
[Abolition of] . . . the Texas Rangers
Registration of all firearms
Repeal of the right-to-work law
Liquor by the drink
. . . [Authorizing] . . . drivers' licenses for drunk drivers
[Legalizing] . . . abortion

The handbill closed with, "Fred Head says he's proud of being part of the Dirty Thirty. Is this the kind of representation you want in Austin?" Campaign workers telephoned voters and made similar charges. Head angrily denounced the handbills, calling them "vicious lies." In the end, Price's alleged Mutscher connection, whether fair or not, proved more decisive than the accusations he leveled against Head. Head's lead shrank significantly by the day of the June runoff, but he still won by 309 votes.[60] As Price later said: "Nineteen seventy-two was a real interesting year for me and my family. My second son was born, I was elected speaker, and then I was defeated—all in '72 . . . Oh, it was a roller-coaster year. Up, down. As a matter of fact, there was a runoff, and the runoff was on June 3, which was mine and my wife's anniversary. So when we got the final result of the election, we had champagne celebrating our anniversary but not the election."[61]

Surprisingly, in spite of his conviction on bribery charges, Mutscher also ran for reelection. Stripped of his speakership and abandoned by top politicos who had helped with his earlier campaigns, Mutscher organized a grassroots effort that emphasized his service to the district. During the campaign, Mutscher took credit for killing Preston Smith's grocery-tax plan, even though he had worked the House floor heavily for its approval. Mutscher actually finished first in the three-candidate primary, with 40 percent of the vote, while attorney Latham Boone III, a thirty-two-year-old native of Grimes County with a long family history of political involvement, finished second. Boone, however, wound up beating the former Speaker in the runoff by about 2,500 votes.[62]

Overall, the Texas Legislature experienced about a 50 percent turnover, with 76 new House members (out of 150) and 15 new senators (out of 31). Although no investigation linked Barnes to Sharpstown, he had presided over the Senate when the legislation benefiting Frank Sharp passed. The suspicion of corruption crippled him during his long-anticipated gubernatorial race against Governor Smith. Barnes failed to make the runoff in a heated four-candidate Democratic primary. Dirty Thirty leader Sissy Farenthold, running an insurgent campaign, finished second, with 28 percent of the ballot, behind rancher-banker and former state representative Dolph Briscoe of Uvalde, who carried 45 percent. Barnes struggled to a distant third, and Smith a dismal fourth, the worst-ever finish for a sitting governor. Smith won only 9 percent of the vote and failed to carry a single one of Texas's 254 counties. Barnes received only 17 percent of ballots cast. The much better financed Briscoe defeated Farenthold in the runoff and won the governorship in November. Republican gubernatorial candidate Henry Grover of Houston and Raza Unida Party candidate Ramsey Muñiz of Waco, however, carried enough votes to make Briscoe the first Texas governor to win office with less than 50 percent support.[63]

The Second Speaker Daniel

Sharpstown-related events shaped the agenda of the regular legislative session in 1973 and the career of the next House Speaker, the moderate Marion Price Daniel, Jr., of Liberty. No person seemed more destined to fill the post of Speaker than Daniel. His mother, Jean, was the great-great-granddaughter of Sam Houston. His father, Marion Price Daniel, Sr., the former House Speaker, state attorney general, U.S. senator, and governor, was, by 1971, serving on the Texas Supreme Court. The younger Daniel was born in 1941 and grew up in the town of Liberty, in Liberty County, near Houston. Daniel studied law at Baylor University and received his degree in 1966. He felt impelled toward public life, and after passing the bar exam, he successfully ran for justice of the peace in Liberty.[64]

Daniel won a seat in the Texas House in 1968. The press characterized his voting record as liberal, though Daniel preferred the label moderate or independent. He emerged, however, as a favorite Speaker candidate among the liberal faction of the Dirty Thirty.[65] Daniel enjoyed distinct advantages in the Speaker's race, according to his friend Bill Bass. "He came with a famous name, and he wasn't particularly apparent," Bass said. "I mean, he didn't get on the microphone a lot. But when it came down to voting . . . he did what he thought was right . . . he voted in a genuinely independent way."[66]

Bass said that he approached Rayford Price about aligning himself with House independents, but Price worried that he would alienate too many if he was seen working with the Dirty Thirty. At this point, Bass said, he began to ask, "Why not Price Daniel?" for Speaker in 1973.[67] Bass said that he and his allies in the House already fondly regarded Daniel's father "as the person who fought the sales tax." Bass did not know that Price Daniel, Jr., having grown disillusioned with the House under Gus Mutscher, had decided to drop out of politics. Unaware of Daniel's frustrations, Bass and John Hannah, a representative from Ben Wheeler, ate ice cream cones in an Austin Baskin-Robbins, where the two discussed which member of the progressive faction they could back in a race against Gus Mutscher.[68] "They came up with the name of Price Daniel Jr. and instantly decided it was the best idea since Rocky Road," Molly Ivins reported in the *Texas Observer*.[69] Neither legislator knew who would support Daniel's candidacy or where money for a race would come from, Bass said. All they had was Daniel's name, and they hadn't even approached him about running. "Later on, when we persisted in encouraging Price to run, he was reluctant, almost derisive of the idea," Bass said. "He would say to his secretary, 'The two movers and shakers in the Texas House of Representatives are here to talk me into being speaker.' . . . It took a while to get Price on board."[70]

Daniel had not endeared himself to all of the Dirty Thirty, having failed to fight against Mutscher's redistricting plan or to support Farenthold's call for a full investigation of Sharpstown. He had, however, sided with most of the Dirty Thirty on twelve of nineteen key reform votes. The AFL-CIO scorecard for Daniel credited him with casting twenty-five "right" votes, five "wrong" votes, and four absences, enough for him to earn the union's endorsement in his Speaker's run.[71] Enough people, Bass said, whispered in Daniel's ear for the legislator to reconsider his retirement plans and openly campaign for the 1973 speakership during the 1971 regular session.[72]

According to reporter Dave Montgomery, Daniel's supporters "cajoled, coaxed and—some say—even lied to get votes" by exaggerating the number of House members pledged to Daniel to make his speakership appear foreordained.[73] Meanwhile, Bass said, several of the Dirty Thirty made an alliance of convenience with the "Mutschercrats," as they were called, to derail Rayford Price's chances of getting reelected Speaker. The two factions mapped out a strategy to keep Rayford Price tied up with procedural votes and other time-consuming matters to prevent him from campaigning in his legislative district for reelection. Tom Moore of Waco, John Hannah, and Bass met with top Mutscher allies to iron out details in a room at the Stephen F. Austin Hotel. As Bass relates the story:

> We believed that if Rayford was elected speaker, he would be unbeatable in his home district and Price Daniel's chance to be speaker would evaporate. We knew that Mutscher and his loyalists were, out of pure vindictiveness, anxious to prevent Rayford's election as speaker. So [Rep.] Tom Moore of Waco, John Hannah, and I were delegated to meet with Mutscher's henchmen to select a compromise candidate who would agree to hold the office for the balance of the present session but not for the next.
>
> We met a roomful of Mutscher's people in a smoke-filled room in the Stephen F. Austin Hotel. We had hardly sat down when Tom Moore got up and said, "I thought when I came here that I could stand being around you bunch of whores, but I see now that I can't take it." [*laughs*] And he walked out the door leaving John and I to negotiate a deal.
>
> We agreed to nominate Dewitt Hale of Corpus Christi . . . He had generally voted with the speaker, but he wasn't a member of Mutscher's

inner circle. And he agreed to hold the office for only the balance of the session.

However, our compromise was not well received by a substantial part of the Dirty Thirty, who were appalled by the prospect of voting for a compromise candidate so tainted by Mutscherism, even if the result was the election of Rayford Price, who had almost the same voting record on reform issues as Dewitt Hale. That group supported the nomination of Zan Holmes for speaker. Zan was one of the two African American members and a great gentleman. When the vote was taken, we lost seventeen of the purist, ultraliberal members, who were thrilled silly at the opportunity to vote for the first black candidate for speaker of the House. So the seventeen purists remained undefiled, and the loss of their votes resulted in Rayford Price's election as speaker.[74]

Bass and Hannah's larger plans, however, returned to life after Fred Head's victory over Price in the primaries. With Price out of the way, Daniel started campaigning for the speakership in the second half of 1972. Daniel's aggressive reform platform included limiting Speakers to one or two terms, limits on the powers of conference committees to rewrite bills, establishing a limited seniority system to reduce the Speaker's powers over committee membership, and reduction of the number of committees and the size of the Speaker's staff.[75] "A speaker does not need 28 aides (which Mutscher has), if he's only going to preside, rather than try to run the floor," Daniel said. Daniel went one step further than his rivals, suggesting that a one-term limit would be critical to curbing the tyrannical excesses that had characterized the Mutscher speakership. With only one term, Daniel said, "the temptation or motive for a speaker to hold up a member's bill, threaten to gerrymander his district, stall a meritorious appropriation, or otherwise deny fair treatment until the interested member signed a pledge for the speaker's re-election" would be removed.[76]

On June 16, 1972, Daniel released the names of seventy-seven House members pledged to support him in the Speaker election, enough to win, and said he had backing from twenty-six others. Frank Calhoun of Abilene, Daniel's chief opponent in the Speaker's race, dropped out in August 1972, five months before the election.[77] Daniel revealed the extent of his sweeping reform agenda a month before he officially won the speakership post. In addition to democratizing House procedures, Daniel declared that his priorities for the 1973 legislative session included reducing the penalty for first-time possession of marijuana from a felony to a misdemeanor, instituting stronger pollution controls, and setting up a transit system for the state's major urban areas. In one of the strongest repudiations of the Mutscher era, he also called for a shield law that would allow Texas reporters to protect the identity of confidential sources. That last proposal would win him the Friend of the Press Award from journalism fraternity Sigma Delta Chi in March 1973. On January 9, 1973, the House elected Daniel unanimously. In one of his first moves as Speaker, he cut the size of the Speaker's office staff from twenty-seven to eight people.[78]

Seasoned political observer Sam Kinch, Jr., noted that Daniel's mild personal manner and moderate politics had not prepared Austin for the depth and breadth of his agenda. According to Kinch:

> All Daniel did was propose about the straightest-arrow ethics code we've seen in these parts. It's a gutty little fellow, full of goodies like a ban on legislators who are also lawyers doing triple duty by making piles of money practicing before the very state agencies that the Legislature controls. That sort of reform. And like the financial disclosure part: it doesn't just cover the state official or candidate. It goes to his wife or kids, so he can't hide a bunch of income that he gets from an oil lease that a lobbyist bought him at a fire sale.[79]

Sam Kinch and Bill Bass, however, eventually believed that the wealth and protection that marked Daniel's childhood left him more out of touch than even other children of comfort who had entered politics. Bass recalls Daniel as, at times, being idealistic to the point of lapsing into pie-in-the-sky unreality. This unworldliness, combined with Daniel's small stature, convinced some that the up-and-coming Speaker need not be feared. At one point, Bass said:

> [Rep. R. C.] Nick Nichols was a member from the Gulf Coast, from somewhere near Houston, and he was a big hulking bear of a man. And a real nice guy too. And not just a labor union stooge. Price was very small and dainty in his suit. Nick was hulking alongside him on the sidewalk in front of us. John [Hannah] and Diane [Daniel] and I were coming along behind while Price was making this pitch to Nick. And somehow it occurred to me that, "It's Pooh Bear and Christopher Robin." So everyone, at least the three of us, saw it.[80]

As Sam Kinch wrote, Daniel, like the fictitious Christopher Robin, was a visionary "surrounded by characters who are always entertaining if not always understandable . . . There is also something of . . . Gus Mutscher in Daniel. Like the former speaker . . . Daniel has a scarcely suppressed streak deep within him to succeed, build, achieve. Unlike the Machiavellian Mutscher, however, Daniel does it with style—a style that puts the emphasis on, well, style."[81] Style would not always prove to be enough, as Molly Ivins observed. "Some of the tougher old boys around the Capitol refer to Daniel as 'Little Price,'" she wrote. "In a value system heavy on being macho, he suffers on first impression from being a slight, slender man, not tall. He is only thirty-one, his face is almost pretty, and he can probably be out-orated by a fourth of his members."[82] From these friends and acquaintances emerges a portrait of a man somewhat shielded from the outside world who nevertheless had a steel will and committed himself to cleaning up a dirty system. Because of his confidence in his vision, he expected others to follow him.

Daniel desired a genuinely democratic House and sometimes ruled with a light hand, especially in comparison to his immediate predecessors. Many of his peers interpreted his podium style and his pledge not to run again for Speaker as weakness. "Daniel does not interfere in the committee process or in floor debate," reporter Bill Collier of the *Houston Chronicle* observed. "Everyone gets his say. He does not pressure the House in any way. There is no 'Daniel team' working under the whip to pass his reforms."[83]

A New Constitution?

In the 1973 session, Daniel took on big reform projects, only to be frustrated by the more conservative Texas Senate, but none of his efforts proved bigger than his attempt to shelve the cumbersome, outmoded 1876 Texas Constitution. Daniel emerged quickly as the likely president of the 1974 Texas Constitutional Convention. He said he favored leaving out of a new constitution anything that could be covered by statute, and he opposed inclusion of the state's right-to-work law in the document, saying that had already been provided by legislation. Representative Ray Hutchison, a Republican, and Roy Orr, a Democrat, were already lobbying for the inclusion of a right-to-work measure. Unions strongly opposed this. Labor hoped to win the right to declare work sites closed shops, a battle that would be made only harder if repeal of the right-to-work law required a constitutional amendment. The battle over this issue would prove fatal to Daniel's efforts.[84]

Bass believes that Daniel overstepped when he made the transition from being a reform Speaker to president of the constitutional convention. In guiding a controversial and potentially politically damaging convocation, Daniel hoped to live up to his father's illustrious legacy.[85] "All sorts of people tried to persuade him against it," Bass said. "I'd mention it to him, that it was going to be a major disaster . . . I wish I had done more."[86]

In preparation for the convention, set to begin in January 1974, the thirty-seven-member Constitutional Revision Commission, appointed by the governor, lieutenant governor, attorney general, and Speaker of the House, traveled the state, visiting nineteen cities and holding thirty public hearings to get voter feedback. The commission then broke into nine committees to suggest different articles of the proposed document to the convention.[87]

Enthusiasm for a new constitution remained tepid at the public forums convened during the commission's ninety-day term, according to Bill Hartman, the vice chair of the local governments committee, who at that time worked as the editor and publisher of the *Beaumont Enterprise and Journal*. "There wasn't a groundswell of people clamoring for a change," Hartman said. "We didn't have thousands of people show up for our public hearings, but we had hundreds of people."[88]

Among the commission's recommendations was a call for a shorter, more broadly worded constitution that would provide general guidelines for governance and descriptions of powers for constitutional offices. The commission suggested increasing the power of the governor, holding annual rather than biennial legislative sessions, reorganizing the judicial branch, and deleting matters from the constitution better covered by legislation.[89]

"This may sound self-serving, but from our position, everything was fine until we handed the ball over to the legislature," Hartman said. "Politics took over then. As a commission, we were not particularly bothered by lobby or interest groups."[90] That changed once the proposed constitution went to the convention. Hartman said that it was a mistake to let the legislature serve as the constitutional convention and that it would have been better to select through a special election. "The commission presented what we felt was far better than the existing Texas Constitution," Hartman said. "The one that was going to come out in the convention, we as interested members of the commission who followed it felt, was inferior to our product and probably inferior to the existing Texas Constitution, because whoever had the biggest gun was getting the biggest portion of what they wanted, and it just became a special-interest document."[91]

The convention eventually hammered out an eleven-article constitution in July 1974. By this point, though, as several convention members began positioning themselves to run for Speaker and as the atmosphere became poisoned by wrangling between prounion Democrats and their corporate-friendly peers, the assembly descended into acrimony. Daniel tried to run the convention the way he ran the House, allowing delegates to speak at length and trying not to impose his constitutional views on the gathering. He had appointed opponents to key committees and tried also to make each committee reflect the number of Republicans, African Americans, Latinos, and women in the legislature. Liberals, however, bitterly attacked Daniel when, realizing that business conservatives had a majority, he gave in to demands and placed a right-to-work provision in the final draft of the constitution. Members of the African American caucus, such as Mickey Leland and Craig Washington, also bitterly denounced Daniel when he allowed conservatives to water down a section that would have guaranteed health care to every Texan. The revised provisions made universal health care a goal, not a guarantee.[92]

The fate of the draft constitution remained unclear during the convention's final day. Capitol aides kept moving the clock back to give delegates more time to forge a compromise on issues like right-to-work, but to no avail. Standing at the gavel, realizing that his hopes for a new constitution probably had died and that his political future probably would suffer as a result, Daniel allowed a vote to take place. By three votes, the convention failed to approve the constitution and thereby to place it on the ballot for public approval.[93]

A clearly saddened Daniel bitterly blamed delegates already campaigning for speakership of the next session, labor unions, and Governor Dolph Briscoe, who declined to support the constitution, for the failure of the convention. "We missed that constitution by three votes," an aide to Daniel told a reporter. "You tell me the governor of this state can't deliver three votes."[94] Daniel reserved his harshest words for the AFL-CIO. "Right-to-work was a bitter pill for a lot of us to swallow," he said. "I don't care what any special interest thinks—I think the appropriate question is will the people of Texas ever forgive labor. In so many instances, delegates would tell me they thought right to work was a phony issue but they had to think of their political future."[95]

Daniel clearly did not appreciate the difficulties facing union organizers in Texas. Daniel rejected criticism that he didn't guide the convention with a firmer hand, saying that conflicted with his belief in democracy. "I read somewhere that if Ben Barnes had been president of this convention, the delegates would have gone home wondering what was in the document," Daniel said. "And if Gus Mutscher had been president, they would have spent the rest of their lives defending it. Well, Price Daniel, Jr., was president and we didn't get a constitution. But we came close, and we did it the right way."[96]

Daniel advocated that the next legislature place the convention's constitutional draft before the voters in a referendum. Daniel's successor as Speaker, constitution supporter Billy Clayton, did that. The legislature proposed eight constitutional amendments that would do the same work as an entirely new constitution. Daniel and Clayton both campaigned hard for the amendments, which had consumed so much metaphorical sweat and blood. The passion for reform had waned, however. Labor unions actively campaigned against the ballot measures, and Governor Briscoe opposed them. The eight amendments went down in flames, rejected by a 3–1 margin.[97]

"I think we tried to take on too much, to write the whole Constitution," Clayton said years later. "If you took a section or article at a time, then you wouldn't get so many [opposed] . . . If you write the whole Constitution and . . . say, somebody was against Article Five, but for the rest of it, they'd vote against it because of Article Five . . . If you're ever going to [adopt a new Constitution], and I think that we probably should, just take smaller chunks at a time."[98]

Bass said the reasons for the constitution's failure went deeper than that. Opponents won, he said, because of the simple fear of change and widespread distrust of politicians.

> [For instance] . . . you've got the schoolteachers' retirement plan written in the Constitution. Schoolteachers are always the ones coming up with the idea that we need a new Constitution. "Look at this silly thing. It's just a body of laws and it's unreadable." But when the time comes to approve a comprehensive revision, somebody tells the schoolteachers, "Do you want that bunch of drunken womanizing slugs in the Legislature to be able to change your teacher's retirement with a majority vote, or leave it in the Constitution, where it takes a two-thirds vote in the Legislature and a majority vote of the people to change it? Do you want to turn that over to that bunch in Austin?" That's all it takes to lose an important group that would ordinarily support revision.[99]

Daniel's chances at future public office faded with those of the proposed constitution. AFL-CIO bylaws prohibited the organization from endorsing any politician on record as voting for right to work. Even though Daniel personally opposed that provision and accepted it only to get approval for the whole constitution, the former Speaker would be denied the campaign support of what had been one of his most important constituencies. In any case, too many union members felt too much anger at the man from Liberty for him to make amends. This became abundantly clear in 1978, when he suffered a sound defeat in the Democratic primary for attorney general to future governor Mark White.[100]

Daniel's speakership opened with the high promise of a fairer, more open political process that would be less beholden to wealthy special interests. In the end, however, Daniel tilted at windmills. He left the Capitol, and the lobby remained as influential as ever. The next two Speakers, Billy Clayton and Gibson D. "Gib" Lewis, witnessed the prolonged battles that had raged from Sharpstown through the ill-fated constitutional convention. They sensed a need to move to other issues. They retreated on reform, expanded the power of the Speaker's office, increased the Speaker's support staff, and extended the Speaker's control of the legislative process. As the speakership grew in power, so did lobbyists' influence, even as the state continued to cope with an increasing population and the resulting greater demand for services. However, alleged improprieties and scandals centered on influence peddling became as frequent in the next fifteen years as they had been in the Gus Mutscher era. Successive Speakers not only needed to expand their knowledge and skills in crafting legislation, they also had to learn to defend themselves in court and in public during turbulent times.

CHAPTER 7

The Executive Speakership, Part One

1975–1983

One of the most anxious nights in Delma Clayton's life came on October 21, 1980, when the jury deciding the fate of her husband, Texas House Speaker Bill Clayton, recessed after deliberating for two hours without reaching a verdict. Clayton had been charged with accepting a bribe as part of an FBI sting operation called Brilab, and Delma expected a quick acquittal. "I had felt confident, all during the trial, that when the jury had all the evidence, they'd find him innocent," she told author Jimmy Banks. "The only thing that bothered me was the fact that some people think all politicians are crooks—and I was afraid there might be someone like that on the jury, someone who would decide he was guilty before hearing the evidence."[1]

The assumption that politicians lie and enter public life to get rich deepened in Texas after the Sharpstown scandal, Watergate, and unrelated congressional scandals. This suspicion of public officials is a tradition dating back to the earliest days of the American republic. In addition, conservative political culture frequently preaches that government is not a solution to society's ills, but the problem. A belief that all government is corrupt creates an expectation that any social program aimed at solving deep-rooted problems, such as racism or poverty, is doomed to failure because of the stupidity and dishonesty of officeholders and bureaucrats. Texans traditionally have relished their outsized reputation for being the biggest, the loudest, the bravest, and the rowdiest. This self-promoted mythology has proved to be a double-edged sword for politicians. Texas folklore tends to paint the state's post-Alamo, post–Civil War leaders as the dimmest and most venal in the country. As the Austin Lounge Lizards put it in their "Stupid Texas Song":

Our accents are the drawliest / Our howdies are the y'alliest,
Our Lone Star flag's the waviest / Our fried steak the cream-graviest,
Our rattlesnakes the coiliest / Our beaches are the oiliest,
Our politicians most corrupt . . .

Texans joke that the constitutional provision calling for the legislature to meet for 140 days every two years should have called for them to meet two days every 140 years. Carl Parker, a liberal leader who represented Port Arthur in the House from 1962 to 1977 and in the Senate from 1977 to 1995, once quipped that if you took all of the fools out of the state legislature, it would no longer be a representative body.[2]

Over the past century, the House chamber has occasionally erupted into fistfights. Bored with interminable debates, members have relieved the tension with nonsense resolutions, such as one passed during the 1971 session that commended Albert DeSalvo, the Boston Strangler, for his efforts at population control. Another resolution passed by the House two years later required lawbreakers to give twenty-four-hours notice before they committed a crime. Also in 1973, members of the Apache Belles drill team, from Tyler Junior College, cheered on ethics legislation by wearing letters on their posteriors that spelled out the word "reform."[3]

For whatever reason, debates of the Texas Legislature frequently turn uniquely provocative and amusing. During an open session of a conference committee, Jim McWilliams, a Democrat from Hallsville, stunned those in attendance when he proclaimed that, "I know the health department doesn't do its job, because ten years ago I had gonorrhea, and nobody talked to my wife."[4]

During the 1954 session, one Houston lawmaker made a habit of keeping a six-gun in his desk on the House floor. As former House member Chet Brooks, who was a reporter at the time, said, it had "a long barrel . . . like an old .45, something out of a Western movie. If he'd get excited in arguing, he'd reach in his desk and pull that gun out and wave it around. He never shot anybody . . . Of course, the speaker (Senterfitt) would just get terribly upset . . . and try to get him to put that gun away or take it away from him or something."[5]

Such tales may have led some Texans to believe the worst of those who served in the state House. Aside from the fun and frivolity that frequently made headlines, governing the growing state in the post-Sharpstown era created more challenges for elected officials and state administrators alike. This led an energized media to focus more attention on the proceedings in Austin throughout the entire year, not just during biennial legislative sessions, and the coverage became increasingly critical. However, as Rayford Price, the former Speaker, pointed out, Texans' contempt for politicians was not universal. "People usually are mad at the Legislature, but they usually like their legislators," Price said.[6]

That was certainly true in Billy Clayton's case. After retiring for the night, a jury found him not guilty of bribery the following day. After announcing the verdict, the jury joined the general cheering in the courtroom, and several members came up to Clayton to shake his hand and those of his attorneys. Marge Hudock, a juror from Houston, said that she hoped Clayton would be "our next governor."[7]

Clayton's long trip to that Houston courtroom began with his birth in the West Texas town of Olney on September 11, 1928. Clayton spent most of his childhood in Springlake, where he discovered a dislike of farmwork.[8] "He started out with his Daddy on the combine when he was so little his feet would just hang in midair," Clayton's mother later recalled. "He used to come in from the fields and tell me, 'Mamma, when I get through school, I'm not gonna farm.'"[9]

Texas A&M University provided an escape from a life on a farm. The conservative College Station institution offered him a rough-and-tumble introduction to the hypermacho world he would later encounter in the Capitol. Aggies revered as a longstanding tradition the verbal and physical harassment of freshmen, or "fish," as they were called on campus.[10] "In those days, nobody ever forgot their freshman year, because hazing was pretty rampant," Clayton recalled in a 2004 interview. Clayton remembered having to go to the showers with fifteen or twenty other freshmen wearing "heavy wool army overcoats, and then they'd turn the hot water on, just as hot as they could get it. They'd make us stand over in a corner, in the steam, and 'grab butterflies'—standing on our toes and reaching into the air. They had upper classmen holding single-edged razor blades under our heels, so we had to stay on our toes. You'd just stand there and do that until you'd fall out . . . I've done so many knee bends at night that I'd start to class the next day and just fall down. I couldn't help it."[11]

Clayton earned a degree in agricultural economics in 1950, but his father's heart attack on October 16, 1949, had brought the future Speaker back to Springlake prematurely. For a time, Clayton ran the family farm.[12] Clayton became politically active in the local Democratic Party and served as a delegate pledged to presidential candidate Lyndon Johnson at the 1960 Democratic National Convention.[13]

Clayton perceived Johnson as a more conservative alternative to John Kennedy. "Come to find out, Johnson was more liberal than Kennedy, really, in actions," Clayton said later. The former Speaker admitted that he had reservations about Kennedy other than the Massachusetts Democrat's liberalism.

> Being brought up in a very religious community and particularly Protestant, the big concern was, basically, Kennedy and the Catholics. . . . And, before my father died, he said, 'We'll never elect a Catholic.' Of course, when I went out to the convention and met Kennedy, and when he won the nomination, I got to escort him around to the Texas delegation, and begin to know him a little more, I kind of liked him. I came home and campaigned for him, after the convention . . . He was really easy to get acquainted with. He was very easy to talk to.[14]

Clayton said the Texas Democratic delegation to the 1960 Democratic National Convention split between the liberals, led by Ralph Yarborough, and the conservatives. The more conservative delegates backed Johnson, but the liberals adamantly opposed the Texas senator. According to Clayton:

> I never will forget the evening before the nomination. Johnson came there . . . before us and said, "You know, we never will take a second position, and we're going to take it all or nothing."
>
> Well, sure enough, it was nothing. And then he came back, and said the same thing to us again with big ol' crocodile tears in his eyes . . . And that night Sam Rayburn got hold of him and got hold of the Kennedys, and the deal was cut, and it was cut and dried. He was going to [get] the vice presidential nomination. And I don't think Kennedy would have gotten elected if it hadn't have been for Rayburn.[15]

Clayton caught the political bug, running successfully for the state House. In 1962, at age thirty-four, Clayton represented a district that included Bailey, Castro, Deaf Smith, Lamb, and Parmer counties. He served in the Texas House for the next twenty years.[16] Clayton joined an unusually large freshman class that had been elected by voters angry over the sales tax approved by the previous legislature. After making opposition to the tax a key point on the campaign trail, Clayton sensed that he and other newcomers could make a big impact on Capitol politics.[17] On December 8, 1962, Clayton wrote an ill-advised letter to his fellow freshmen. "I am writing all the freshmen members of the House, to see if you would be interested in forming a freshman members' organization for the coming session," Clayton wrote. "With sixty new members in such an organization, we certainly could demand our share of recognition. By helping one another we could stand a good chance of passing prime legislation, projects that may be hard to accomplish individually."[18]

Clayton's independent streak irritated Byron Tunnell, who had already cinched election as the next Speaker. Tunnell worried that Clayton's letter represented the launching of an incipient rebellion from the House rank and file before the incoming Speaker had even been sworn in. Tunnell sent word to Clayton that a "freshman members' organization" would be unnecessary, and that aborted the effort.[19] Tunnell later said, however, that Clayton's initiative impressed him. "It was an indication that he was not an ordinary farmer," he said.[20]

In spite of this rough start, Clayton and Tunnell became close. On January 8, 1963, when Clayton joined 140 other House members voting in Tunnell as Speaker, the freshman representative visited the new Speaker in his office and had a premonition of his future. "Joan Hollowell was his secretary," Clayton said. "And she tells the story—and I vaguely remember—that I walked in there, looked around the office, and said, 'Someday this office'll be mine.'"[21] Hollowell, who later became Joan Whitworth, said she recalled being impressed that Clayton sounded confident rather than cocky.[22]

Clayton certainly demonstrated that he was going places as a key part of fellow conservative Tunnell's team. The future Speaker became one of only four freshmen to serve on the critical Appropriations Committee. He served as well on the Committee on Conservation and Reclamation, which dealt with water issues, later Clayton's signature issue. Clayton's instinct for attaching himself to up-and-comers did not fail when Tunnell became a Texas Railroad Commissioner. Tunnell tipped off Ben Barnes, and Clayton joined Barnes's phone team at Austin's Driskill Hotel, which blitzed House members to lock up the Speaker's race. For his efforts, Barnes awarded Clayton with choice office space.[23]

Clayton never earned a reputation as a skilled orator, and as Speaker would became famous for his occasional potshots at a defenseless English language. Speaking of pending legislation, he once urged members to "do this in one foul sweep." Trying to shut down a session, Clayton declared, "It's the sediment of the House that we adjourn."[24] "Clayton butchers the English language as if it were a hunk of mutton," one Capitol observer noted.[25] His clumsiness with the language, however, deceived opponents, and his House peers came to call him a "country slicker" (as opposed to a "city slicker"). Clayton didn't have to be a great orator, because he tirelessly worked the floor in support of his priorities. "By the time he got a bill up on the floor, he'd probably have talked to at least 100 of the 150 members about it—so that he didn't have to be that good on the mike," said fellow Representative Randy Pendleton, who represented the West Texas county seat of Andrews from 1963 to 1969.[26]

Clayton distinguished himself as one of the most conservative members of an already extremely conservative House. He repeatedly introduced a resolution opposing court-ordered school busing to achieve racial integration. He wanted to make it a misdemeanor to teach bilingual classes above the third grade; he also opposed any gun-control bills and the federal constitutional amendment granting eighteen-year-olds the vote. He also resisted a 1971 state constitutional amendment to increase Texas's small welfare payments. "Bill Clayton has a voting record that only Attila the Hun could appreciate," Representative Neil Caldwell of Angleton said.[27] Finally, Clayton voted no on the Equal Rights Amendment and the creation of a holiday honoring Martin Luther King, Jr., thus rounding his image as a social and economic conservative.[28]

In the 1960s and 1970s, Texas spent more on highways than other needs. Although prosperity allowed Texas and other southern states to increase expenditures for public services, their efforts still fell below the national average. In a 1975 study of the "business climate" of states, those rated highest were those with "low taxes, low levels of public assistance, restrictive labor legislation, and a low level of government spending and debt." Texas ranked near the top of such lists. The vast majority of House members and other state leaders in Austin agreed with this philosophy. Yet thanks to federal civil rights legislation, blacks, Mexican Americans, and women began to make inroads into the once solidly white male political system.[29]

Representing an always-parched region of West Texas, Clayton spent much of his House career obsessed with development of a state water plan, a focus that earned him the nickname "Mr. Water." Clayton pushed for legislation to develop irrigation in West Texas, to purchase water from other states, and to encourage water conservation. Environmentalists, however, sharply criticized him for pushing development schemes that would have devastated the landscape, endangered wildlife, and caused pollution.[30]

Water arose as a dominant political issue in the High Plains during a prolonged drought in the 1950s. The legislature created the Water Pollution Control Board and the Texas Water Research Committee to examine the state's water usage. The recommendations of these groups led to the widespread construction of manmade lakes and the creation of local water districts.[31] Many West Texas farmers opposed a state water-conservation program, arguing that such regulations violated property rights. By the late 1960s, however, Clayton (representing a region of the state where 3 percent of the population used 30 percent of the water resources but produced an even larger percentage of the state's agricultural output) became chief advocate for a Texas water plan. His plan called for the transfer of water from the Mississippi River through North Texas to the High Plains and then to the Rio Grande. The Mississippi water would have flowed through a series of canals and aqueducts and would have required the construction of sixty-seven dams.[32]

Critics called Clayton's cost estimates for the project unrealistic and deemed the chain of proposed dams harmful to the environment. Dr. Daniel Willard, a University of Texas botanist, warned a legislative committee that implementation of Clayton's Texas Water Plan "would completely destroy the face of Texas."[33] He predicted that the proposed reservoirs in East Texas, a region with high evaporation rates, would actually produce drought-enhancing climate changes in West Texas. Nevertheless, Clayton enjoyed the support of Lieutenant Governor Preston Smith, another West Texan, and other powerful state officials. The legislature placed the plan on the ballot in 1969 in the form of a constitutional amendment. It narrowly failed; the no vote in Houston was large enough to provide the margin of defeat.[34]

In 1974, Clayton called for a similar plan to import water from out of state and to construct twenty-seven new reservoirs, but voters also rejected this proposal. In 1981, the state enjoyed a budget surplus, and Clayton, then House Speaker, called for half of the money to be placed in a permanent water fund, but this time he did not submit a comprehensive water plan, and water supply competed with other budgetary needs, such as education. Voters shot down this proposition by a 4–1 margin.[35]

Speaker Clayton

With his campaign for a state water plan, Clayton again demonstrated leadership, forging close relations with powerful lawmakers, such as Preston Smith, proving his talent for prodigious fund-raising, and garnering $100,000 (more than $500,000 in today's dollars) for an advertising campaign on behalf of the water-plan amendment. And although Speakers tended to come from East Texas and Central Texas, it seemed that Clayton might be able to fulfill his prophecy that he would occupy the Speaker's office.[36] Clayton bided his time, but as the Sharpstown scandal erupted, he quickly emerged as a contender for the top House post. On September 24, 1971, the day after a grand jury indicted Speaker Gus Mutscher, around forty members of the legislature met in a Dallas hotel to discuss possible replacements. Clayton's name came up in the conversation. Mutscher resigned March 28, 1972, and was succeeded by Rayford Price. When Price lost in a runoff for reelection to the House in June 1972, he became a lame duck. Clayton nearly entered the Speaker's race, and even wrote a letter to his House peers announcing his candidacy, but never released its contents. Instead, a fellow West Texas conservative, Frank Calhoun, announced his bid.[37]

Under Speaker Price Daniel, Jr., Clayton maintained high visibility as a member of the Elections, Intergovernmental Affairs, and Natural Resources committees. Daniel had announced that he would serve only one term, and the 1975 race for the speakership began even before the 1973 legislative session started. On June 6, 1973, Clayton publicly announced his long-acknowledged ambition to run for Speaker of the 1975 session.[38]

Clayton immediately contrasted his vision with that of Price Daniel, announcing that, unlike his predecessor, he would not pursue a specific legislative agenda but would make the legislative process more efficient. "I don't think it's the speaker's prerogative to get involved in a legislative program," he told the *Dallas Morning News*. Clayton pledged to stress "economy and efficiency in the operation of the House . . . a more orderly system of scheduled committee and subcommittee meetings" and said he would seek more office space for House operations.[39]

As would be the case later with Speakers Gib Lewis and Tom Craddick, Clayton became entangled in an interlocking web of personal and political interests. Even as he announced his candidacy for the speakership, reporters posed questions about a land deal involving property along Lake Austin in which Clayton partnered with Texas Railroad Association lobbyist Walter Caven. Reporters also asked why Clayton, a director of Olton State Bank, voted to raise interest rates on consumer loans and supported a bill that would have allowed state officials to file financial disclosures in secret, sealed envelopes, even as he voted against legislation calling for lobbyist regulation. Clayton denied there was any conflict of interest regarding his votes.[40]

Clayton entered a heated three-way race. His opponents included Fred Head, the maverick who had successfully challenged Rayford Price's bid for reelection to the House. The third major candidate, Carl Parker (acknowledged as a liberal leader in the House), nevertheless had angered labor Democrats with his support of the 1974 proposed constitution, which had included a right-to-work clause.[41]

The 1974 Constitutional Convention, or "Con Con," as it was known, profoundly affected the Speaker's race. Daniel, elected convention president, appointed Clayton, Head, and Parker to the important Committee on Legislative Provisions. During the convention, a bitter battle broke out between Head and Parker, who accused each other of campaign dirty tricks such as issuing phony press releases announcing that certain House members had pledged their support for one of the candidates. Meanwhile, Clayton floated above the fray and, to many of his peers, increasingly looked better than his opponents.[42]

The convention proved to be a political disaster for both Head and Parker. Parker once declared, "No one can get on a liberal like a bunch of other liberals. If you don't agree with them one hundred percent of the time, they figure you are bound to have sold them out."[43] Parker's support of the new constitution proved fatal. Head, meanwhile, emerged as the only major Speaker candidate to vote against the proposed constitution. Two-thirds of the convention delegates (121 out of 181) had to endorse the proposed constitution for it to be brought to the voters. As mentioned in the last chapter, proponents fell three votes short, and Head came in for a large share of the political blame for what the United Press International called a "seven-month exercise in futility that cost the Texas taxpayers $5 million." Price Daniel in particular blamed Head, who he claimed was owned "lock, stock and barrel" by organized labor. Shortly afterward, nine House members previously committed to Head announced they were withdrawing their pledges because of the "lack of leadership" he had shown during the convention.[44]

Head's campaign collapsed, and his bitterness toward Parker meant that Clayton received the fallen candidate's endorsement. Borrowing the tactic that Ben Barnes used so successfully when he got the scoop on Byron Tunnell's appointment to the railroad commission, Clayton organized a telephone blitzkrieg of members and rapidly secured a number of endorsements from former Head supporters. Clayton built an odd coalition of conservatives, liberals, African Americans, and Mexican Americans who found him more trustworthy than Parker. "If I had chosen the person who would have been closer to me philosophically, it would not have been Billy Clayton," said Dallas state representative Eddie Bernice Johnson, who later served in Congress. "But I felt that I could trust what Billy Clayton said or did, and on that basis I decided to go with him."[45] In the end, enough liberals and moderates agreed with Johnson to provide Clayton with an easy 112–33 victory over Parker on the opening day of the 1975 legislature.[46]

After the post-Sharpstown reform movement fizzled in the early 1970s, it was perhaps inevitable that the Speaker's office would continue on its trajectory toward greater power and that lobbyists would continue to extend their influence over state politics. Under Clayton, the Speaker's fingerprints would appear on almost every action of the House. Beyond guiding the fate of legislation, Speakers became responsible for managing the Capitol grounds and gained hiring authority over an expanding number of jobs under the dome. In his inaugural speech, however, Clayton promised a sharp break from the leadership style of the Mutscher years. "I stand before you today to say the days of iron-handed rule are gone," Clayton told a cheering House. "The public won't stand for it, the members won't stand for it and, most of all, I won't stand for it."[47]

It didn't seem as though Clayton was ushering in a new era of democracy, however, in the opening days of his speakership. On the one hand, he distanced himself from the imperial trappings of the office by declining to live in the Speaker's apartment, converting the space into offices. He also contradicted expectations by releasing substantial financial records. On the other hand, he tightened access to public records. He required both a written request and his personal permission before information on "the operations, records, employees, or deliberations of the House of Representatives and any of its committees or departments" could be released to the public.[48] Challenged on the legality of blocking access to public records, Clayton told the *Fort Worth Star-Telegram* the move would stop "nosy employees checking on a colleagues' salary and precipitating a feud."[49] State attorney general John Hill ruled that Clayton's restrictions did not violate Texas's Open Records Act. Clayton also tried to ban all nonmembers from the House floor, even though the Capitol press had traditionally been granted access to this area. Outrage forced Clayton to abandon this plan. These actions, however, probably created a rocky relationship with the Capitol press that grew only pricklier.[50]

The major legislative controversy of Clayton's first term came with his advocacy of the so-called Bentsen bill, designed to give the junior senator from Texas a leg up in the 1976 Democratic presidential primary. First elected to the U.S. House of Representatives in 1948, Lloyd Bentsen served until 1955. The South Texan proved predictably conservative, participating enthusiastically in the Red Scare and pledging to ferret out "Reds" in the Truman administration. Bentsen retired from public office for fifteen years, but conservative Democrats like former governor John

Connally persuaded him to challenge Ralph Yarborough, the incumbent liberal Senator, in 1970. The well-funded Bentsen upset the favored Yarborough in the Democratic primary, and then won against Republican nominee and future president George Herbert Walker Bush in the November election.[51]

Bentsen announced in 1975 that he would run for president in 1976, and Lieutenant Governor Bill Hobby immediately endorsed him. The same day, the Texas House Elections Committee approved a bill, written by Bentsen's staff, that created the state's first-ever direct presidential primary. This "Bentsen bill" included a so-called winner-take-all provision that actually would award 75 percent of the state's Democratic National Convention delegates to whoever carried a plurality in the preference primary. The bill also set stiff requirements for out-of-state presidential candidates trying to get on the Texas ballot, and prohibited delegates from remaining uncommitted, which would have made it more difficult for liberals to pool resources in an attempt to gain control of the Texas delegation from the Bentsen supporters. The law also allowed Bentsen to appear on the primary ballot as a candidate for both president and senator. Hobby, Clayton, and other state party leaders pushed for the bill's passage.[52]

In spite of all these advantages, however, Bentsen lagged far behind the surprising underdog campaign of former Georgia governor Jimmy Carter. Bentsen's well-financed effort completely sputtered before the Texas primary, although he announced he would stay on as a favorite-son candidate to "see that the Texas viewpoint is heard at the Democratic convention."[53] Unfortunately for him, many conservatives in the Democratic Party voted instead in the Republican primary in order to back Ronald Reagan's challenge to incumbent president Gerald Ford. As a result, liberals constituted a disproportionate percentage of Democratic-primary voters May 1, 1976. The main beneficiary of the Bentsen bill turned out to be Carter, who won ninety-two of the state's ninety-eight delegates after the May primary. Bentsen got the remaining six.[54]

In June 1976, Clayton expressed worry over the 350,000 or more conservative Democrats who opted to vote in the Republican primary. Clayton claimed that conservative Democrats suffered an unfair disadvantage, since the most conservative presidential candidates were on the GOP primary ballot but the Texas Republican Party was not strong enough yet to be competitive in state races. Conservative cross-party voting had proved decisive, he believed, in Bentsen's defeat. Clayton called for combining the two presidential primaries onto one ballot so voters could choose a candidate without picking a party affiliation.[55]

This effort never gained traction, but Clayton and Lieutenant Governor Hobby continued to experiment with party-primary laws in order to strengthen conservatives in both major parties. In 1979, Hobby pursued passage of the so-called Connally bill, which was designed to give an advantage to former Texas governor John Connally, who had officially defected to the GOP in 1973 while serving as Richard Nixon's secretary of the treasury. In 1979, Connally already had begun his campaign for the 1980 Republican presidential nomination. Hobby asked the state Senate to pass a bill that would separate the presidential primaries from other races on the ballot. A voter under this system could vote in the Republican presidential primary for Connally, or perhaps Reagan, and then back conservatives in a Democratic primary for down-ballot races. Like Clayton's "unitary primary" concept, this system would have been without parallel in the United States.[56]

To defeat the Connally bill, a dozen of the more liberal senators ducked out of the chamber's back door to break the quorum required for the Senate to conduct its business. They hid in an Austin garage apartment, playing cards and napping while the press and the Texas Rangers combed the city looking for them. Senator Gene Jones of Houston, tired of the cramped quarters, fled home. Texas Rangers armed with a faxed photograph of the senator showed up at his door. Rangers asked the man who answered the door whether he was Jones. The man said yes, and the Rangers arrested him and flew him back to Austin. Only after the group got back to Austin did the Rangers discover they had arrested Jones's look-alike brother. When the Rangers had arrived at his residence, the real Senator Jones fled to the backyard, hopped the fence, and remained invisible for another day. The escaped senators became known as the "Killer Bees," named after the Africanized honeybees causing hysteria in Texas because of their alleged lethality and aggressiveness and their rapid approach toward the United States border from Mexico. The Bees triumphed after Hobby gave up on reaching a quorum. In the end, Connally spent more than $10 million and won just one delegate to the GOP national convention, dropping out of the race long before the Texas primary.[57]

The Republicans' Return

Democratic conservatives like Clayton and Hobby tried to preserve the dominance of conservatives in the Democratic Party, but the political world had already substantially changed. The two-party era in Texas began with the election of William P. Clements as governor in 1978. The

Democratic Party primary that year produced a surprise when Attorney General John Hill, a relative liberal, defeated incumbent Democratic governor Dolph Briscoe. Hill's campaign alienated the governor's rural supporters, who opted instead to support the Republican nominee that fall, Bill Clements.[58]

The multimillionaire founder and chief executive of an oil drilling company, Clements was nominated by President Richard Nixon as under secretary of the navy and served for four years before he returned to Texas and announced plans to run for governor. He promised to cut taxes and slash state programs to balance the budget. The age of progovernment conservatives had ended. Cultivating an image as a tough, no-nonsense "Texan to his toenails," Clements won over many Briscoe Democrats. Historian Randolph Campbell also attributes much of Clements's success to white anger against programs such as affirmative action, which had been supported by past Democratic administrations in Washington. "The Republican Party's 'southern strategy'—based on backlash against the civil rights movement and federal support of minority interests—had come into its own in Texas," Campbell writes. "Republicans in the 1976 primary, for example, voted overwhelmingly [in a nonbinding referendum] against busing to achieve school integration, whereas Democrats refused to put the question on their ballot. The Democratic party continued along the road to becoming the refuge of minorities, a high percentage of whom did not vote, and Republican candidates such as Clements benefited from a steady influx of whites into their party."[59]

Clements's victory in November 1978 sent shock waves through Texas's political world comparable to those registered by John Tower's Senate victory almost two decades earlier. The number of Republican Party primary voters increased from 158,403 in 1978 to 265,851 in 1982, signaling a deeper shift in sentiment toward the GOP. Clements lost his reelection bid to Democrat Mark White during a recession blamed on Republican president Ronald Reagan, and mostly progressive Democrats swept the statewide races in the executive branch. With the popular and deep-pocketed Senator Lloyd Bentsen leading the ballot, Democrats capitalized on a massive, coordinated campaign that elected one of the most diverse groups of statewide officeholders in Texas history. Yet when Tower retired from the Senate in 1984, Republicans held onto the seat with the victory of former Democrat Phil Gramm. An oil bust in 1986 eroded state tax revenues, allowing Clements to recapture the governor's mansion from White and opening the door to Republican dominance of the state for the next decade.[60]

The varied efforts of men like Clayton to alter the state primary system shared an undemocratic essence. The idea behind these schemes was to make the primary voter base significantly more conservative than the general electorate and to parlay even a minor victory by a conservative favorite son into a delegate rout. Yet in spite of his role in these failed efforts, Clayton received high marks from his peers—even liberals who disliked his agenda—for his fairness toward members. Eddie Bernice Johnson gave Clayton only tepid support during his first Speaker's race, yet Clayton rewarded her by making her chair of the Labor Committee, a key post. "When he called me to ask me to take the chairmanship, I said I was not philosophically on the same side as he was and I wasn't sure how comfortable I would be on his team," she said. "He told me he wanted me to do whatever I needed to do to abide by my principles."[61]

Clayton's Achievements

Clayton exhibited the characteristics of other successful southern white Democratic politicians of the era. While accommodating the new voices in the legislature and expanding and modernizing the services provided by state government, he focused on promoting businesslike management and economic development. Regardless, critics emerged when Clayton won an unprecedented third term as Speaker in 1979. Although he had been hailed as the man in the white hat by some after his election in the wake of Sharpstown, by the end of the 1970s, his opponents derided him as the second coming of Gus Mutscher. "Speaker Bill Clayton is spending state money at the rate of more than $192,000 per year to pay for a staff that he admits may help him formulate key legislative programs and retain leadership of the House for years to come," Andy Welch of the *Denton Record-Chronicle* observed in a 1976 analysis.[62] Clayton's staff of eighteen, significantly larger than those enjoyed by Speakers in the 1960s, included a full-time press secretary, George Works. This indicated that Speakers made news year-round, even when the legislature wasn't in session.

Even if he presented himself as a limited-government conservative, Clayton instituted a professionalization of the state legislature and its staff that was unprecedented in Texas history. Drafting legislation now became a year-round affair, and there were no off years. Clayton allocated money so members had more support services, and the House used computers extensively for the first time in its work. To provide members more room, he moved some offices and agencies out of the Capitol to other state-owned property in Austin.[63] "We were the first ones who put the House on computerization," he said. "I wanted to see [the state government] operate efficiently, and I wanted to see everybody be pleased with the way it operated."[64]

As Speaker, Clayton also expanded the role of standing committees, which met in between sessions. He would direct the chairs of these committees to examine certain bills or legislative issues while the House was in recess so solid research could be provided earlier in sessions. He also gave these standing committees and their chairs greater budgetary authority over agencies. Finally, Clayton allowed members to file bills in advance of a session.[65]

No Speaker before had asserted such authority over Capitol staffing. At the time of his computerization drive, Clayton fired four senior staffers whom he said were standing in the way of progress. Clayton removed about thirty janitors, many with long years of service, replacing them with a cheaper custodial service.[66] While the budget for the Speaker's office increased, Clayton instituted tighter limits on members' postage and telephone-call expenses. Dallas representative Paul Ragsdale said this move made members more dependent on the Speakers' staff for research and information. "I think we're turning the clock back to the Gus Mutscher days," said liberal House member John Bryant of Dallas. "I think he's trying to set himself up as an absolute power so that we can't do a dadgum thing about it."[67]

In a majority-urban state, representatives from Texas's largest cities complained about the legislature's dominance by Clayton's men, known as the "rural mafia" or "Billy's Boys." "If you're not on the team, you're not in the game," one member complained to the *Dallas Times Herald*.[68]

The cohesion of Billy's Boys, who included James "Pete" Laney, a future Speaker, increased as Clayton began holding Sunday-night briefings in the space formerly used as the Speaker's apartment. Committee chairs would munch snacks and down drinks as they swapped status updates on pending legislation. The extent of Clayton's power, however, became clear in March 1977. He announced he had enough votes to be elected Speaker a third consecutive time, in 1979, and that he planned to remain Speaker through a fourth term. He noted that in 1981 he would be able to enter the race for governor, state comptroller, or some other statewide position in 1982.[69]

Brilab

Those hopes crashed in 1980 when the FBI announced it was investigating Clayton as part of a sting operation involving corrupt union officials trying to bribe politicians. The scandal came to be known in the press as Brilab (bribery and labor). On October 19, 1979, Clayton had met with L. G. Moore, regional director of the Operating Engineers International Union and former member of the Texas Constitutional Revision Commission, and Joe Hauser, identified to Clayton as one of the top people with the Prudential Insurance Company.[70]

In fact, Hauser, previously convicted in California and Arizona on insurance-fraud charges, had been sent to Clayton as part of an FBI sting. During his meeting with Clayton, Hauser complained about the State Employees Retirement Board's acceptance of a bid from the Metropolitan Insurance Company and claimed that Prudential could save the state $1 million a year. At the end of their conversation, Moore and Hauser said they wanted to make a contribution to Clayton's political fund. Clayton admits he was handed $5,000, and then Moore and Hauser said they could contribute up to $600,000 in the future. Clayton later said he told his secretary to put the money in an envelope in a safe place because he intended to return the money, believing it would be a political embarrassment for him to receive so much from a liberal labor leader and for Moore to be seen by his union colleagues as backing a conservative. Clayton never reported the receipt of cash, because, he said, he intended to return it. He said he didn't refuse the money, however, because he didn't want to embarrass his friend Moore.[71] In a 2004 interview, Clayton said:

> I would've done the same thing again had I been approached the same way. A friend of mine brought this guy in my office, and he said we could save the state a million dollars if we can open the bidding so he can bid . . . I couldn't see anything wrong with that . . . My friend wanted to give me a $5,000 contribution at that time. I said, "No, you don't—you can't afford this and I don't want it." And he just *insisted*. So I took the cash and put it in the . . . credenza drawer. And it lay there and lay there . . . And consequently . . . the only violation that . . . really occurred, because we didn't do anything to benefit the guy, was to not report that $5,000 . . . And I didn't report it because I was going to give it back . . . So that cost me about $400,000 and a six-week trial to prove my innocence.[72]

On February 9, 1980, the *Dallas Times Herald* ran a front-page story that led with this explosive paragraph: "FBI agents posing for a year as Prudential Insurance Co. agents paid thousands of dollars to union leaders, organized crime figures, and elected officials in four Southwestern states in connection with an insurance kickback scheme . . . Political leaders involved in the investigation included . . . Billy Clayton, Speaker of the Texas House."[73] Clayton's five-year sway over the House weakened immediately after the Brilab allegations were aired, and members started floating their names as possible replacements. Potential Speakers included Fort Worth representative Gib Lewis, who began collecting pledges of support from House members in case Clayton should step down. "I don't see how Clayton could remain a candidate under indictment regardless of his guilt or innocence," said Representative Bob Maloney, a Dallas Republican. "We couldn't have a speaker under that kind of cloud."[74]

An extraordinary meeting of twelve leading lobbyists convened in Austin to see whether they should cut off the momentum of a liberal Speaker candidate, John Bryant of Dallas, by anointing a successor. The committee decided that Clayton's defense seemed plausible. "We decided, kind of informally, that God-almighty, let's hang loose for awhile," Durward Curlee of the Texas Savings and Loan League told the *Dallas Times Herald*. "Clayton's looking better. This is not a Sharpstown." Amazingly, the *Times Herald* did not comment on the spectacle of lobbyists holding a private meeting to contemplate whether they should handpick a new Speaker.[75]

Clayton's position became more perilous when a federal grand jury indicted him on June 12, 1980. During Clayton's trial that fall, his performance on the witness stand impressed jurors. Defense lawyers even turned the ten minutes of wiretapped conversation between Moore and Clayton to their advantage. Clayton could be heard saying during a November 8 meeting with Moore and Hauser, "You know, our only position is we don't want to do anything that's illegal or to get anybody in trouble, and you all don't either."[76] Jurors later said they could not identify any specific illegal act Clayton supposedly had committed, and they accepted Clayton's story that he had considered opening up bidding for a state contract only as an attempt to save the state money. By contrast, jurors were heavily put off by Hauser's criminal record, which undercut his credibility. Prosecutors made a monumental goof when they called to the stand Assistant Secretary of State Chip Holt, director of that office's campaigns and ethics division, who told jurors that Clayton had not violated the law by failing to either report or return the $5,000 given by Moore. Jurors were also swayed by the fact that Clayton had put the money away and never deposited it in his campaign fund.[77]

A jubilant jury acquitted Clayton on October 22, 1980. Several jurors said they felt Moore and Hauser had entrapped Clayton.[78] The jury's decision freed Clayton to win a fourth term as Speaker. Clayton felt so confident after his acquittal that he hinted he might seek a fifth term in 1983, a statement that caught Gib Lewis, planning to run for Speaker that year, completely off-guard. "That's entirely the reverse of what he's told me," Lewis told the *Fort Worth Star-Telegram.*[79]

House dissidents made a last stab at limiting Clayton's powers, apparently undiminished by his Brilab ordeal. Frank Gaston of Dallas introduced a package of House rule changes that would have allowed members to select the committees they serve on, based on seniority; curbed the power of committee chairs appointed by the Speaker, by not allowing them to pass legislation on to subcommittees without the consent of other committee members; and required the House Administration Committee and the Speaker to submit itemized reports of expenditures to the House. Gaston argued that committee chairs answerable to Clayton had too much power to kill legislation by referring bills they didn't like to unfriendly subcommittees. Clayton's allies dismissed Gaston's faction as "termites," and the House rejected the proposals 89–48. Another proposal would have ended the Speaker's power to appoint the House parliamentarian, chief clerk, and sergeant at arms, requiring these posts to be voted on by the full House, but a majority also rejected that measure.[80]

The power of the Speaker's office had so grown that Clayton could snuff a full rebellion in utero even after the humiliation of an indictment and trial. Nevertheless, Clayton's chances of winning statewide office suffered a serious blow in 1982 when voters rejected, 57 percent to 43 percent, a state constitutional amendment setting aside half the state's budget surplus to create a water fund. Clayton had campaigned heavily for the amendment, and analysts believed the proposition's failure reflected general voter distrust of Clayton after the Brilab trial. Clayton's support among Democrats statewide also declined sharply because of the perception that he had cooperated too willingly with the congressional redistricting demands of conservative Republican governor Bill Clements during the 1981 session.[81]

In early December 1981, Clayton announced his plan to run for state land commissioner the following year. But by late January he had dropped out of the race, which was eventually won by liberal Democrat Garry Mauro. The power of the Speaker's office played a role in Clayton's decision. He apparently decided that the Brilab trial had destroyed his chance of winning a gubernatorial race, but incumbent Democrats Bill Hobby and Bob Bullock already filled the positions of lieutenant governor and state comptroller. State Democratic chair Bob Slagle said that Clayton probably viewed serving as land commissioner as "at best a lateral move" and probably a "rung down" from the Speaker's post.[82]

By expanding the Speaker's authority over House administration and effectively using his appointment authority to guide legislation, Clayton created an office that could be seen as a step up from the governorship. Clayton's personal power ended up diminished, but two of the men who followed him as House leaders—Gib Lewis and Pete Laney—would expand the foundation the Speaker from Springlake had laid and make the office one of the most powerful in the United States.

CHAPTER 8

The Executive Speakership, Part Two

1983–2002

Texas leaders often feel as if they are in a hole, either from deficits or from attempting to keep up with the ever-increasing demands for services from a booming population and diverse business community. In 1990, the entire legislature stood side by side in an honest-to-goodness hole that was more than 100 feet deep, just north of the Capitol. The dramatic renovation of the Capitol and its expanded underground office facility saved the venerable structure from literally collapsing because of neglect and misuse. This moment also stood as a metaphor for the decade of the 1980s, since state leaders were fighting to recover from a devastating economic recession. The first representative to serve five terms as House Speaker, Gib Lewis, presided over some of the most dramatic changes in state government. Equally momentous, he also pushed a reluctant legislature to renovate and expand the 100-year-old seat of government.

Although he would represent the Fort Worth area in the Texas House for more than twenty years, Gib Lewis, like his predecessor Billy Clayton, grew up in small-town Texas. Born in a log cabin in 1936 in Oletha—described by *Fort Worth Star-Telegram* reporter Mike Ritchey as "an eyeblinker of a town in East Central Texas"—Lewis grew up in the Central Texas community of Mexia, which in the 1950s had a population of less than 7,000.[1] His parents divorced when he was two. Lewis describes his family as struggling occupants of the lower middle class. "Kind of like a comedian said one time," Lewis recalled. "'I was raised poor but I didn't know it . . . I really wasn't poor. My mother was poor, and she just kind of drug me around with her.'" Everyone worked in Mexia, he said, and the lack of general prosperity served as a social equalizer: "I remember working from the time that I was eight, nine, ten years old, from sacking groceries at the local grocery store, to hoeing and picking cotton with everybody else out in the fields, and at the same time having the paper route and doing it because everybody else did . . . Every kid had some kind of a job, and I remember the incentive was, if you picked enough cotton, you could always get your choice of school clothes."[2]

Lewis attended Sam Houston State University in Huntsville before signing up for a four-year tour of duty in the air force, which he spent flying on B-36 and B-52 bombers. While stationed at Carswell Air Force Base in Fort Worth, he began attending Texas Christian University. After his military service, Lewis brought his extensive work experience to the Olmsted-Kirk Paper Company in Dallas, which hired him to work in its Fort Worth office. The job turned out to be a turning point in Lewis's life. "I guess this was where I got involved in my politics," Lewis said in a 2004 interview. "They wanted their salespeople to be very visible in the community . . . and to do that, they wanted you to be involved in the civic activities. They wanted all their people to be members of the Kiwanis Club, the Lions Club, the Rotary Club, or the advertising club."

> And that is when I got really involved in politics. I was president of the Lions Club one year and president of the Junior Chamber of Commerce the following year. And they have a couple of craftsmen clubs, which were industry clubs, and I was also president of these clubs. So pretty much through civic activity politics, you learn how to cut a deal . . .
> I used to say that through my civic activities and involvement in Fort Worth, I knew almost everybody in town. I mean, I could go to downtown Fort Worth and people would tell you, they were amazed that I would know everybody on the street.[3]

Lewis said that when he served in the legislature, he was surprised to find how many of his House peers he had already met through his club activities. Because so many members had worked in a nonpartisan environment before they wound up collaborating and colliding on controversial legislation, Lewis believes, a convivial atmosphere was easy to establish in the state House. The intense partisanship of recent legislative sessions, he believes, is in part a product of the decline of civic clubs. "When I got elected to the Legislature . . . I had a good relationship already established. Of course, once you establish a relationship outside of the Legislature, it gives you more credibility. They know who you are, and they feel more like they have something in common with you," Lewis said.[4]

In 1964, three years after starting at Olmsted-Kirk, Lewis opened his own firm, Lewis Label Products, Inc., which specialized in manufacturing pressure-sensitive labels and decals. The company made Lewis a millionaire. Lewis entered politics in 1969, winning election to the city council of River Oaks, a Fort Worth suburb. Fort Worth voters elected him to the Texas House of Representatives in 1971, the tumultuous session that saw Gus Mutscher step down as Speaker and Rayford Price emerge as his successor only to lose his reelection bid.[5] Watching Sharpstown unfold, Lewis said, taught him to be suspicious of a press he believed to be dominated by antiestablishment reporters who had been "hippies" and "demonstrators" during the 1960s.[6] Later on, when Lewis became Speaker, he came to call the Capitol press corps "the wolf pack."[7]

Preparing to Be Speaker

Luck frequently played a role in Lewis's House career. For instance, occupying a desk near Price Daniel, Jr., may have played a role when Daniel, as Speaker, named Lewis chair of the important House Committee on Natural Resources in 1973.[8] Achieving high visibility early in his career, Lewis became Billy Clayton's choice to head the House Committee on Intergovernmental Affairs in 1977, a post he held for four sessions. Lewis and Clayton clicked. Like Clayton, Lewis considered himself a business-oriented conservative who drew a broad spectrum of members to his leadership team. He added to this a vastly more gregarious personality that made him highly attractive as a possible replacement Speaker when Clayton ran into legal difficulties from Brilab. To many legislators, he presented an attractive alternative to liberal legislator John Bryant.[9] "Gib Lewis is a man who can appeal to more Democrats and at the same time to more Republicans," said Frank Gaston, a Republican from Dallas. "I expect that a lot of Republicans, knowing that there is little opportunity for one of their own in the race, might support Gib."[10]

Lewis shied from taking the microphone on the House floor, which allowed him to avoid unpleasant disagreements with legislators possessing long memories. "Dapperly dressed with a long cigar jammed between his teeth, Lewis is a shrewd operator—a politician to the quick," a *Dallas Morning News* story said. "A glad-handing back-slapper with the finesse of a snake-oil salesman, Lewis has nurtured long and fast political friendships by going to great lengths to avoid offending anyone. A fence straddler, he's a political pragmatist, unburdened by any overwhelming passions to right social wrongs."[11]

These same eager-to-please traits, however, aroused the suspicions of the Capitol press, which described Lewis as "lacking brains."[12] Lewis's predecessor, Billy Clayton, became well known for committing an occasional verbal faux pas. Reporters found Lewis's way with words worthy of its own name: "Gibberish." As Speaker, Lewis would proclaim particularly auspicious events to be "mon-e-mentus," and once introduced England's Prince Charles by saying, "Let me welcome you to Texas and tell you how thankful you are to be here." Web sites today recall the more legendary gaffes of Lewis's speakership, such as when Lewis told an assembly, "I am filled with humidity." Other classic "Gibisms" included:

"This is unparalyzed in the state's history."

"I want to thank each and every one of you for having extinguished yourselves this session."

"There's a lot of uncertainty that's not clear in my mind."

"The budget can be cut by employee nutrition."

"This problem is a two-headed sword."

"They're just beatin' their heads against a dead horse."[13]

Lewis acknowledged that he had committed verbal miscues during his tenure as Speaker, but credited the Capitol press corps with stressing these statements. "The problem I had was that I never realized that it was such a detriment to my career that I had a lot of colloquialisms and a lot of expressions."[14]

Appearances were deceiving, Lewis's many friends in the House noted. "Fortunately we don't have to take an intellectual test to run for political office or a lot of us would fail," said Representative Chris Semos, the Dallas County Democratic chairman. "The only test we have to take is with the voters. Gib Lewis is as intellectually sound as most members and probably more so than most. Those who know him, love him for what he is. That's better and more advantageous than us getting a Rhodes scholar as speaker."[15]

Even as Lewis ran his first Speaker's race, newspapers asked questions about his fund-raising. Although Clayton's fate remained unclear in 1980, Lewis raised approximately $21,000 by the end of that June for an anticipated Speaker election the following January. In a problem that would plague him through his decade as Speaker, he failed to report as an in-kind contribution the free use of fellow legislator Charles Evans's airplane. Flying to meet legislators across the state, Lewis spent 94 hours in Evans's plane between March 1 and June 30. Lewis also failed to properly report the free use of other lawmakers' planes and some 200 hours of volunteer work from state lawmaker Mike Millsap. Lewis raised eyebrows as well when he presented members of the Intergovernmental Affairs Committee, which he chaired, with gold-colored watches paid for by lobbyists for pari-mutuel betting interests and other political contributors with pending legislation before the House. Lewis initially claimed he had paid for the watches himself, but when he was unable to produce a cancelled check, he admitted lobbyists paid for them.[16]

These miniscandals erupted in 1980 while Billy Clayton battled prosecutors in a Houston courtroom. Lewis set aside his speakership quest when a jury acquitted Clayton, and the Speaker came back for a final term. Lewis's long journey toward the speakership finally ended on November 12, 1981, when he announced that he had received written pledges from 113 of 149 House members. In Lewis's view, the speakership represented the ultimate political prize and constituted the most powerful office in the state. The Speaker, he said, "can push or defeat any proposal that he wants to get involved in . . . Every piece of legislation has to filter through his office . . . He has life or death [power] over what happens in the legislative process. The only thing a governor can do is veto a bill or sign it. But it has to go through the speaker's office before any of that can happen."[17]

Lewis barely had time to celebrate. Two weeks after announcing that he had the speakership locked up, Lewis made the headlines again, this time because of an embarrassing hunting trip. The Speaker-to-be fired at a covey of quail and ended up peppering a man with birdshot. The man, who remained unidentified in press reports, suffered a bloodied cheekbone. "They were little old pellets hardly big enough to hurt anybody," Lewis said.[18]

In spite of two years of bad press, Lewis had raised $430,000 for his Speaker race by January 1982, about twenty times that of his opponent, Grand Prairie Democrat Carlyle Smith. Maintaining a large campaign account was now part of the Speaker's arsenal for defending his position and supporting friendly legislators. Fort Worth oilman Perry R. Bass became Lewis's chief financial lifeline, contributing $10,000. The fund-raising paid off handsomely: Lewis won the speakership in mid-January 1983 by an overwhelming 144–2 margin with one abstention, the first Speaker elected from an urban district since W. O. Reed of Dallas in 1947.[19]

Speaker Lewis

If many saw Lewis more as a hunting companion or fellow country-club member, they were shocked when, in less than a month, he acquired even more institutional control for the speakership. Having won a comfortable mandate in the Speaker election, he successfully persuaded a compliant House to give him the power to fire committee chairs and employees of House members. Robert W. Calvert, a former Speaker and former chief justice of the state supreme court, expressed amazement that the House rank and file would surrender so much authority to Lewis. Calvert declared: "[In the 1930s] . . . there was no such thing as the speaker and his close friends completely dominating the process in the House. There were too many strong-willed, strong-minded people who were totally independent. It seems to me today that the 'good-old-boy' philosophy is dominant. The 'good-old-boy' philosophy says, 'Look, you can get more done being a good old boy than you can by fighting.' . . . We thought that the way to get things done was to fight for them."[20]

Lewis's inaugural session as Speaker ended with another controversy. Lewis made one more "inadvertent" move when he neglected to mention that he had invested in a firm that held interests in liquor-related businesses. This drew notice because Lewis had been accused of assigning liquor-regulation bills to hostile committees. Bills aimed at raising the Texas drinking age from nineteen to twenty-one, to ban open containers in motor vehicles, and to strengthen penalties for driving under the influence numbered among the legislation in question. Midsession, Lewis announced the omission of forty-nine business interests from his financial-disclosure statements, sparking a House Ethics subcommittee inquiry. Eventually, in July 1983, the state ethics panel exonerated Lewis of wrongdoing for filing incomplete financial-disclosure forms. By then, Lewis had already paid the state an $800 fine.[21]

House Bill 72

After a tentative start, Lewis made his mark on state government when Democratic governor Mark White called for teacher pay hikes. Lewis said he would agree to raises, but only if they were tied to education reform.

> Mark White had promised [when he was elected governor that] school teachers would get a raise. And so he came over to my office and said, "Here's what I want" . . . and I said, "Mark, I'll tell you what. Number one, to do that, you're going to have to have a tax increase. And before you have a tax increase for schoolteachers, you'd better sit back and get some better-quality education."
>
> What had happened . . . I had gone through about four [receptionists]

who couldn't spell, or you couldn't read what they'd written . . . These were recent products of the Texas educational system. And I said, "We're going to have to do something to teach these kids how to read and write and do arithmetic." . . . I said, "I think I had a better education when I was in the sixth grade than some of these kids who are getting out of high school . . . I'm going to tell you, you're not going to get me to sign off on it until we have a complete overhaul of our education system."

. . . We got Ross Perot to head it up, which was great, because that gave him the visibility he wanted . . . I think he did a great service to Texas by taking the time and energy that he took . . . and I think the recommendations of the committee turned out to be good.[22]

When Lewis, Hobby, and White began mulling school reform, Texas ranked thirtieth in the nation in teacher pay and forty-ninth in expenditure per pupil. Texas students also ranked near the bottom nationally in Scholastic Aptitude Test (a type of college entrance exam) scores and forty-second in percentage of high school graduates attending college.[23]

White, Hobby, and Lewis impaneled a citizens' committee headed by eccentric billionaire Perot, who ran as a third-party presidential candidate in 1992 and 1996. Examining education from top to bottom for a year starting in 1983, the committee sought to reverse the perceived lax school standards of the 1960s and 1970s and presented a package of reforms known collectively as House Bill 72, changes to Texas education as significant as the earlier Gilmer-Aikin laws. The recommendations, costing a total of $4.2 billion, were approved by the legislature during a thirty-day special session on July 3, 1984.[24]

The reforms attempted to equalize state funding formulas for school districts; the 151 poorest districts received a 44 percent per capita funding increase, while the 151 richest saw their state funding cut by 25 percent. The bill raised teachers' salaries and instituted a career ladder for educators based on years of service (though this was not funded by the state). The new law also required teachers to take so-called competency tests and to meet tighter certification standards. The state would fund prekindergarten for economically disadvantaged children and free summer school for students who spoke English as a second language, and it required schools to provide tutorials for failing students. Undergraduate degrees in education at state colleges and universities were replaced by degrees in specific subject areas like history or science. Standardized tests were also implemented to measure school performance. The most controversial aspect of the bill, besides the teacher competency tests, however, was the bill's "no pass, no play" requirement. The legislature raised the minimum passing grade to 70, and students who failed a class would become ineligible for extracurricular activities, including sports, unless the grade report for the next six weeks showed passing marks.[25]

That the legislature implemented such major changes in a mere month, as opposed to the marathon wrangling over school funding that would happen in the early 1990s and at the start of the twenty-first century, can be credited to the cohesion of the top leadership, many observers of the 1984 education special session agree. "We had a consensus among the leadership on what direction we were going to take on the major issues," said Bill Haley, who led the House Public Education Committee and sponsored the Perot reforms in the lower House.[26]

"One thing the Perot committee did do right was we covered this whole state and we worked hard," added Carl Parker, the Senate sponsor of the Perot reforms in 1984. "We listened to everybody who had an ax to grind about education. We had a plan when we got there (for the session)."[27] Many also credit Perot, who spent a great deal of his own money to promote the reforms, hiring his own political consultants to ensure public support. "Ross Perot of course is an absolute tornado of energy," said political columnist Molly Ivins. "And . . . among other things, [he] went all over the state preaching to businessmen and business groups and chambers of commerce. 'Look y'all, if we don't improve the public schools, y'all aren't going to have workers who are worth anything. Your businesses will go to pot.' And of course it's a perfectly legitimate argument and nobody can make it . . . with more vigor than H. Ross."[28]

Opposition to the reforms was fierce. The most conservative Republicans in the Texas House, such as Tom DeLay (later elected to majority leader of the U.S. House) and Tom Craddick (later elected Texas House Speaker) voted against the Perot reforms and the taxes to pay for them. Parents of public school athletes and coaches organized campaigns to reverse "no pass, no play." Other parents objected to high-stakes standardized testing, and teachers protested the competency tests and the increased bureaucracy that would be required to monitor school progress.[29]

The reforms did move teacher salaries upward so Texas matched the average nationwide for the first time, but teacher resentment remained deep. The Texas State Teachers Association, one of the largest organizations for educators in the state, refused to endorse White in 1986, as it had in 1982. Many teachers ended up staying home when White faced former governor Bill Clements in a rematch in November 1986. By then, oil prices, which fueled an economic boom in the state in the early 1980s, had collapsed from $35 a barrel to $10, requiring White to call a special session of the legislature to close a $2 billion state deficit. State employee pay raises were revoked and taxes were raised just months before the state ballot.[30] Clements returned to the Governor's Mansion with 53 percent of the vote, although many political commentators noted that his margin over White was surprisingly small, given the awful circumstances surrounding the incumbent.[31]

The School-Funding Mess

The oil bust, combined with a collapse of the real estate market and the savings and loan crisis of the late 1980s, placed state government in desperate straits.[32] These crises made a mockery of the attempts by House Bill 72 to equalize desperately uneven school spending across the state. The state's school-funding system had already faced a long series of legal challenges, beginning in the late 1960s, by parents living in poor school districts. On May 16, 1968, 400 students walked out of predominantly Mexican American Edgewood High School in San Antonio to protest poor funding and inadequate facilities. Edgewood schools lacked up-to-date textbooks, chalk, and in some cases toilet paper. Parental protests led the Mexican American Legal Defense and Education Fund (MALDEF) to challenge the constitutionality of school funding in *Rodríguez v. San Antonio ISD* (1971), a case filed in federal court.[33]

MALDEF lawyers demonstrated that Alamo Heights, San Antonio's richest school district, could raise $413 per capita, while the Edgewood district could only levy $37 per pupil, an 11–1 ratio. On March 21, 1973, the U.S. Supreme Court ruled 5–4 that Texas's financing system did not violate the Constitution and that funding inequities would have to be resolved by the state of Texas.[34] The battle moved to the state courts in 1984 with *Edgewood ISD v. Kirby*. This time, MALDEF lawyers argued that unequal school funding violated the provision of the Texas Constitution requiring the state to provide an "efficient and free school system." Following five years of wrangling, the case finally reached the state supreme court, which in October 1989 ruled in favor of the plaintiffs. Funding inequities had only worsened since the U.S. Supreme Court dismissed *Rodríguez v. San Antonio*. The Texas Supreme Court noted that Alamo Heights held property wealth of $570,109 per student, compared to $38,854 per student in Edgewood, a 15–1 ratio. The court ordered the state legislature to implement a fair system of funding by 1991.[35]

Governor Clements ended up calling three separate special sessions to consider school finance. He himself proved to be the sticking point by insisting that any increase in funding for poor districts be paired with a reduction of state regulations and standards for public schools. A fourth special session finally produced a bill that increased school spending by $528 million. An increase in cigarette taxes and a quarter-cent increase in the sales tax provided the revenues. This legislation did not, however, address the inequities created by Texas's reliance on property taxes as the main source of school funding. Legal challenges to the finance system continued in the courts.[36]

In 1991, the state supreme court ruled that the new school-funding scheme also failed to meet constitutional requirements. Once again, it gave the legislature the summer to come up with an equitable funding plan or face a court takeover of the school system. The legislature developed a plan that shifted tax funds from high-wealth school districts to poorer ones. In response, the courts extended the legislative deadline. In a 1992 special session, Republicans killed a proposed constitutional amendment that would have reduced administrative costs by consolidating school districts, and in 1993, Texas voters rejected a constitutional amendment that would have equalized school funding to a limited degree. With one month left before a court takeover of state schools, the legislature passed a "Robin Hood" law that took "surplus money" from the state's 100 richest school districts and distributed it to poorer districts throughout the state. (There are 1,045 school districts in Texas.)

The state supreme court upheld this approach in 1995. However, more and more school districts faced a crisis when they no longer qualified as poor districts because of their per capita wealth and when they reached the legislature's cap of $1.50 per $100 of property valuation. As enrollments expanded and the cost of food, fuel, health insurance, and other necessary expenditures increased, more districts had to slash programs, cut staff, and delay purchases in order to balance budgets.[37]

Those Pesky Ethics Laws

Although he received well-deserved credit for his leadership on the education issue, Lewis still generated controversy with his personal finances and his use of state property. In 1987, reporters discovered that the Texas Parks and Wildlife Department had stocked 187 deer over a four-year period on two ranches owned by Lewis. As reported in the *Austin American-*

Statesman, state law requires landowners who want deer to find the animals themselves and pay for trapping and transportation expenses. State law also requires Parks and Wildlife to inspect and approve any privately owned ranches to be stocked. Lewis's ranches apparently had never been inspected, and the Speaker never paid for the deer. Trapping and transportation of the deer cost the state $12,425. Officials later discovered that Parks and Wildlife transported 100 black bass from an East Texas lake to the Speaker's Williamson County ranch. Hoping to quiet negative coverage, Lewis returned the deer and three elk.[38]

The new flap began as press concerns rose over the high number of lobbyist-paid trips taken by state legislators. The *Austin American-Statesman* reported in November 1989 that the House parliamentarian co-owned a sporting lodge with lobbyists. About 800 registered lobbyists spent $1.86 million to entertain legislators during a five-month period in 1989, and 25 lobbyists accounted for a third of that amount. In 1984, Lewis had taken a golfing vacation in New Mexico, paid for by trucking and horse-racing lobbyists; traveled to apartheid-era South Africa for two weeks at the expense of the racist regime in Pretoria; and vacationed for four days in New York City in 1986 at the expanse of Dallas businessman Jess Hay. The ludicrous weakness of Texas ethics laws reached comic heights in 1989 when millionaire chicken processor Lonnie "Bo" Pilgrim passed out $10,000 checks on the Senate floor as the body debated bills pertaining to work-related injuries (which tend to be rampant in chicken-processing plants). Concerns about what increasingly looked like lobbyist bribery sparked debate over the need for a new ethics bill. Previously opposed to lobby reform, Lewis sought to mend the damage to the legislature's image. Elected to an unprecedented fifth term as Speaker in 1991, Lewis changed course and declared he would support new ethics rules.[39]

Lewis's legal and political problems increased in 1990 when a Travis County grand jury in Austin, at District Attorney Ronnie Earle's direction, investigated ties between the Head, Goggan, Blair and Williams law firm in San Antonio and several legislators, including the Speaker. Allegations arose that Lewis and other members of the state legislature received gifts, including free trips and political contributions, from the firm in return for protecting the law office's lucrative, exclusive contract for collecting delinquent property taxes. The San Antonio firm paid half of a delinquent $10,433 tax bill owed by Shooter's Palace, a bankrupt gun store co-owned by Lewis, and paid for a trip to Mexico that was attended by several lawyers from the San Antonio firm, former legislator Bill Harrison, lobbyist Dean Cobb, and six women, including a Houston stripper who went by the stage name "Chrissee."[40]

In December 1990, the Travis County grand jury indicted Lewis on two misdemeanor counts, including one charge of illegally accepting a gift and another of failing to report that gift as required by state disclosure laws. In spite of the indictment, Lewis won a fifth term as Speaker on a 146–1 vote on January 9, 1991, and used the occasion to call for tighter ethics laws. "Practices that were once acceptable in the past now raise doubts about the integrity of our system," Lewis said. "We must understand that it is no longer enough to be innocent. We must be above suspicion."[41] During that session's Speaker's Day, in April, lobbyists showered lawmakers with $120,000 worth of food, entertainment, and presents.[42]

Lewis's support eroded in October when he failed to show up on time for a court hearing on the two pending misdemeanor charges and Judge Bob Perkins ordered him arrested. Perhaps his House peers disliked the spectacle of the Speaker emerging from the Travis County jail and being harangued by a gaggle of reporters. Lewis didn't help himself when he hinted he might not seek a sixth term, a statement he quickly retracted. In any case, several members of the Lewis leadership team, including Pete Laney of Hale Center, began to openly campaign for the speakership.[43] On January 7, 1992, Lewis announced that he would not seek reelection to the House. "I had pretty much made up my mind two years ago that this would be my last term," Lewis said.[44]

The Lewis Legacy

In spite of constant controversy, Lewis's fingerprints remained on every important piece of legislation passed in Texas from 1983 to 1993, including the signature bill of that decade, House Bill 72. Under Lewis's leadership, the House passed laws establishing an indigent health-care system, creating a state lottery, legalizing pari-mutuel betting, reforming worker's compensation, providing a set of tax increases that prevented the state government from shutting down in the oil-bust days of 1987, and increasing school funding in the cash-strapped early 1990s. He also appointed a record number of female, African American, and Mexican American House members to leadership positions.

Nevertheless, Lewis's record remained clouded by accusations of ethical laxity. Even as colleagues sang his praises at the beginning of his last year as Speaker, Lewis entered into a plea bargain on January 22, 1993, with prosecutor Earle, pleading guilty to two campaign financial-reporting violations and paying a $2,000 fine. Earle revealed that he had demanded Lewis's resignation as part of the plea arrangement. When Lewis left the legislature in January 1993, several political accounts he had opened held about $1 million, most of which he was free to use as he pleased. Lewis pledged to use the money to start a scholarship fund before pursuing a lucrative career as a lobbyist. He earned $600,000 his first year in that position.[45]

Regardless of the long-lasting impact of legislation Lewis successfully supported, the legacy he bequeathed to the speakership will probably prove more durable. By extending the Speaker's authority over the makeup of committees, he gave that office nearly complete control over legislation in the House. Lewis also became the first Speaker to see the office as an end unto itself and not as a stepping-stone to a supposedly higher position. The Speaker's office had come of age and, in Lewis's view, surpassed the governor's and lieutenant governor's powers.

Lewis and Clayton also played an important role in easing the state's transition from one-party Democratic rule to a brief period of competitive two-party power sharing. Both came from the Democratic Party's conservative, business-oriented wing. They found common cause with Republican members of the House in their opposition to liberal Democrats. As Republicans became sufficiently powerful to warrant attention, both Speakers appointed Republicans as heads of committees and subcommittees. What appeared as bipartisanship to the outside world functioned as an alliance of conservatives, independent of party label. Clayton and Lewis both enjoyed amiable relations with Republican governor Clements and seemed more than sympathetic with the GOP during redistricting years. Clayton essentially endorsed Clements in his 1982 race against Mark White. Clayton surprised no one when he switched to the Republican Party in 1985, though he later characterized himself as an independent.[46]

Clayton and Lewis represented change within tradition, a condition that Texas and the rest of the South experienced during the period after the civil rights movement of the 1960s. The region became more urbanized as its economy expanded. Hoping to promote economic development, the region's leadership class pushed for increased public-school funding and greater expenditures for infrastructure to accommodate business and population growth. Political leaders also developed strong support networks as the region's businesses expanded and diversified. However, these contributors often caused ethics problems as attempts to gain influence increased. As the power and the influence of the Speaker grew, so did the attention paid to the person who occupied the position.

At the same time, southern Democrats and Republicans came to be more closely identified with their national parties. The vitriolic debates over segregation disappeared, to be replaced by more cordial race relations (although mistrust and misunderstanding between whites on one side and African Americans and Mexican Americans on the other continued). Southern Democrats moved toward the liberalism of their Northern peers, while the national Republican Party increasingly assimilated the ideology of its southern wing.

Bill Bass, a former Democratic legislator aligned with the Dirty Thirty in the early 1970s, said that the Democratic Party in Texas became culturally tone deaf by the 1980s.

> I went to the Democratic State Convention in 1986, and there was a motion to censure all of the Democratic members of Congress who had voted for aid to the Contras. You know, Iran-Contra.[47] Well, that included all the Texas delegation. And so the debate was on. And a Latin American woman delegate spoke against the censure motion. She argued, "I think you ought to fight communism in Nicaragua rather than on the Rio Grande," and instantly, some delegates started booing a little bit.
>
> The lady continued, "I've got a son, a corporal in the United States Marine Corps." BOOO! And the booing became intense and mean, and one lady next to me got up in her chair with her hairy armpits and her big sandals and she shouted, "Get in the other party, where you belong." And they are booing a mom, and the United States Marine Corps. I felt uncomfortable, alienated from a Democratic Party whose state convention boos the Marine Corps and their mothers.[48]

Speaker Laney

This political climate inevitably made Democrat Pete Laney a transitional figure for the speakership. Born on March 20, 1943, in Hale Center in Hale County, James E. "Pete" Laney still lives 200 yards from his first childhood home. The Laney family worked as farmers.[49] Hale Center had a population of about 2,000 people when Laney grew up, and he graduated from high school in 1961 in a senior class of fewer than 40 students. Laney attended Texas Tech University, where he earned a bachelor's degree in agricultural economics.[50] After graduation, Laney became a successful cotton farmer and first won a seat in the Texas House in 1972.

Laney beat an incumbent in the throw-the-bums-out mood that swept the state in the first election following Sharpstown.[51] Laney's victory came as Price Daniel, Jr.'s campaign for the speakership was already in high gear. Laney recalls that "thirty minutes after I was elected, Price Daniel, Jr., and Diane, his wife then, landed at the Plainview airport, and I visited with them about an hour." The lightning visit would be Laney's introduction to the intense world of speakership politics. Laney already knew the man who would next serve as Speaker after Daniel, Billy Clayton, and said that he was probably the first or second member of the Legislature to pledge support for Clayton's speakership campaign. This put him in a good position to assume an important position in the House by his sophomore term.[52]

Laney served four terms as chair of the House Administration Committee under Clayton.[53] That post proved key to Laney developing a close relationship with a broad roster of House members. This committee assigns members' offices and parking spaces. When a fellow member of the Clayton team, Gib Lewis, landed the speakership in 1983, Laney remained in the leadership, serving as chair of the State Affairs Committee for the next decade. "Laney made a habit of mentoring new members, helping them understand and work the system, even if he disagreed with what they were trying to do," longtime Capitol reporter Dave McNeely wrote. "That personal attention helped elect him speaker."[54]

After almost two decades as a team player for Clayton and Lewis, Laney was elected as Speaker in 1993. By the end of Laney's first regular session at the helm, members could tell a difference from the Lewis years. Perhaps because of his tendency to not take up the reins until the end of a session loomed, or perhaps because a rocky economy made legislative options more difficult, Lewis presided over a House that met in seventeen special sessions during his ten years as Speaker; the Seventy-first Legislature, which convened in 1989–1990, met a record six times. By contrast, no special session needed to be called by governors Ann Richards, George W. Bush, or Rick Perry during Laney's ten years as Speaker.[55]

In the Lewis years, the end of legislative sessions brought a frenzy of bills, usually read into the record and voted on before any pretense of debate or discussion took place. "Those mad scrambles (with members on the final night sometimes setting the clock back to allow more bills to pass before the midnight deadline) had the ambience of the Oklahoma

Land Rush and the decorum of tag-team mud wrestling," McNeely wrote. "They produced a lot of adrenaline and testosterone, some great sine die (end of session) parties and some awful legislation. Laney said when he passed an important bill on the last night of the regular session, with only a handful of people having any idea what was in it, he realized something had to change."[56]

Laney moved the deadlines for submitting bills to earlier in regular sessions in order to give representatives more time to think before they voted. "The main reason [for the rule changes] was to make sure the members had their say-so," Laney said. "The end-of-the-session rules were very important to me because I got an ethics bill passed in the last 30 seconds of the last night of the 1991 session. That's not fair to those people. I could've screwed up real bad."[57] Under Laney's rules, all major bills had to win at least tentative House approval eighteen days before a session concluded. Important Senate bills were required to win tentative House approval six days before the end of the session, and conference committee reports had to receive a final up-or-down vote by the next-to-last day. Laney set aside the final day for corrections and additions to legislation.

House business proceeded more smoothly not only because of rules changes, but also because Laney's subdued personality provided some quiet repose after Lewis's larger-than-life presence. After a twenty-one-year period that saw one Speaker go to prison, another stand trial on bribery charges, and a third spend almost a decade facing questions about ethics, the Laney years proceeded scandal free.

That does not mean that the lobby's influence on the House diminished. In fact, Laney, along with five of the most powerful Democratic committee chairs—Hugo Berlanga, Mark Stiles, Rob Junell, Clyde Alexander, and David Counts—were each able to raise more than $200,000 from July 1, 1995, to the end of 1996, according to a report by the citizen's lobby Texans for Public Justice. About 37 percent of the contributions came in increments of $1,000 or more. Businesses and political action committee (PAC) contributions accounted for 62 percent of all itemized political donations received by House candidates. These numbers indicate that a narrow group of business special interests dominated campaign fund-raising in Texas House races and strongly shaped who entered the House leadership.[58]

Texans for Lawsuit Reform (TLR), a corporate PAC that aimed to limit jury awards paid to consumers who had been cheated, injured, or killed by business products and services, led the way by contributing more than $600,000 to House races during 1995–1996. TLR also donated $700,000 to George W. Bush's 1994 gubernatorial campaign. Businesses got a return on their investment. Already one of the toughest states for consumer plaintiffs to win a verdict, Texas furthered tightened tort restrictions under Laney and once again under his successor, Tom Craddick. For the politicians, the TLR cash flow proved decisive in campaigns. Out of sixty-six campaigns examined by Texans for Public Justice in the 1995–1996 period, only seven were won by candidates with less money than their opponents, and only two of those were upsets against an incumbent.[59] As Patrick Kelly Graves noted in his study of campaign finance in Texas, "Most citizens are relegated to spectator status while wealthy economic interests duke it out to persuade the Legislature into favorable action or to prevent it from taking action contrary to their well-being.[60]

The Mediator

In spite of his success in raising PAC money, Laney's ethics record remained squeaky clean. Add the lack of scandal to the continuation of Clayton's and Lewis's policy of including Republicans in the House leadership team, and Laney's tenure may have been one of the most harmonious of the century. He appointed not only Republicans to chair committees, but also supporters of Jim Rudd, his opponent in the 1993 Speaker race. "After it's over, everyone's in the same room for 140 days," Laney explained.[61]

In his first term as Speaker, Laney frequently mediated between Lieutenant Governor Bob Bullock and Governor Ann Richards, both Democrats. In a short time, relations between Richards and Bullock completely soured, but Laney said he was able to maintain his friendship with both.

> My involvement with Bullock was probably different than a lot of people, because, first of all, he and I were friends, but he knew that I was not afraid of him, and I think he respected me for that. Bullock was not a person who *tried* to intimidate, but whether he did it purposely or not, he intimidated a lot of people.
>
> He and I got along because we disagreed, but we disagreed . . . then we resolved the problem . . . When I became speaker, he . . . already had succeeded in becoming estranged with Ann Richards . . . The breakfast meetings were few, with her presences . . . few, and short . . . I was more of the mediator in that, because Ann was a good personal friend, and it was just that . . . Bullock had decided that they had a problem and they didn't get it fixed.[62]

Laney generated goodwill in the lower chamber by ensuring that the House authors of bills got final credit for passage of the legislation. John Moritz, a former *Fort Worth Star-Telegram* reporter and longtime Capitol observer, calls this an important part of "inside baseball" that outsiders might be unaware of, but that richly enhanced Laney's reputation with lawmakers.[63] Laney said he never asked his members to take a vote that would be politically costly to the member back home. "In fact, on more than one occasion, I have suggested to members that they vote against what I was trying to get done in the legislative process because of their district," Laney said.[64]

Even if he had not been a conservative Democrat who was willing to mediate between Republicans and Democrats, Laney would have had to act in an evenhanded, bipartisan way to get anything accomplished. The state GOP had finally arrived as a fully competitive force. In 1992, the Republican caucus in the state House grew to fifty-nine members, and the GOP held thirteen of thirty-one Senate seats. In 1993, state treasurer Kay Bailey Hutchison won election to the U.S. Senate, where she joined fellow Republican Phil Gramm.[65]

In 1994, Republican George W. Bush beat Ann Richards in her quest for another term as governor. The son of a former vice president and president, Bush had dabbled for years in the oil business in Midland. Just before his entry into politics, his father's business connections led Bush, in return for a relatively minor investment, to be named the figurehead leader of a consortium of businessmen who bought the Texas Rangers baseball team, in Arlington. Bush and company convinced the city to underwrite the construction of a new, expensive, state-of-the art stadium, and then used this platform to project an image of him as a successful, decisive businessman. Richards, meanwhile, suffered from a backlash against Democrats prompted when President Bill Clinton failed to pass a promised national health care program, broke a campaign pledge to cut taxes for the middle class, and, with almost exclusive Republican help in Congress, passed an unpopular free-trade agreement with Mexico and Canada. In spite of Richards's close cooperation with Texas businesses, Bush successfully tagged her as a liberal. Democrats and Republicans remained racially polarized in Texas: 90 percent of African Americans and 75 percent of Mexican Americans supported Richards, but a majority of Anglos, including those in lower income brackets, supported Bush, who carried 54 percent of the vote.[66]

In congressional elections in 1994, Republicans moved from holding just eight seats in the twenty-seven-member Texas delegation in the U.S.

House of Representatives to twelve out of thirty (Texas gained three seats in the most recent federal census). Bush took full advantage of the Republican high tide. Collaborating with moderate-to-conservative Democrats such as Laney and Bullock, Bush successfully lobbied for bills allowing Texans to carry concealed handguns. Welfare payments in the state were slashed. A property-tax rollback approved by the legislature allowed Bush to claim credit for the biggest tax cut in state history, amounting to $11 billion. In fact, the change forced local school districts, city governments, and county governments facing rising costs to boost property valuations in order to make up for the revenue shortfall.[67]

The legislative process went more smoothly when Bush arrived as governor, Laney said, largely because Bob Bullock got along better with the new, Republican chief executive. "I think that Governor Bush decided that he wanted to let us help make him a good governor," Laney said. "So he took the concepts that Bullock and I had been working on for several months during the interim and laid down his goals, which was fine, and passed most of it because we already had most of it in the oven already, which was good political sense for him. It made our job a whole lot easier when the governor was touting the programs that we were trying to take care of."[68]

Bush proclaimed education as his chief concern. Again, with the support of Laney, Bullock, and the Democrats, the legislature passed bills requiring schools to give yearly standardized tests to students and allowing parents whose children attended low-performing schools to transfer to other schools in the district.[69]

An End to Bipartisanship

Laney remained so friendly to Republicans that the night when the U.S. Supreme Court declared George W. Bush the winner of the hotly contested 2000 presidential election, the president-elect made a national address from the Texas House chamber and picked Laney to introduce him. For the country, Laney became the face of Texas-style bipartisanship. During his tenure, Laney appointed Republicans as the chairs and vice chairs of committees and flew across the state to attend fundraisers for both Democrats and Republicans he liked. "Some Democrats have felt Laney's bipartisanship actually wounded their party: He has refused to help the campaigns of Democrats running against incumbent Republicans who have been part of his team," reporter Dave McNeely noted.[70]

Unfortunately for him, state politics got caught up in Washington-style partisanship. The legislature's failure to approve a redistricting plan in 2001 sealed Laney's fate as Speaker. The 2001 redistricting legislation "was a bill that most of the members had drawn themselves for their districts, even the Republicans, but it was not necessarily what the new [Republican] leadership wanted, so it became very confrontational to say the least," Laney stated. "The Republican Senate blocked the redistricting program that we passed, and that was the catalyst that changed the numbers drastically in the Legislature, in the House."[71] When the legislature fails to draw new district lines after the decennial census, the task falls to the Legislative Redistricting Board, which Republicans that year dominated for the first time. The new district lines were aimed at undermining several Laney lieutenants, who faced uphill election challenges or decided to retire rather than end their legislative careers on a losing note.

"The vote of the Legislative Redistricting Board was a three to two vote," Laney remembered. "I was the only Democrat on the redistricting committee, and with one Republican and one Democrat voting no and three [Republican] statewide office holders [Comptroller Carole Keeton Rylander, General Land Commissioner David Dewhurst, and Attorney General John Cornyn] voting yes. [Lieutenant] Governor Ratliff and I both voted against both the House and Senate plans . . . The other three members were doing everything for pure political purposes and did severe damage to rural Texas and severe damage to even some of the Republicans. I mean, they sacrificed some Republican members' districts to do damage to Democratic members."[72]

The chief force behind Republican efforts to wrest control of the House from Laney and the Democrats was Representative Tom Craddick of Midland, who had served in the Texas House since 1969 and had been a member of the Dirty Thirty, who bedeviled and eventually overthrew Gus Mutscher. Craddick had devoted his career to creating a Republican majority in the Texas House, and the 2000 elections placed him on the cusp of success. For decades, Craddick had acted as an "unpaid consultant to party hopefuls," according to one *Texas Monthly* profile. "We recruited the candidates, helped them with their mailers, helped them with their media, and helped them to lay out their campaigns," Craddick told the magazine. "We even monitored their efforts. We had a sheet I devised where they had to report how many phone calls they made, how many signs they put out, how many doors they knocked on every week."[73] Setting up PACs supported by big-ticket donors, Craddick created a cadre of Republican legislators who owed their success directly to him.

Laney named Craddick chair of the Ways and Means Committee, but the Midland representative's partisan electioneering and his open desire to replace Laney finally exasperated the Speaker, who stripped him of the post in 1999. "When you have individuals who are trying to make this a partisan place, divide the aisle and want to unseat you, it's hard to put much trust in their judgment," Laney explained.[74]

By 2000, Republicans held all twenty-nine statewide offices and achieved majority status in the state Senate. In 2002, the Texas Association of Business and the Texans for a Republican Majority Political Action Committee (TRMPAC), created by U.S. House majority leader Tom DeLay, distributed about $2.5 million to back Republican candidates in targeted state House races, hoping to complete the GOP takeover of the legislature. Republicans captured 88 of 150 House seats, and the membership elected Tom Craddick, by a 149–1 margin, as Texas House Speaker, the first Republican to hold the post since William Henry Sinclair, who served from 1871–1873.[75]

Craddick began his Speaker campaign more than a year before the general election that gave the Republicans a House majority. Beginning in October 2001, he and his wife, Nadine, gathered pledge cards. Unlike previous candidates, he solicited pledges of support from all primary candidates for the state House, Democrats and Republicans. In Collin County, he sought the support of eleven different candidates. The strategy was to lock up the support of whoever won House races. "Everybody else thought they could wait until after the primaries were over and then come by and see members and say, 'Now that you are the nominee, how about voting for me?'" Craddick later told a reporter. "But most of the candidates said, 'I already committed to Craddick.' It was over."[76] Immediately after the election, on November 7, Craddick surprised the political world by announcing he had already cinched the speakership.

A nonpartisan Speaker could not last forever in so partisan an age. Laney in effect declared that party loyalties should play no role in how members voted on key issues. After he lost his position as Speaker, Laney remained in the legislature and reflected on his tenure: "My style was not a power style. I didn't think it was the job of the speaker to exert his or her will on the membership. I thought that the speaker was there to make the job of each member easier and let them represent their district."[77] By contrast, Craddick saw his ability to advance the Republican agenda as the key to his effectiveness. The political cultures of Austin and Washington, D.C., were increasingly similar. Craddick's strategy clearly prevailed in the electoral arena. The new challenge would be to lead the House of Representatives and maintain the influence of the "executive Speaker" in a dramatically changing, Republican-dominated political environment.

CHAPTER 9

"Hell on Horses and Women": Gender and Family Life under the Dome

Few of the approximately one million people who visit the state Capitol each year know that the landmark is not only the seat of state government but also a residence. Tucked behind the Texas House chamber, on the western end of the Capitol's second floor, is the Speaker's apartment. The Texas House Speaker is the only presiding officer of a state legislative body to have an official residence on the Capitol grounds, in this case, an apartment that in 2004 contained an office, a reception area, a kitchen, a living room, an upstairs library, three bedrooms, and two bathrooms.[1]

The story of that residence provides an excellent metaphor for the growing empire called the Texas speakership. For more than half a century, House members claimed the right to also reside in the Capitol or attempted to evict Speakers from what was seen as a royal perch. Through it all, the apartment was expanded, modernized, and made more sophisticated. In this way, the Speaker's apartment parallels the development of the speakership itself in the twentieth century. Starting in the 1980s, the Speaker could no longer be considered simply a steward among his peers in the House, but was instead on the way to becoming primus inter pares (first among equals) when joined with the governor and lieutenant governor. By the time Tom Craddick became Speaker in 2003, the apartment served as the symbolic locus of power within state government.

The Speaker's apartment dates back to completion of the Texas Capitol. After a fire destroyed its predecessor, the new Capitol was constructed from 1881 to 1888. The Capitol's original architect, Elijah E. Myers, set aside two rooms each for the Speaker of the House and the lieutenant governor, on opposite ends of the second floor. Myers designed an open corridor of geometric clay tiles running perpendicular to the second-floor hallway behind the House chamber. The room to the south of the open hallway was to be the office of the Speaker, along with an adjacent "private room" that included a water closet.[2]

It was unclear under Texas law at the time whether it was legal for the Speaker or the lieutenant governor to live in these private rooms. An act of 1884 allowed judges of the Texas Supreme Court and the Texas Court of Criminal Appeals to take up residence within rooms on the third and fourth floors of the Capitol. The same law, however, said that with the exception of the judges, "no room, apartment or office in [the Capitol]" could be used "by any person as a bed room or for any private purpose whatever."[3]

It seems that early on the area was used for informal meetings and late-night naps, but there is no official record indicating when Speakers started using the private rooms as an apartment. No furniture was initially provided by the legislature.[4] By 1891, however, the *Austin Daily Statesman* complained about the Capitol being turned into a "cheap lodging house," noting that visitors to the Capitol saw "red blankets and soiled sheets aired in the windows."[5] The newspapers complained that allowing members to live in the Capitol not only compromised the dignity of the place, but also exploited taxpayers and fellow legislators. "The fact is these members who lodge in the capitol are taking advantage of all other members in grabbing state lodging rooms free," the paper noted. "If there is not room enough in the capitol building for all of them we protest against a few of them taking this advantage of all the others."[6] In 1897, the *Statesman* noted that two years earlier, "eighty odd beds" filled space in the Capitol, but that the building superintendent had begun enforcing the 1884 law and for the 1897 session began turning away members' "trunks and other equipment . . . and politely refused to receive their baggage."[7]

This ban on living in the Capitol still did not apply to Speakers or lieutenant governors. In 1899, the superintendent of public buildings and grounds reported that the "Speaker's Room" contained, among other items, a desk, couch, dresser, wardrobe, four tables, sixteen chairs, two beds, three mattresses and various linens. Presumably, the private room was used as a bedroom so work could be conducted in the outer office. Whether these items were bought by Speakers themselves or with state funds is not clear.[8]

No one is sure when the Speaker's rooms became a full-time residence. In *The Capitol Story: The Statehouse in Texas* (1988), Mike Fowler and Jack McGuire suggest that Sam Rayburn in 1911–1913 became the first Speaker to use the rooms full-time. Considerable evidence, however, suggests that House Speakers had begun living in the Capitol at least a decade earlier.

The year 1903 marked the beginning of Pat Neff's speakership. That same year, a "foot tub," along with bath and face towels, had been installed in the Speaker's apartment.[9] This suggests that the Speaker's rooms were already considered a private space used for personal hygiene and relaxation. Neff is the earliest Speaker to have indicated that he lived in the "private rooms." In 1938, a researcher asked Neff whether he knew which Speaker started the custom of living in the Capitol apartment. "I occupied an apartment there when I was speaker in 1903," Neff responded. "I think I am safe in saying that it has been successively occupied by the Speaker. I do not know if it was occupied during the two years prior to my speakership."[10] No kitchen had been installed in the apartment yet, which forced the Neffs to find meals elsewhere.[11]

As previously mentioned, a scandal erupted over Speaker Austin Milton Kennedy and his wife's furnishing of the apartment. Testimony before the House suggested that the Kennedys spent a great deal of time in the apartment, as did Lieutenant Governor Asbury Davidson in the apartment at the opposite end of the Capitol. In spite of the controversy, the tradition of a live-in Speaker survived.[12]

Improvements continued at the Speaker's apartment even as its existence faced repeated legal challenges. A floor plan from about 1916 showed that the Speaker's rooms by then consisted of an office and a private room that included a bathtub and a water closet. Nevertheless, in 1925, the Texas Legislature reaffirmed the statute prohibiting the use of any room in the Capitol for private use by anybody except judges of the state supreme court and court of criminal appeals.[13]

Finally, in 1943, the legislature provided legal cover for both apartments, formally recognizing the second-story apartments as the official residences of the House Speaker and the lieutenant governor. Yet challenges continued. In the late 1950s, voters rejected a constitutional amendment sanctioning the Speaker and lieutenant governors' residences. This prompted one state senator from East Texas, Joe Hill, in 1957 to file a series of lawsuits aimed at forcing House Speaker Waggoner Carr and Lieutenant Governor Ben Ramsey to vacate the premises. The Texas press dubbed this legal struggle "the battle of the bedroom." Hill asked a district judge to block Carr and Ramsey from using state funds to pay the maids, cooks, and other staffers who worked at the apartments. Other suits sought to block state funds from being used to pay bills for furniture in the apartments. Hill argued that the living quarters provided a form of financial compensation beyond what was allowed by the Texas Constitution. A court rejected Hill's suit in April 1957 before it went to trial.[14]

One last challenge to the legality of the apartments came in February 1974, in the aftermath of Sharpstown, when Senator Bill Moore proposed to amend the state constitution to prohibit living quarters in the Capitol. Though Moore's efforts failed, complaints continued. Representative Bill Heatly, angered when Speaker Daniel stopped the state from reimbursing him for charter flights between Austin and his home base of Paducah, raised a protest during the 1974 state constitutional convention because a previously approved appropriations bill supposedly permitted Daniel to "hire two cooks, a babysitter, and a $9,500 a year bartender who serves whiskey in the state Capitol." Heatly apparently was referring to the staff at the Speaker's apartment. Heatly also attacked Daniel for not reporting "free rent" on his financial disclosure forms and argued that nothing in the state constitution allowed Daniel to live in the Capitol. Nevertheless, the Speaker's apartment became permanently established as the modern speakership evolved in the post–World War II era.[15]

Throughout the first half of the twentieth century, life inside the apartment could be uncomfortable and noisy. In a 1947 interview, Mrs. W. O. Reed noted that the apartment sat next to a corridor filled with thirty legislative stenographers who busily typed away from eight to five. Jean Houston Daniel, the wife of Price Daniel, Sr., Speaker from 1943 to 1945, also recalled the many inconveniences posed by that secretarial pool. "There was no back elevator and I had to choose between climbing up and down the long back stairs and or going through the House Chamber with children and groceries," she later recalled.[16]

Walls inside the apartment were either "super-stout or non-existent," according to a 1949 *Austin American* story. At that point, the newspaper reported, an unattractive "eight-foot high temporary partition" separated the dining room, bathroom, and kitchen, compromising privacy in a space with thirty-foot high ceilings.[17] Living conditions at the apartment remained surprisingly spare. For instance, there was no garbage-collection service. According to one news account, the maid who cleaned the apartment had to carry the garbage down a flight of stairs, and, if she were lucky, she would find a porter who would carry the garbage to some uncertain destination outside. The apartment was also not air-conditioned, which made the quarters incredibly stuffy in Austin's often overheated summers, when temperatures hit more than 90 degrees about 80 percent of the time.[18]

In 1948, the legislature provided funds to modernize the lieutenant governor's apartment. The next year, the legislature authorized renovation of the Speaker's apartment, the first major remodeling of the apartment since the Capitol opened in 1888. Architects reconfigured the apartment, which had consisted of a living room, a small dinette, a bath, a kitchenette, and two bedrooms. The new layout included a living room, three bedrooms, two baths, a dining room, and a modern kitchen. Workers removed an estimated twenty to thirty coats of varnish from the walls, added new doors, and replaced the paper-thin partitions with two-foot-thick walls. Furniture purchased for the apartment during Speaker Durwood Manford's term remained in use in the mid-1960s.[19] Workers also installed a 5,000-ton air-conditioning unit. Manford balked, however, at furnishing a new room, added under W. O. Reed, and at spending $400 (about $3,200 today) for drapes to hang over the apartment's twenty-one-foot windows. "Durwood doesn't want to spend the House's money," Joyce Manford told the *Dallas Morning News*.[20]

Even following the redecoration, the aging Capitol sometimes proved a dangerous place to live. "While we were moving into the Speakers' Apartment, some plaster fell off the back bedroom and almost killed my parents," David Carr, the son of Speaker Waggoner Carr, remembered. "The ceiling caved in . . . [and the debris] landed a foot from the tops of their heads."[21]

Not yet open for public tours, the apartment often changed design as each new Speaker's family moved in, an aspect that underscored the still relatively short tenures of Speakers until the late twentieth century. Under Jim and Moja Lindsey, "18th century or late Georgian décor" marked the residence. Green silk brocade curtains with interlaced triple swags and ball fringe trim draped the apartment's massive windows. Hand-carved wooden doors with large, heavy brass hinges stamped with the words "Texas Capitol" marked the entryways to rooms decorated with eighteenth-century mahogany and damask-upholstered furniture.[22] In 1963, under Byron Tunnell, the Capitol staff painted the apartment walls in magnolia, described in a Capitol report as a "lovely off-white color," even as a like-hued nylon carpet in a sculptured design replaced the apartment's fraying fabric carpets.[23]

A Ramshackle Place to Work

As Speakers began to routinely serve more than one term, they were increasingly acknowledged as power brokers. Simultaneously, the Speakers' apartment came to symbolize the office's rising importance. The contrast between the ever more comfortable official residence and working conditions in the rest of the Capitol could not escape the attention of rank-and-file members. Originally designed to house offices for all of state government, including the Texas Supreme Court, the treasurer, the comptroller, and various agencies, in addition to the chambers of the House and Senate, the Capitol became noisier and more ramshackle as the size of government expanded. The mushrooming population, new communications technology, and growth in state services created a maze of offices in a building constructed to meet the needs of a citizenry in the horse-and-buggy days of the late nineteenth century.[24]

Only House leaders had offices; senators had to share space. Secretaries and other staffers made phone calls and typed in a crowded corridor near the Speaker's apartment or in a big room in the Capitol basement. Secretaries fought for space on the House floor, where they elbowed for room with state representatives, pages, reporters, and special guests. House members lacked desk phones, so Capitol switchboard operators directed calls to a bank of phone booths in the hallway behind the chamber, adding to the incessant noise, which at times rose to a barely decipherable din.[25]

Jimmy Turman said he did very little to redecorate the Speaker's apartment when he rose to House leadership in 1961. Turman said that he placed greater emphasis on improving working conditions for House members and their small staffs and upgrading the House chamber's appearance and comfort. Joe R. Greenhill, a former chief justice of the Texas Supreme Court, remembered the Capitol as "just a granite barn" in those days, a place "as hot as hell in the summer and cold as hell in the winter." Summer heat forced Texas justices to forgo traditional black robes while in session in the sauna-like Capitol. By the 1960s, however, the legislature had authorized the construction of new buildings for the supreme court and other state agencies, and those departments began to move out. As space opened, Turman convinced the legislature to acquire it for House members' offices, making life more bearable inside the Capitol.[26]

"So we took those old . . . *huge* . . . tall offices. And we double-decked them, and started making individual members' offices," Turman said. "I had about 97 of them completed by the time my speakership ended."[27] Space remained severely cramped: two members shared a space little larger than a closet. State representative Chet Brooks, who represented Pasadena in the House from 1963 to 1967 and in the Senate from 1967 to 1993, said later that when constituents came to visit his office mate, "I'd get up and go outside so they could all get in there and talk to him. When people came to see me, he'd do the same thing."[28]

Under Turman, the House Chamber gained air-conditioning and

underwent redecoration. "I spent a half million dollars air-conditioning that," Turman said. "And I put our new carpet down, a new gold carpet. They're back now to what it was a hundred years ago, and I like that idea . . . So I decorated the chamber for the members and for people."[29]

Nevertheless, quality office space remained at a premium. Seniority generally bought members the choicest offices. Such was the case with Richard Slack of Pecos, who had reached the number one post in seniority by 1980. That year, however, Slack suffered an upset loss to Republican Jerry Cockerham during the Ronald Reagan Republican landslide in the November general election. Bill Heatly of Paducah called Speaker Billy Clayton to mourn Slack's loss. "Mr. Speaker, I can't believe they beat my old friend Dick Slack," Heatly reportedly said. "I know better. I know that the people of West Texas want him to represent them. I think he should demand a recount. And I think he should sue if he loses the recount."[30]

"But Mr. Speaker," Heatly continued, "if Dick Slack loses that recount, I want that office with the bathroom." As trivial as such matters seem to the outside world, offices and parking spaces represented the trappings of power under the Capitol dome. Freshmen and other junior members of the House entered at the bottom, consigned to the legislative Siberia of the Capitol basement, once home to the secretarial pool. "The basement stinks," said former legislative staffer Sara Speights in the late 1980s. "It's mildewed and the ceilings are low. And outside your windows you have to look at dead crickets."[31] The contrast between such a setting and the Speaker's apartment, even with all its flaws, could not be more sharply drawn.

Billy Clayton, who became Speaker in 1975, presented a paradox. The most powerful Speaker up to that time, Clayton nevertheless eschewed the trappings of an imperial speakership. Clayton refused to live in the Speaker's apartment and converted most of the space back to offices. "I felt like I needed the [office] space, and I didn't feel like Texas owed me a place to live," Clayton said.[32] His stance had a pragmatic ground. Clayton had the largest staff of any Speaker to that time, a measure of the office's growing, full-time bureaucratic responsibilities. There were few other places to put the extra personnel. Clayton said that it was a relief to leave the Capitol and return to his home in northeast Austin each night. He arrived at his office at eight each morning and usually called it a day by eleven at night. Clayton probably was no less a workaholic than Ben Barnes, but he wanted to return to the days when a Speaker could have a private life amid public duties.[33]

That division was impossible to maintain, and it disappeared during the administration of Gib Lewis, from 1983 to 1993. A disastrous fire that struck the Capitol in 1983 transformed the official residence while accidentally adding to the speakership's prestige.[34] On the morning of February 6, 1983, a short in a television set in the lieutenant governor's apartment in the Capitol's east wing sparked a fire. "For what seemed an eternity, the flames climbed elusively inside the plaster walls and through a maze of false ceilings, the result of years of makeshift remodelings," Michael Ward wrote in his history of the Capitol. "But thanks to modern equipment and some old-fashioned luck, firefighters were able to stop the fiery advance before the attic was engulfed."[35] Matt Hansen, a friend of Lieutenant Governor Bill Hobby's daughter Kate, died in the fire. In addition, eleven firefighters and police officers suffered injuries, and damages to the Capitol topped $2.5 million.[36]

Sadly, the death and injuries could have been prevented. As early as 1931, state senator George C. Purl said, "That the Capitol in Austin is a firetrap is obvious to any casual observer. I have several times during the last eight years made a sincere effort to make this structure as nearly fireproof as is possible to do so, but must confess that I have never been able to get through the necessary appropriation." Later, a committee recommended fire-safety improvements to the building, which were subsequently rejected by the legislature as too expensive. "Should this building be destroyed by fire, priceless archives, records and data would be destroyed, and the members of the Legislature would stand convicted of negligence for failing to recognize the conditions that surround them," one committee report warned.[37]

Lewis remembered that he had also worried about the possibility of a major fire before the February 1983 tragedy. "We would find live wires just coming out of the wall [in the Capitol] that were still hot, and it was a tinderbox," Lewis said in 2004, "The next morning [after the fire], I said, 'We need to do a major, major renovation of this whole Capitol and get it done.'"[38]

Shortly after the fire, Lewis persuaded the legislature to create the State Preservation Board. The board's first major project became to replace the Goddess of Liberty statue on the Capitol dome. A new statue, made of aluminum and shaped by molds from the original zinc statue, was placed, after numerous unsuccessful tries, on the dome in June 1986. The new Goddess of Liberty cost about $450,000, which was raised from private donations.[39]

Additions and Restorations

By 1988, work had commenced on a master plan to restore the Capitol and construct an underground office annex north of the building.[40] Even Lewis's critics concede that the Speaker took the lead in the successful Capitol restoration. He proposed the innovative solution of building an underground office annex that would relieve crowding in the Capitol, which had reached critical proportions before the fire. By the early 1980s, the Capitol on a normal day housed about 1,300 workers, even though the building had been designed with fewer than 350 in mind.[41]

Funding the renovations proved to be a difficult task, especially as the early-1980s oil boom began to collapse in the second half of the decade. As Michael Ward notes, "The state's boom times had gone bust, and the budget was drenched in red ink. Taxpayer money for a complete overhaul was out of the question, and private fundraising could not collect enough for all the work that was needed to be done."[42]

Renovations began under Democratic governor Mark White, who had thwarted Bill Clements' bid for reelection during the recession in 1982. By 1986, their fortunes were reversed, and Clements, eager for political payback, won the Republican nomination and defeated his nemesis. Clements saw successful completion of White's restoration project as a way to complete his political vengeance and so made it a top priority. The leadership team of Bill Hobby, Gib Lewis, and Bill Clements worked together to persuade the legislature to spend what was necessary to restore the Capitol to its 1888 glory. They recruited the aid of Allen McCree, an architect with the University of Texas system, who began taking legislators on "deficiency tours," enthusiastically treating reluctant lawmakers to sights of the Capitol's leaky pipes, exposed asbestos insulation, and patchwork wiring. The legislature approved a master plan in 1989.[43]

Restoration began in 1990, and construction crews completed the extension by January 1993. The restoration of the Capitol ended two years later. Costs for the extension and restoration reached $200 million. Crews also restored and improved the Speaker's apartment. Lewis asked the architects and crews to return the apartment to its appearance "when Sam Rayburn slept here." Lewis said the lowered ceilings were removed, woodwork was cleaned, and the apartment was decorated with paintings featuring state scenery done by Texas artists. Lewis also added a second-story Texana library, accessed by a spiral staircase, to the den. With patchwork repairs and renovations cleared away, an unprecedented elegance graced the quarters. Lewis's leadership in the restoration confirmed the rising stature of the Speaker, a fact underscored when Hobby insisted that the lieutenant governor's apartment not be rebuilt but be replaced with a reception area. The result was that the Speaker now joined the governor as the only two officials in Austin awarded official state residences. When Pete Laney, the Speaker from 1993 to 2003, and his successor, Tom Craddick, opened the rooms to tours, the Speaker's apartment began its career as a state icon, granting the speakership even more visibility.[44]

Living in the Capitol

In the 1980s, Lewis sensed that the accessibility of the apartment could be a weapon in the Speaker's political arsenal.

> We utilized that apartment a great deal. We held election watches up there all the time. Members really utilized it. I even had a bar set up. We had members there at night . . . I'd have a Christmas party every year for all of the staff people in the Capitol.
>
> We had a kitchen staff that worked for the speaker's office . . . Certain mornings, we would have breakfast meetings with various members of the Legislature. We'd always have lunches in there all the time with various people . . . My wife was probably as good as anybody as far as entertaining members. Members' wives like to come to the Capitol because they could always go back to the speaker's office and hang around and do whatever they wanted to do and feel free to do it.[45]

The apartment's accessibility sometimes resulted in embarrassing encounters with the public. In the days before entrances to the residence were locked, and because most tourists were unaware that the Capitol included two private apartments, the threat always existed that a stranger might wander into the Speaker's residence at an inconvenient time.

"If I ever had complete privacy, I wouldn't know how to cope with it," Martha Barnes told the *Dallas Times Herald* in 1969 as her family prepared to move from the Speaker's apartment to the lieutenant governor's residence across the Capitol. According to the *Times Herald,* the Barnes family was the first to live in the Speaker's apartment year-round.[46] One time Barnes ran into a state representative who told her that she had made him feel "real at home" that morning. "I couldn't remember seeing him that morning, so I asked him what he meant," she said. The legislator told her that he had been in the House post office that morning and could hear Barnes scold one of her children. "It reminded me of home," he said. "You don't do anything but that everyone knows about it," Barnes told a reporter.[47]

In his book *Texas Politics in My Rearview Mirror,* Waggoner Carr recalled a time when he got too casual in the official residence.

> There was a metal plate sign on the speaker's apartment door to identify those quarters, but the general public sometimes paid no attention to the sign and just walked in unannounced if the door was not locked.
>
> After a long day of presiding, early in my first term as Speaker, I was sitting alone in the apartment enjoying some much needed relaxation. I had stripped down to my undershorts, was having a cool drink, and watching television, when I was startled by the sound of strange voices. Some public visitors had obviously entered the apartment and were headed my way. I quickly crouched behind the largest chair, hoping for the best, and trying to think of something witty to say in my defense.
>
> Fortunately for me, the uninvited guests only paused a moment and continued on their way. Unfortunately for them, they missed what could have been the highlight of their tour.[48]

The inconveniences of living in a public building continued through the twentieth century. Pipes in the 1880s building at times thunderously rattled.[49] "The first night we were there in the apartment I worked till about three-thirty or so, working on committee appointments, and we finally got to bed, got to sleep," Jim Lindsey remembered. "Just as we got to sleep, about five o'clock in the morning, the heat came on. Well, they're these great, huge pipes and they were reverberating and made this clanking, terrible noise. And we woke up. We didn't sleep much that night."[50]

Even well-intentioned Capitol staff members sometimes posed a hazard for the Speaker and his family. Because of space limitations in the 1950s, the Lindseys plugged a deep-freeze refrigerator into a socket controlled by the bedroom light switch.

> We didn't have any money much to buy things with, so [friends] . . . would send us occasionally a brace of pheasant or some quail or venison if they killed a deer. And we had a cook who had been with Governor Moody years ago, and she could marinate that venison and make it taste like good steak.

So we'd serve that. Well, we went on a trip somewhere, and we were gone two nights. And while we were gone, the guard of the rotunda saw the light burning in the bedroom. So he went in and turned the switch off. But it was the switch to the deep freeze. We got back, and of course you know how all that smelled. What an odor there was. We got back, and my wife like to have never gotten those odors out of there. She had a tea planned for the next afternoon, with all the ladies coming in from everywhere . . . and here's that tremendous odor.[51]

Noise joins a lack of privacy as constants in the lives of Speakers' families under the dome. As Nadine Craddick put it in a February 2005 interview, "It is a building that never sleeps. There is something going on all night long. There are either the mail people coming, or they are refurbishing or refinishing or restoring or doing whatever they do here. It is pretty noisy to live here."[52]

The embarrassments and inconveniences of living in a public space seem to have been magnified for the children of Speakers, who lived lonely lives in the adult-centered, empty caverns of the Capitol. Slightly more than a year before Reuben Senterfitt assumed the speakership in 1951, the state representative and his first wife, Maurine, adopted three children, Shirley, age five, Linda, age four, and Ronnie, age two. The pressures involved with gaining an instant family, having a husband and father acquire a position that required his attention from sunrise to after midnight, and managing the family in the public limelight placed extraordinary pressure on Maurine Senterfitt and the children. As the youngest in the family, Ronnie Senterfitt had the toughest time adjusting to life in the Capitol. "He misses our home in San Saba," Maurine Senterfitt told the *Dallas Morning News*. "He says, 'Mamma, please—back home—now,' but he will get used to it."[53]

Rueben Senterfitt recently admitted the family found itself under more pressure than it could bear. "Well, I had marital problems," Senterfitt said. "You know, it's not easy to be in politics . . . And I think . . . the pressures of those three adopted children [added to our stress] . . . Their parents were in the service, and they just abandoned them, and they were in foster homes. So we took them all, and I think the pressures of the children and the pressures of politics was a little too hard for her [Maurine] to handle . . . [It was an] atom-smasher."[54]

In numerous cases, the Capitol turned out to be a less-than-warm place for children to grow up. "The lack of playmates is the biggest drawback for the children," Martha Barnes told the *Dallas Times Herald* in 1969. "They think it would just be the greatest thing in the world to live in a regular house in a regular neighborhood—they think that children would just come out of the woodwork. We try to raise them as normal as we can—but we have to try twice as hard here."[55]

In another interview, she admitted that the pressures of public life at times caused her children to withdraw. "Gregg and Amy both went through periods when they wouldn't talk to anyone," she told the *Houston Chronicle*. "They wanted to be left alone and would just tune everybody out. They both did it at about the same age. There are days when I walk out in the hall and feel like Amy and Gregg, days when I don't want to talk to anybody or smile at anybody. But you have to be friendly. You never know who will be out there."[56]

Gregg Barnes worried that a picture of him in a tuxedo during his father's inaugural as lieutenant governor might end up in the hands of cruel classmates and "make him the laughing stock of Casis Elementary." Gregg relieved boredom by playing loosely organized games of catch in the hallways or by going to his father's office, where he volunteered (for allowance money) as a page, filed documents, and learned to run the "robotype machine."[57]

David Carr said that when he was a child during his father's speaker-ship, he stretched his imagination to turn the Capitol into a playscape.

Well, it was pretty empty. It was an empty feeling because it was a large place with high ceilings . . . My parents were usually gone to some party or some banquet or some speech or sometimes a trip. So I was there lots of times with some babysitter, just staying by myself. And then that place was huge! After everybody leaves every day, it becomes a great big huge building with nobody in it, except the guards in the rotunda.

So to keep myself occupied, I would just simply roam the Capitol at night. And one of my favorite things to do, when the guards would go to sleep down in the bottom of the rotunda, I'd get on about the fourth-floor banister and drop some Dixie cups full of water down there and try to hit them on the head. And they knew I was up there, and they'd try to find me. But they couldn't find me because I had more places to hide than you can imagine.

The other thing I used to do was take paper airplanes and get as high up there and open up the windows in the House of Representatives and fly them out the window and see how far I could get them to fly down to the Capitol grounds. And the other thing was getting a bicycle and just riding around and around and around the Capitol grounds.[58]

A lack of neighborhood children meant that Carr struck up friendships with the adults in the Capitol and with the pages who were closer to his age.

> And during those days, too, it was a big deal ostensibly to have some cigars. I went to Pease Elementary, and I would come home [and] there wasn't anything to do back in the Capitol, so I would just be a page boy and not get paid for it. But I'd sit with the page boys until the light would come on, and then I'd go see what the representatives needed. Then I'd run an errand, just to have something to do.
>
> That was cool, because all my memories of that are pretty vivid, because I remember a lot of activity. Smoke everywhere, cigars just going full blast . . . Spittoons, brass spittoons, below each member's desk so he could spit his snuff in there . . . [and] Stetsons hanging everywhere. You have no computers. A bathroom going toward the speaker's apartment that had swinging doors on it. And you go in there and there'd be a shoe-shine going on all the time, and guys [were] doing shoeshines for all the representatives. There'd be spittoons everywhere, and people spitting and chewing tobacco and cigarin' and [*laughs*], it was a whole different time.[59]

Political Women

An old joke says that Texas is "hell on horses and women." The women who have lived in the Speaker's apartment shared with their children the hardship of loneliness, and in addition faced the heavy burden of managing a very public household and serving as an unpaid campaigner and consultant for their husbands. They did all this even as they faced the daily condescension of the male-dominated, macho-saturated world of Texas politics and the Capitol press corps.

In newspaper stories, Speakers' wives received loaded compliments that made it seem as if writers were required to assess any woman's attractiveness, whether she occupied public office or was married to a politician. Thus, readers learned that Joyce Manford was a "beautiful brunette," that Jim Lindsey's wife, Moja, was a "petite brunette," that Ben Barnes's first wife, Martha, was "pretty [and] bubbly," and that Ben Barnes's second wife, Nancy, looked "tiny" next to her six-four husband and was a "fragile-looking, blue-eyed blonde."[60] Such descriptions diminished Speakers' wives by depicting them as vulnerable and physically weak and treated the physical appearance of these women as being more important than their ideas. Light feature stories on Speakers' wives also marked most of the rare occasions that female reporters from the 1940s to the 1970s got to venture near the heavily male world of the Capitol press corps. These reporters got to ask Speakers' wives about child rearing, recipes, and their wardrobe plans for inauguration day. If the women expressed ideas about integration, public schools, or tax policy, their thoughts were never shared with the reading public.

The *Houston Post* asked "Mrs. James Turman" (the *Post,* following a typical press convention of the day, referred to women by their husbands' names, a practice that eroded the individual identity of women) "to what extent does your husband influence your opinion on political issues?" The *Post* did not ask Marlene Wallace Turman whether she influenced her husband. Readers found out that the Turmans "generally agree" on political issues, but the newspaper never shared either specific opinions held by the Turmans or their areas of disagreement. Readers were informed in detail, however, about Jimmy Turman's favorite recipe, which was for lemon pecan cake. (The *Post* asked all the wives of the lieutenant governor candidates in 1962 to share their favorite recipes.) Mrs. Turman then offered that her "share" in her husband's campaign was "encouragement, a good listening ear, and accompanying him whenever he deems it best."[61]

Of course, even such insipid press coverage revealed that Speakers' wives contributed much more than passive wifely support. "The first time he ran, I worked my heart out," Martha Barnes told the *Austin American* in 1969. "I even made speeches for him and handed out cards." Barnes made campaign appearances, although she disliked making speeches, the newspaper reported. "I thought it would be terrible working door to door . . . But everybody was so nice and invited me in for a Coke or a coffee," she said. She ended up handing out 65,000 cards as her husband beat his better-known opponent by a 5–1 margin.[62]

Barnes's second wife, Nancy, also brought extensive political involvement and experience to the marriage. Nancy de Graffenried majored in political science at the University of Texas, where she met her first husband, Scott Sayers, a senior law school student. She married Sayers, earned a political science diploma, and took graduate courses in education before the couple moved to Fort Worth, where she started a career as a political science teacher. Her husband won two terms in the House as a representative from Fort Worth. Nancy Sayers served as Tarrant County Democratic chair and became Governor John Connally's administrative assistant. While in Austin, Scott Sayers opened a law practice. After his death in 1968, Nancy resumed her busy political career. She served on all of Connally's inaugural committees. She was a member of the state Democratic executive committee from 1966 to 1968, and served as chair of the Texas Employment Commission, the first woman to ever head a major state commission. All this before she became "Mrs. Barnes," wife of the new lieutenant governor. Nancy Barnes briefly forced the state press to reevaluate its stereotypes concerning political wives, although the media reverted to form after the high point of feminism in the midseventies.[63]

In 1925, Miriam "Ma" Ferguson shattered a barrier by becoming one of the first women to be elected governor in the United States, and the first in Texas. In her wake, women won terms in the state House and Senate, served as chairs of legislative committees, and captured seats in Congress and the U.S. Senate. In 1991, Ann Richards became the second woman to occupy the Governor's Mansion. Yet not only has the state House speakership remained an exclusive Anglo preserve, but as of 2009, all the Speakers in the state's history have been men. Part of this no doubt stems from the boy's-club atmosphere that has sometimes reigned in the House chamber and in the social networks created by the members. Women who defied conventional gender roles and ran for office faced a brutal reception from their male political peers and from the press. Eddie Bernice Johnson of Dallas, who served in the Texas House (1983–1987) and Senate (1987–1993), said that "booze, beefsteak, and broads" represented the "three B's" of lobbying.[64] The three Bs also served as a formidable barrier between women and the House speakership.

Women who entered politics encountered a hostile environment. "The opinion seemed to be that any woman who would get out and run for public office would have to be a sort of fishwife type with a sharp tongue," said Margaret Gordon, a Waco state representative from 1939 to 1941. Nancy Baker Jones and Ruthe Winegarten, in their groundbreaking work *Capitol Women: Texas Female Legislators, 1923–1999,* argue that to survive, female legislators often accommodated their sexist male colleagues by acting "ladylike."[65]

Even accommodating female representatives had to operate under severe political handicaps. While she strove to appear as if she had no chips on her shoulder, Gordon held picket signs of protest in the House chamber when the Houston Chamber of Commerce held a "stag party" and invited only male legislators to attend.[66] The exclusion of women from these male-bonding retreats further weakened the already marginalized position of women in the House. As Wilhelmina Delco put it, "In Texas politics, power politics often is played out away from the public eye—in backroom, after-hours meetings." Delco said that as speaker pro tem, she suffered in her relationship with Speaker Gib Lewis because she "wasn't one to sit around and sip coffee and drink a beer." Lewis threatened to "unappoint" her when she supported bills he objected to, but her persistence caused him to back off. "He clearly understood that I wasn't giving up my sex or my ethnicity or my principles for the honor of being speaker pro tem," Delco said.[67]

Given the sexist condescension women faced in Texas's political culture, it is ironic that women played a central role in building the state's Republican Party into a competitive force in the second half of the twentieth century. Affluent, conservative women began to flock to the GOP banner in the 1950s and 1960s, in part because they believed the national and local Republican Party supported smaller government and that the Democratic Party's monopoly on political power had led to corruption. "In the 1950s, the backbone of our effort was the women," said Peter O'Donnell, a Republican Party leader in Dallas County. "At the time the business community by and large was conservative Democrats and men, but women . . . worked hard. They were dependable . . . We had a huge volunteer effort. We knew that they could perform. There weren't as many women in the work force then as there are today."[68]

Republican women played a significant role in John Tower's victory in the 1961 senatorial special election. Virginia Eggers, who was active in GOP circles in both Dallas and Wichita Falls, recalled her time as a "Tower Belle." "We were all dressed up in our little red vests," she said. "They were red felt and we had these little red pillbox hats. We would wear our navy blue skirts and our white blouses. We got on a bus and we just drove down the highway. We would stop in any town. We went in the billiard parlor one time. There were groups in the back playing cards. Not one of them did a thing. They just raised their eyes to us and watched as we paraded around the room. We want you to meet John Tower . . . they never moved—their eyes just followed us around the room. We are lucky they didn't shoot at us."[69]

In spite of the state's long history of sexism and paternalism, Texas became one of the first states to pass the Equal Rights Amendment. Besides being a driving force in the Republican movement, women played key roles among liberal Democrats as well. Voters approved the ERA as part of the state constitution, a measure cosponsored by Democratic state representatives Barbara Jordan and Frances "Sissy" Farenthold, by a 4–1 margin in 1972.[70]

In spite of the immense political talent displayed by so many women, those running for public office in the late 1960s and the 1970s still ran a gauntlet of sexism at the state House. Sissy Farenthold later described herself as "naive" when she arrived in Austin to serve as a House member representing Corpus Christi. Farenthold initially refused to sponsor a state equal rights amendment in the House, she said, because of her loyalty to the Texas Bar Association, which opposed it. But she quickly lost her innocence after repeated brushes with sexism in the political world. During her first campaign for the legislature, a voter confused by her androgynous first name proudly told Farenthold he had voted for her husband. She told the voter that he had voted for her. "If I had known that, I wouldn't have voted for you," he replied. Capitol guards, assuming she was not a member of the legislature, repeatedly blocked her entry to the House and Senate chambers and questioned her when she tried to use her official parking space. Fort Worth senator Don Kennard, upon meeting Farenthold, asked her who she worked for. The House sergeant at arms marched into her office and removed her male secretary.[71]

When the Constitutional Amendments Committee, which included Farenthold, chose to hold a meeting at the men-only Citadel Club in Austin, fellow committee members took no action when the club barred her entry. Farenthold's peers on the committee bought her chocolates, but neglected to tell her what had been discussed at the Citadel. Farenthold didn't laugh this off. She objected loudly, and she was never barred from another committee meeting. "In the beginning, I could have been a pet," Farenthold later recalled. "There was a sort of pethood ordained for you, if you accepted it . . . If I had quietly gone about what was expected of me, I probably would have had a few perks . . . But I wasn't up here as a guest. I was up here as an elected representative."[72]

The persistence of all-male retreats as part of the legislative culture became a formidable obstacle to the election of a woman as Speaker. Garland representative Anita Hill, who served as a Democrat from 1977 to 1979 and as a Republican until 1993, encountered discrimination for the first time in her life when, in 1981, she was barred from entering the Citadel Club, as Farenthold had been years earlier. Hill had hoped to meet with the rest of her legislative delegation and Garland city officials, but was told by attorney and club president Clint Smalls that the Citadel was "just not set up to handle women at noon" and that "a gaggle" of women would sound like "magpies" and annoy the male customers. Hill said the experience increased her sensitivity to the discrimination suffered by African Americans and Mexican Americans. "I'm just upset enough to look at things very differently," she said. Hill, Wilhelmina Delco, and other women in the House pushed through a resolution pledging that no member would attend a function excluding other members on the basis of race, ethnicity, or gender.[73]

On the surface, the 1980s and 1990s represented a political watershed for Texas women. In 1982, Travis County commissioner Ann Richards surprised political pundits when she was elected state treasurer, becoming the first woman to win statewide office in Texas since "Ma" Ferguson won the governorship. Eight years later, Richards became the first Texas woman to win the Governor's Mansion in her own right and not as a proxy for a man, as happened when Ferguson governed Texas as a stand-in for her husband, Jim. In 1986, three women won election to the state Senate, whereas previously no more than one had served in any legislative session. Democrats and Republicans both nominated women for state treasurer the same year, and the winner, Kay Bailey Hutchison, became the first Republican woman to ever win statewide office. Three years later, Hutchison again made state history, this time by becoming the first Texas woman elected to the U.S. Senate. She prevailed in a special election against Bob Krueger, the man appointed to the Senate by Governor Richards when President Clinton appointed Lloyd Bentsen secretary of the treasury. In 1993, Judge Rose Spector broke another barrier with her election to the Texas Supreme Court. The speakership of the Texas House of Representatives, however, has remained an exclusive male preserve.[74]

As the number of women in the House and the Senate grew in the 1990s, the institutional culture nudged forward. Although the three Bs of lobbying previously mentioned were shunted aside in favor of golfing trips, women were still not included in the game. In the 1990s, the agenda of conservative women and their male allies, not that of their liberal, openly feminist peers, ascended triumphantly. The priorities of socially conservative men and women included placing severe restrictions on abortion, adding an anti-gay-marriage amendment to the state constitution, and restricting the awards litigants could win in the civil courts, even in sexual-harassment cases. Equal wages for equal work, affirmative action for women, and legislation helping poorer women obtain child care were not up for consideration.

The exclusion of women from legislative decision making survived, in spite of the increased visibility of women in the House. "The [golf] trips [attended exclusively by male legislators] are bad politics," Johnson said, "but I don't even hear about them until I read about them in the papers." Johnson said legislative men still condescend towards women. "When you look at the important huddles, the important power positions, the people the big legislation is taken to and who gets all the big [campaign] checks, they're all men."[75] Without those big campaign checks and the other political perks that came with possessing a Y chromosome, the Speaker's apartment remained beyond reach for any woman not married to the presiding officer.

CHAPTER 10

The End of an Era? The Executive Speakership under Tom Craddick

2003–2009

At the dawn of the new millennium, one person embodied the confluence of social and economic conservatism that drove the Republican conquest of state government. Born in Beloit, Wisconsin, on September 19, 1943, Thomas Craddick later earned bachelor's and master's degrees in business administration from Texas Tech University. The Midland resident decided to run for the legislature in 1968 while a PhD candidate, beating his high school government teacher in the Republican primary. Craddick thus became one of only nine Republicans then serving in the 150-member House of Representatives. He has represented Midland in the House ever since.[1]

Craddick displays a relentless drive both as a businessman and a politician. As an undergraduate at Texas Tech, he formed a business partnership with his finance professor, George Berry, and Coley Cowden, the son of a powerful and wealthy Midland family. They launched a seven-store gas station–car wash chain called Scrub-a-Dub. Using profits from that enterprise, the threesome bought 7 Up and Dr Pepper bottling plants and invested in duplexes in the Midland area. By this point, Craddick was only in his midtwenties and entering graduate school.[2]

Craddick's intensity made him wealthy, but sometimes difficult to know. As a graduate student, he staked out a library table as his personal workstation, and was startled one day when he found fellow student Nadine Nayfa of Sweetwater sitting there. Nayfa, the child of Lebanese immigrants who ran a dry-goods store, was pursuing a teaching degree. As Craddick recalls: "I really spent a lot of time at the library and in the student union . . . I would just leave my books over at the library on a certain table, and I really never took them back to my apartment . . . So I had all my stuff stacked on a table over there, and one day I came over and

Nadine was sitting at the table. And I told her 'You're sitting at my table.' And that is how we met."³

Nadine Craddick remembers the encounter slightly differently: "I was in the library, and I was very young, very new to the school, when I sat down at his table. And somebody's books were there, but I did not know which was his table, so to speak. And he came back and informed me that I was sitting at his table and that I needed to move. And I think he took my pencil and broke it, or maybe I took his pencil and broke it."⁴

From such unromantic circumstances, an enduring relationship flowed. "I built a car wash with some other people. And she was involved in sorority rush, and her lodge was next door to the car wash we built," Tom Craddick said. "And so one summer she was out there for prerush, and I was working in the car wash, and I saw her one day and asked her for a date. What is interesting, she fell asleep on our first date, but other than that it worked out pretty well."⁵

Before his twenty-fifth birthday, Craddick told a friend that he wanted to leave any children he might have a million dollars. He was already well on his way toward his financial goal when he ran a successful campaign against two-term Republican House incumbent Frank Cahoon in the 1968 primary. Craddick entered the race as a Republican even though his father was a Democratic precinct chair at the time.⁶

> Actually, both parties offered me a chance to run on their ticket. And the Democratic chairman in Midland County wrote my announcement because he thought I was going to run as a Democrat, and I ran as a Republican. I went before this [Republican] candidate's committee, and at that time I weighed seventy-five pounds more than I do today. And the main question, they said, was that they didn't think I could win because, one, I was Catholic and they did not think I could win in that community. And two, they thought I was too young to run [at age twenty-five]. And the third question was, "Can you lose twenty pounds in order to look better on television?" So I lost seventy-five pounds. I met that goal, but the other two I didn't work too well on.⁷

Craddick ultimately won because he worked harder than his opponent, running a retail, door-to-door campaign. With a master's degree in business administration already in hand and a Texas House seat awaiting him, Craddick never finished his dissertation. His life dreams had seemingly been met well before he hit thirty.⁸ "I wanted to make a bunch of money and I wanted to go into politics and I was doing both," he told *Texas Monthly*.[9]

While he was learning the legislative ropes, he expanded his business empire by entering the oil business, eventually forming Mustang Mud, a firm that supplied lubricants for oil drilling. He adopted a political goal he chased as resolutely as he did wealth. Craddick devoted himself to building the Republican Party and, along the way, his power base. Republicans were an oddity when Craddick first arrived in Austin, in January 1969. In thirty-three years of uphill struggle, Craddick dedicated himself to dismantling the Democratic Party. As detailed earlier, he took a lead role among the Dirty Thirty, who forced the Sharpstown investigation that weakened Texas Democrats.[10] In 1975, Speaker Bill Clayton, then a Democrat, appointed Craddick to chair the House Natural Resources Committee, making Craddick the first Republican committee chair in 100 years. Craddick subsequently chaired the Public Health Committee under Speaker Gib Lewis and the House Ways and Means Committee under Speaker Pete Laney.[11] In the 1990s, Craddick's long-held dreams of a Texas Republican majority began coming true. George W. Bush became governor in 1994 as the party made steady gains in the state House and Senate and in the Texas congressional delegation. Bush benefited from holding the Governor's Mansion during a national economic boom fueled by a high-tech bubble and became increasingly popular as his term went on.[12]

By the time of Bush's reelection in 1998, his triumph seemingly presaged a multihued GOP in which blacks and browns would add color to what had been a monochromatic monolith. Bush carried what was an unprecedented, for a Republican gubernatorial candidate, 40 percent of the Hispanic vote that year.[13] Looking ahead to the 2000 presidential campaign, he aimed at expanding the GOP base to include African Americans and Mexican Americans. Craddick also sought to solidify the Republican hold on Texas, but his approach differed sharply from that of the purported party leader. As a House member, Craddick opposed affirmative action in state contracting, voted against a state holiday honoring Martin Luther King, Jr., and fought against a state hate-crimes bill numerous times. On the vote regarding the King holiday, Craddick, four other Republicans, and a House Democrat insisted that their no votes be recorded, even though the measure was passed on a voice vote. Craddick would seek support from disaffected Democratic black and Latino House members in his later Speaker races, but in building the GOP caucus, he did little recruiting in minority communities and focused more on securing the overwhelmingly white Republican base and forming a firm alliance between fiscal and social conservatives.[14]

Craddick remained hard to know. "He is not a good old boy," a *Texas Monthly* article noted. "He does not play golf . . . He doesn't drink or smoke or even partake of coffee . . . He rarely does lunch. He does not go out much at night."[15] Nevertheless, Craddick commanded loyalty from fellow Republicans at least in part because of his access to wealthy Republican donors such as James Leininger of San Antonio. Although the Catholic Craddick could be more accurately described as a business conservative rather than a member of the Republican Party's religious right, he astutely followed the GOP donor dollars. He formed a tight alliance with the multimillionaire Leininger, who expressed his fierce pro-school-voucher, pro-tort-reform, anti-gay-rights, and antiabortion politics by providing the most conservative Republicans an endless flow of cash. Leininger, who grew rich manufacturing hospital beds, also owned the Promised Land Dairy and was at one time part owner of the National Basketball Association's San Antonio Spurs. He held personal wealth estimated at $340 million. Probably more than any other Texan, he has bankrolled the GOP's rise in Texas since 1994. The *Houston Chronicle* estimated that Leininger's campaign donations to conservative Republicans reached $550,000 in 1997 and that the total take in 1998 probably exceeded that amount.[16] More than $1 million of the $10.3 million raised by Republican lieutenant governor candidate Rick Perry before the 1998 general election came from a loan guaranteed by Leininger and two other businessmen.[17]

The firm alliance between culture warriors like Leininger and businessmen like Craddick proved formidable. To Craddick, the differences between the social and fiscal conservatives in the GOP paled compared to the liberal-conservative split in the old Democratic Party: "I do not think the division in the Republican Party is like it was in the Democratic Party because the Democratic Party was *the* party, so you have a conservative aspect and you have middle-of-the-road aspect, then you have the liberal faction in there. But the Republican Party today has a conservative faction, plus there are some who are more conservative than others. But you don't have a liberal faction, so you kind of go from the middle of the road to conservative."[18]

In spite of Craddick's disavowals, the Republican Party would soon divide among social conservatives focused on issues like gay rights and abortion, fiscal conservatives determined to reduce the size and power of state government, business conservatives who still expected tax breaks and subsidies from Austin, and libertarians who wanted less governmental regulation of business but also less governmental intrusion in private matters like sexuality and drug use.[19]

At times, these multiplying Republican factions brought to mind philosopher Thomas Hobbes's description of humanity in its state of nature: a war of all against all.[20] Yet these tatterdemalion camps united against a common villain they blamed for all social ills. Social conservatives expressed nightmare fears of activist judges sanctioning the mass murder of the unborn, public school teachers promoting homosexuality and witchcraft, leftist professors indoctrinating students with warmed-over Marxism, and a sick popular culture promoting orgiastic self-indulgence. Business conservatives dreaded the power of a leviathan state that punished success with confiscatory taxes, smothered innovation with suffocating regulations, and sabotaged profit margins by promoting the efforts of labor unions, consumer advocates, and trial lawyers. The two groups may have differed on their lists of social evils, but behind these ills lay a single bête noire: a mythic "big government" that had supposedly been captured by liberal interests.

The shriller opponents of an activist state government drowned out the voices of those pragmatic conservatives who had been dominant in the 1950s and 1960s, who preferred lower taxes and less regulation, but who still wanted to fund roads, schools, universities, and hospitals as necessary means to economic growth.

Late-twentieth- and early twenty-first-century Texas conservatives at times seemed united more by what they opposed than by their common values. Building a movement on ever-multiplying Venn diagrams of resentment invited instability. In fact, according to Thomas Frank (a nonacademic commentator on the current political scene and holder of a history PhD), modern conservative activists have reduced the concept of freedom to the right to accumulate capital. The state, through taxation and regulation, is seen as intrinsically inimical to that freedom. Many modern conservative leaders, like Governor Rick Perry's friend and GOP antitax activist Grover Norquist, believe that government functions best when it functions not at all.

"Believing effective government to be somewhere between impossible and undesirable, conservatism takes steps to ensure its impotence," Frank writes. More to the point, Frank quotes a 1920s conservative whose attitudes reflect the philosophy of many conservative ideologues in the twenty-first century: "If public officials are and remain inefficient, the public will sicken of incompetence and rely exclusively upon corporate enterprise."[21]

Speaker Craddick

Under Craddick, Perry, and other Norquist-influenced Republicans, the wheels came off the legislative process. To begin with, Craddick turned the position of House Speaker into a virtual executive, and House members came to resent what they saw as a usurpation of authority. His first term, beginning in 2003, was marred by controversy. A nationwide recession had created a $10 billion state budget deficit. In Rick Perry's most successful assertion of authority, the governor framed the budget debate with his pledge to veto any appropriations bill that increased property taxes, sales taxes, or business franchise fees. Income taxes, of course, were not even considered. This position was aligned with Craddick's, so the House and Senate faced few viable options except deep budget cuts, which Perry called "re-examining the core responsibilities of government and state spending."[22] Norquist, who labored to convince Republican state and federal lawmakers to starve "the beast" of governmental spending, by slashing revenues, deeply influenced Perry and the new Republican-led House. Perry frequently visited with Norquist, even inviting him along for a retreat to the Bahamas. Four state senators, Craddick, and thirty-four other House members signed a national "no new taxes" pledge distributed by Norquist. Despite the state ranking forty-third in per capita hospital, health, and welfare spending nationally in 2000, and forty-first in state aid per pupil in grades K–12, those budget items faced devastating reductions.[23]

Democrats and moderate Republicans scrambled for alternatives to draconian budget cuts. The House Ways and Means Committee debated removing almost all exemptions from the tax code, including sales-tax exemptions for prescriptions and groceries and business exemptions on products used in manufacturing. State comptroller Carole Keeton Strayhorn—formerly a Democrat as mayor of Austin, then a Republican as a statewide officeholder, and then an independent candidate for governor in 2006—proposed hiking the state's cigarette tax from 41 cents to $1.41 a pack in order to raise $1.5 billion in two years. Finally, lawmakers sought to close a franchise-tax loophole that allowed major Texas corporations to dodge taxes by reorganizing as partnerships or creating subsidiaries outside the state. About 4,000 corporations, including such giants as Dell Computer Corporation, SBC Communications, and Cox Texas Newspapers, avoided paying an estimated $200 million a year in taxes between 2000 and 2004 because of this loophole. Perry, Craddick, and others shot down each of these proposals as tax increases and insisted on budget cuts.[24]

With Craddick providing GOP muscle in the House, Perry won a 7 percent across-the-board budget cut paid for by actual reductions in appropriations or delayed payments until after the biennium. These cuts included: slashing the Texas Department of Criminal Justice budget by $300 million, partly paid for by the elimination of 1,000 full-time jobs; chopping about $55 million from three university research budgets and cutting faculty and staff at state-supported schools; reducing a health insurance stipend for school teachers, counselors, and librarians from $1,000 to $500; eliminating the $2.8 million Healthy Families child-abuse-prevention program; and whittling by $835.2 million state spending on Medicare and the state children's health insurance program, which provided families of the working poor with financial aid for medical care.[25]

Most taxes were not raised, although the state hiked fees for various public services, cut other services, and deregulated tuition at the University of Texas and other state-supported universities. The Republican leadership declined to call these moves tax hikes, however.[26] Even when child-abuse-prevention programs were axed to avoid raising cigarette taxes, Republican leaders received relatively little opposition to their budget priorities, since most of the leading House Democrats were conservatives as well.

The Redistricting Fiasco

However, Craddick's attempt to ensure continued Republican domination of the legislature and, by extension, of the Texas congressional delegation proved far more controversial. In 2001, a federal court drew a new congressional district map when the Democratic-dominated House and the Republican-controlled Senate could not agree on a redistricting plan. Although Republicans garnered almost 55 percent of the state's total congressional vote in 2002, they captured only fifteen of the thirty-two seats in Texas's congressional delegation.[27]

Redistricting was little discussed when Craddick gaveled in his freshman session as Speaker in January 2003. *Fort Worth Star-Telegram* reporter John Moritz said that Republicans moved through their legislative agenda quickly that year, leaving time to revisit the issue of Texas's congressional representation. Discussion of taking up redistricting for an unprecedented second consecutive session had moved from theory to reality by April. Outnumbered in the House and Senate and not holding the office of governor or lieutenant governor, Democrats had few parliamentary weapons available to prevent the re-redistricting of both congressional and legislative districts.[28]

U.S. House majority leader Tom DeLay drove the process. During the 2002 campaign, DeLay's long-term goal was to ensure a Republican state House majority that would elect his ally Craddick as Speaker. Craddick, in turn, would seek to increase the number of Republicans elected to Congress from Texas by drawing more new, GOP-friendly congressional districts. In particular, DeLay sought to unseat two of his chief nemeses—moderate-to-liberal Lloyd Doggett of Austin and Martin Frost of Dallas—along with several conservative Democrats from Republican-dominated districts, such as Charles Stenholm of Abilene and Nick Lampson of Beaumont. DeLay's goals were often incompatible with the interests of several large Texas constituencies. Austin had long been represented by a single member of Congress; the DeLay-Craddick redistricting plan split the capital city among multiple districts in order to dilute the Democratic stronghold's strength. Communities like Abilene would lose the services of experienced representatives like Stenholm, who had acquired seniority in the U.S. House.[29] DeLay felt that what was good for the national GOP was good for Texas. "I'm the majority leader," DeLay declared, "and we want more seats."[30]

On May 12, 2003, fifty-five House Democrats fled to a Holiday Inn in Ardmore, Oklahoma, to prevent the House from reaching a quorum. The "Killer Ds" had to maintain their walkout only until May 15, the legislative deadline for House bills to be referred to the Senate. Not trusting the GOP majority, each absent Democrat instructed the House parliamentarian and clerk to lock the voting machines at their desks.[31]

The walkout became a farcical national spectacle. Craddick ordered the Department of Public Safety and the Texas Rangers to arrest any wayward legislators and bring them back to the House. Craddick and Tom DeLay then went much further, requesting the federal Department of Homeland Security to track Pete Laney's plane on its way to Oklahoma; DeLay asked the Department of Justice to enforce Craddick's arrest warrants in Ardmore. The Department of Justice declined to get involved, and the legislature adjourned June 2 without drawing any new congressional lines. Governor Perry immediately called a special session to start June 30 to again consider redistricting.[32]

The Senate, in anticipation of the session, held a series of public hearings across the state at the urging of Lieutenant Governor David Dewhurst, who showed little enthusiasm for the redistricting effort and wanted to establish an "independent record" of public sentiment regarding the issue. The hearings began June 30 and continued through July. The sessions drew boisterous crowds, and Democrats frequently booed GOP officials. On July 28, ten Democratic senators imitated their House colleagues and took flight to Albuquerque, New Mexico, to break the quorum. Democratic resistance crumbled when Houston Democratic senator John Whitmire knuckled under the pressure and returned to Texas. Republicans reminded Whitmire that his Senate seat had been preserved in the 2001 redistricting effort "as a political favor" and that such a helping hand could be withdrawn.[33]

Perry called another special session to complete redistricting. Republican state attorney general Greg Abbott certified that the new congressional maps passed the requirements of the Voting Rights Act. Craddick, ironically, delayed approval of the final redistricting bill until Midland was given its own congressional district.[34]

Craddick played a central role in preserving the Republican majority in the U.S. House in 2004. No Texas Speaker had ever played such a visible role in national politics. The Texas Speaker's national reach, however, went far beyond redistricting. Partly as a result of the "New Federalism" initiated by the Reagan administration in the 1980s, which devolved power from Washington to the states, lobbyists increasingly funneled money into state political coffers and influenced public policy through officials like Craddick. Meanwhile, Craddick, with his access to big-money donors like Leininger, has become a major financial player in the Republican Party, and his impact reached beyond the Lone Star State.

On Not Having It Both Ways

The French historian and philosopher Michel Foucault once observed that "there are no relations of power without resistance."[35] Craddick reached a pinnacle of influence in the redistricting struggle, but the techniques required to succeed—the calling-in of old debts, the arm-twisting to get some members to vote against the interest of their own districts for the greater glory of the Republican Party, the implicit threat represented by a powerful officeholder well connected to wealthy patrons—reaped a harvest of resentment. As Craddick became the state's most powerful Speaker ever, immediate blowback ensued.

The bitterness engendered by redistricting came to a head over the issue of school funding. The state's Robin Hood redistribution plan remained in place in 2003 even as it faced legal challenges by wealthier districts. By that year, any district with more than $305,000 in taxable property per student paid into the state system, while districts below that mark received money. Districts experienced a crisis when they no longer qualified as poor districts and also hit the legislature's imposed limit of $1.50 per $100 property valuation (a limit set to force reduced state spending). As enrollments expanded and costs increased, more districts found it necessary to balance their books by cutting budgets, reducing staff, and delaying needed repairs and purchases. Some districts tried to circumvent the tax caps by regularly raising property valuations, but antitax Republican legislators responded by trying to limit districts' valuation increases to 5 percent, down from the current 10 percent, or to roll back the property tax caps by 33 percent, to $1 per $100 of valuation.[36]

Local school-budget cuts angered residents of wealthier districts, but constantly climbing property-tax rates upset voters across the state. Perry, Craddick, and other Republican leaders tried to tap into this sentiment and ended up making a series of what turned out to be mutually exclusive commitments. "You cannot eliminate Robin Hood, keep equity, reduce property taxes substantially and adequately fund schools back to the level they need to be, and say there will be zero—neutral taxes in the end," Michael Boone, a Dallas lawyer and adviser to state Republican leaders on school finance for ten years, told the *Dallas Morning News*.[37]

Unable to meet these contradictory demands and unwilling to prioritize them, the state's top three leaders and the state legislature ran into a brick wall six times between 2003 and 2005. The legislature debated but failed to agree on school-finance reform during the 2003 regular session, a fourth special session that year (following the three special sessions that wrestled with redistricting), the 2005 regular session, and three subsequent special sessions that year. (Special sessions cost the taxpayers $60,000 a day, or nearly $2 million for a full thirty-day special session.) Perry demanded a property-tax rollback and called for hikes in "sin taxes" on alcohol and sexually oriented businesses. Perry refused to agree to a plan called for by Democrats and moderate Republicans to close loopholes in the business franchise tax. Craddick wanted to shift even more of the tax burden from businesses by raising the sales tax, even though Texans already paid some of the highest sales-tax rates in the country and the state's own budget estimates indicated that this move would raise the tax burden on 90 percent of residents.[38]

Less than a week into the second consecutive special session on school finance, House leaders started the session by introducing a motion that would have cut off all debate and amendments to their school-finance plan, a high-handed move rejected in a bipartisan vote. The Republican leaders introduced their plan, but members slapped it down in an overwhelming 124–8 vote. Before the vote, fourteen rebellious Republicans joined the sixty-two Democrats to amend the plan to provide more property tax relief, larger pay raises for teachers, and twice as much new funding for school districts. The amendments, which shifted taxes to businesses, lost the support of the bill's original sponsors, who then allowed members to tack on dozens of additional amendments without debate. The entire bill became a poison pill that no one in the legislature would swallow. Since revenue bills must originate in the House and since that body was prohibited from introducing new measures that substantially resembled previously rejected bills, the second special session failed before the first week had been completed.[39]

Perry's call for a third special session in the summer of 2005 clearly irritated the House Speaker. When the leadership's school financing plan went down in flames in July, Craddick declared that members were "worn out . . . They're kind of fatigued voting multiple times on the same issue."[40] Craddick expressed a clear preference for waiting until a court ruled on the constitutionality of the state's current system, believing that a finding in favor of the state's system would make moves by the legislature unnecessary, and that a court ruling against the current system would supply the needed pressure to force the legislature to approve a new plan. Lieutenant Governor Dewhurst moved ahead with a plan that increased some business taxes but did not include a cap on the property-tax dollars that rich districts had to pay into the state system, a provision Craddick insisted upon. The Speaker took the unprecedented step of using spare campaign funds to buy radio spots across the state to criticize the Senate plan. Craddick's ads further strained an already tense relationship with Dewhurst. "Speaker Craddick's time and energy would be better spent on solving the state's problems than on . . . misleading advertisements," Dewhurst spokesperson Mark Miner said.[41] The third session failed, however, like its predecessors, after Craddick refused to bring to the floor a tax-swap bill that would exchange cuts in property taxes for increases in sales taxes and some business taxes.[42]

At the beginning of 2006, the legislature knew that it faced a crisis. On September 15, 2005, state district judge John Dietz ruled the Texas system of paying for schools unconstitutional, declaring that the average

38 percent of local school budgets paid for by the state failed to meet the constitution's requirement that the legislature provide "an adequate and suitable education." Furthermore, he ruled that because budget shortfalls forced an increasing number of districts to tax at the legislature's imposed $1.50 cap, local districts had lost "all meaningful discretion," and the state had, in effect, instituted an unconstitutional state property tax. "Texas in 2040 will have a population that is larger, poorer, less educated, and more needy than today," Dietz warned. "Education costs money, but ignorance costs more money."[43]

The collision between ideological purity and depressing fiscal reality ended in legislative failure and fierce criticism of Perry, Craddick, and Dewhurst from the usually complacent state press and fellow politicians. Critics charged that the Republican insistence on tax cuts in all political circumstances painted the party leadership into a corner. "They're up against a painful reality here, and that is you can't have a decent—let alone quality—education system without paying for it," said University of Texas political science professor Bruce Buchanan.[44]

Things Begin to Unravel

A looming scandal clouded the Speaker's efforts during the redistricting and school-financing battles. Travis County district attorney Ronnie Earle indicted Tom Delay and three of his associates for the fundraising activities of Texans for a Republican Majority Political Action Committee. The PAC funneled $190,000 in legally questionable campaign funds to Republican candidates in key state House races during the decisive 2003 general election campaign. Texas law prohibits direct corporate contributions to political candidates. Earle charged that DeLay laundered the funds by transferring the cash to the Republican National Committee, which then distributed the money immediately to Republican legislative candidates.[45]

In September 2004, Earle convinced a Travis County grand jury to return thirty-two felony indictments against several corporations, including Sears Roebuck, Cracker Barrel Old Country Store, and Bacardi USA, and three men with close ties to Tom DeLay: John Colyandro, the former executive director of TRMPAC; Warren DeBold, a top DeLay fundraiser; and Jim Ellis, a key DeLay political aide. In September 2005, DeLay himself was indicted on conspiracy and money-laundering charges in connection with TRMPAC's activities. The indictment forced DeLay to temporarily step down as U.S. House majority leader, a move he made permanent in early 2006 after revelations of his close relationship with Jack Abramoff, who pleaded guilty to charges of conspiring to bribe members of Congress, mail fraud, and tax evasion, came to light.[46]

The DeLay scandal, frustration with the Iraq War begun in 2003, a sexual scandal involving congressional pages in Washington, D.C., and anger over mismanagement of relief and rebuilding efforts in New Orleans after Hurricane Katrina in 2005 created a bad electoral climate for the GOP in the 2006 elections. In Texas, partisan resentments stirred by redistricting and frustration concerning the epic battles over school finances further complicated Republican political ambitions.

The first sign of trouble came on February 14, 2006, when liberal Democrat Donna Howard easily beat Republican Ben Bentzin, 58 percent to 42 percent, in a runoff to fill the unexpired term of retiring GOP lawmaker Todd Baxter. Howard's win, some observers noted, was particularly significant since it came in one of the "Tommy-mandered" districts drawn by the House in 2003 to guarantee a Republican win. During the March 7 Republican primaries, a key Craddick ally, Kent Grusendorf of Arlington, chair of the Public Education Committee, lost to challenger Diane Patrick, a former Arlington school board member and one-time member of the state education board, whom the nineteen-year incumbent derided as an "educrat." Voters, however, blamed him for the ongoing school financing fiasco.[47]

Nevertheless, Texas Republicans entered the summer with some hope for success. An improving national economy that conservatives credited to President George W. Bush and Governor Rick Perry's tax cuts provided the Texas legislature with welcome breathing room and at least temporarily resolved the logjam over school spending. In spring 2006, the state recorded an $8.2 billion surplus. This allowed the Legislature to pass a 33 percent cut in local property taxes, to be replaced in part by increases in state business and property taxes. Teachers also received a $2,000 annual pay raise. Doubts remained, however, whether the new statewide levies would compensate for the reduction in local taxes over the long term.[48]

Regardless, Texas Republicans felt the sting of that year's anti-incumbent backlash. In the November 2006 elections, the national GOP lost control of the U.S. House and Senate, and in solidly conservative Texas, the Republicans unexpectedly lost six seats in the state House.[49] Even though Republicans maintained their majority for a third straight election cycle, some GOP caucus members blamed Craddick's leadership style for the party's reduced majority.[50]

In spite of the ill feeling in the Capitol, Craddick and his wife, Nadine, continued with their $1 million renovation of the Speaker's apartment, a project funded by lobbyists and big corporate contributors to Republican campaigns. The money paid for new wood floors, removal of the loft and spiral staircase in the living room that had been installed by Gib Lewis after the Capitol fire, and two $1,000 commodes. Critics charged that donations to the redecoration effort amounted to influence peddling by lobbyists. This controversy, combined with resentments over GOP election losses, led to an attempted palace coup. The month after the November elections, conservative Republican state representative Brian McCall of Plano announced that he planned to challenge Craddick for the speakership. McCall dropped out, however, when Jim Pitts of Waxahachie announced that he would also seek the speakership.

Pitts's campaign fizzled when his supporters failed on a procedural vote. Pitts's supporters pushed for keeping House members' votes in the Speaker race secret until after the election was decided and the Speaker had made committee assignments. Craddick's backers countered that having House members vote in the open provided transparency in government. Pitts's backers said that House members, worried that they would lose key committee assignments, feared openly rebelling against Craddick. The voting proposal by Pitts's backers failed on an 80–68 vote; fourteen Republicans supported Pitts in the losing effort. Pitts then announced he was dropping out of the race because he didn't "want to put anyone else in jeopardy. It's time to heal."[51] Members dutifully reelected Craddick, 121–27.[52]

In spite of Craddick's reelection, however, it was clear that the Speaker was presiding over a badly divided house. And Democrats remained bedeviled by the racial divides left over from the days of segregation. Ironically, Craddick's victory in the 2007 Speaker's race depended in part on support from a notable contingent of African American Democrats such as Dawnna Dukes of Austin and Sylvester Turner of Houston, and Mexican American Democrats such as Ismael "Kino" Flores of Mission and Armando "Mando" Martinez of Weslaco. Still marginalized in the political process, black and brown Democrats stood firmly behind the leadership of a conservative white Republican like Craddick after he assigned them plum committee posts.[53]

To everyone's surprise, however, Craddick's unexpectedly hard struggle to keep the speakership had not ended. As the legislative session wound toward a dispirited conclusion on May 25, 2007, lawmakers still struggled to pass a $153 billion state budget. Critics charged that Craddick had loaded the budget with pork earmarked for his business supporters. Craddick's opponents introduced motions reconsidering his election as Speaker. On May 27, Representative Paul Moreno, an El Paso Democrat, asked Craddick whether the House could reconsider any vote taken earlier in the session. When Craddick said yes, Moreno said, "I move that the vote by which Speaker Tom Craddick was elected on January 12th of this year be brought back to the floor for a recount."[54] Craddick slapped down the motion immediately. He later outlined a legal theory justifying his refusal to recognize any motion to unseat him. Craddick proclaimed he had "absolute discretion" to ignore any member making such a motion and that such decisions could not be appealed by House members.[55]

House members finally passed the budget, but the last act of the drama had not played out. On the session's final day, Representative Pat Haggerty, an El Paso Republican, made a "personal privilege" speech and began calling out House members' names, asking them to announce whether they wanted Craddick to remain Speaker. Speaker Pro Tem Sylvester Turner, one of the African American Democrats on Craddick's team, tried cutting Haggerty off. Haggerty then called on all representatives who would have voted against Craddick to take their voting keys and walk out. Almost sixty stood up and filed out of the chamber, leaving the House without a quorum and forcing it to adjourn.[56] "I don't think this is an obituary [for the attempt to remove Craddick]," said Representative Fred Hill, a Richardson Republican who had already announced his intention to challenge the Speaker the next session. "It's just the first act. You're going to have 18 months to play out the scenario."[57]

The End of an Era

Hill proved prescient. President George Bush's deepening unpopularity, the collapse of the American economy in the fall of 2008, the failure of Republican presidential nominee John McCain's White House run, and the vast and enthusiastic grassroots crusade behind Democratic nominee Barack Obama's presidential campaign created a national shift in the electorate that touched Texas. Significantly, the Republican majority in the Texas House of Representatives shrank from a commanding majority to a razor-thin 76–74 margin. The election results created an immediate problem for Speaker Craddick.[58] More than half of the members in the 2009 session had been elected after Craddick won his initial term as House Speaker, in 2003. Along with the loss in GOP members, the Speaker's critics on both sides of the aisle sensed an opening for a new presiding officer when the legislature convened in January 2009.

A survey of active voters conducted by the Houston-based Republican polling firm Hill Research Consultants revealed that Texas voters believed that the Republican Party was out of touch and had sold them out to wealthy special interests. Voters rated Democrats as better at representing "homeowners, small businesses and average payers." By double digits, Republicans were more likely to be described as "racist," "arrogant," and "corrupt," while Democrats were significantly more likely to be described as "smart," "fair," and the "party of the future." The poll revealed that few voters cared about Republican social conservatives' top issues, like abortion or school prayer, and hard-line GOP stands on immigration alienated Mexican American voters as well as political moderates.[59] Many Republican members and nearly all the Democratic representatives sensed a shift in the political landscape. In the immediate aftermath of the 2008 Texas general election, the controversy over the House Speaker played only a very minor role. The state's changing demographics, the economic downturn, and the national election undoubtedly played a more important role in the minds of voters. Nevertheless, the national mood shaped a dramatic turn of events in the Speaker's race.

Craddick's fall as Speaker came faster than anyone could have anticipated. On November 19, 2008, he hosted a fund-raiser and political powwow with his supporters at the Lost Pines Golf Resort in Bastrop, near Austin, a gathering intended to scare off potential rivals. Instead of locking up another term, the event generated criticism in the press and additional Republican opponents in the Speaker's race. By December 29, fourteen candidates had filed papers to enter the Speaker's race. The same day, sixty-four "ABC" ("Anyone But Craddick") Democrats signed a pledge promising they would oppose the Speaker's reelection "under any circumstances."[60]

The key moment in the anti-Craddick coup came during a January 3 meeting of ten dissident Republicans at the Austin home of Byron Cook, the Republican chair of the House Civil Practices Committee, who was highly critical of Craddick during the 2007 legislative session. An eleventh dissident, Representative Rob Eissler of The Woodlands, participated in the session via webcam; Capitol reporters camped out on Cook's yard. Craddick had scheduled another caucus with fifty-five backers at Sullivan's Steakhouse in downtown Austin for the evening of Sunday, January 5, and hoped to sew up a narrow majority, but the eleven Republican dissidents hoped to head off the Speaker at the pass.[61]

After four rounds of voting, the dissidents selected as their standard bearer the little-known two-term San Antonio representative Joe Straus over Burt Solomons of Carrollton by a squeaky 6–5 vote. Straus rapidly sewed up the support of the ABC Democrats, and by Saturday morning, Doug Miller, a freshman Republican from New Braunfels who had committed to no candidate, announced his support as well. By 4:30 p.m. on Sunday, January 5, just hours before Craddick's planned steakhouse gathering, Straus announced he would be the state's next House Speaker, revealing pledges from eighty-five House members.

Speaker Straus

Joe Straus was first elected to the Texas House of Representatives in a special election in February 2005. He represents the affluent Bexar County communities of Alamo Heights and northeast San Antonio. His brief legislative experience has revolved on issues related to business and energy. Straus quickly gained a reputation as a moderate, conscientious member. He received recognition from diverse groups such as the Texas Public Power Association and the Sierra Club. In 2008, *Texas Monthly* picked Straus as one of the thirty-five Texans who would shape the future of the state.

A lifelong Republican and San Antonio native, Straus played many roles in the local and state party. In 1986, he managed U.S. Representative Lamar Smith's first campaign for Congress. He served in the administration of President George H. W. Bush from 1989 through 1991 as deputy director of business liaison at the U.S. Department of Commerce. Straus is a principal in the insurance and executive benefits firm of Watson, Mazur, Bennett and Straus, L.L.C. Straus is a graduate of Vanderbilt University with a BA in political science. He is described in his official biography as an avid sportsman with a lifelong interest in Thoroughbred breeding. He is married to Julie Brink Straus, and they have two daughters, Sara and Robyn. Straus's noncontroversial biography was intended to soothe raw feelings within the House. His connection to pari-mutuel betting, however, later raised the ire of some Christian conservatives.[62]

At the evening meeting with his supporters at Sullivan's, Craddick and his allies assessed their chances and quickly reached the conclusion that the battle was over. Adding the latest chapter to the tumultuous history of the Speaker's office, Craddick dramatically announced that he had withdrawn from the Speaker's race.[63]

Angered at the dissidents' disloyalty to Craddick, conservatives briefly rallied around the speakership campaign of Representative John Smithee of Amarillo, even as the Christian Right attacked Straus's conservative credentials. GOP critics also raised questions about Straus's opposition to abortion and his family's investment in the Retama Park horse-racing track. "Joe Straus is very much a Republican in name only," said Cathie Adams of the Texas Eagle Forum. "He will be beholden to Democrats." Straus also drew the ire of Joe Pojman of the Texas Alliance for Life. "He's never been a strong vote for us at all," Pojman said. "We're very concerned about Joe Straus." Nevertheless, the list of Straus's supporters grew to 100 by the afternoon of January 5, and Smithee announced his withdrawal from the race.[64]

Straus became the fourth Republican Speaker in state history, but he won the office primarily through the support of Democrats alienated thoroughly by Craddick's heavy-handed methods. The past served as prologue. When House members rebelled against Democratic Speaker Gus Mutscher in the 1970s, his successors Rayford Price and Price Daniel pledged to reduce the power of the office. Straus made a similar pledge at the start of his term. He initiated rule changes that would increase the power of committee chairs, implement a limited seniority system to fill the powerful House Appropriations Committee, and change procedures so that a majority of House members could force debate on motions to remove a Speaker from office. Raw power politics did not disappear, however. Straus also moved to reduce the number of House committees, an effort that had the political benefit of eliminating committee chairs who happened to be Craddick's key allies. The GOP also returned to pushing divisive, ideological legislation, including proposing a "voter ID" bill that critics charged would reduce Mexican American and elderly voting, and another bill that would have outlawed the "straight-ticket" voting thought to have benefited Democrats on Election Day 2008.[65]

Regardless of the structural reorganization, a sense of elation emerged from the House with the change of leadership and the hope for a more participatory process. The sudden end to the Speaker's race prevented a bloodletting at the Capitol. The political armistice resulted in members turning to address the very serious business of the overwhelming needs of the state and its citizens during a period of economic uncertainty. The future of the Speaker's office and whether it would continue its trajectory toward assuming ever-greater authority remained an open-ended question.[66]

The Speakership in Historical Perspective

Craddick's power was more than 160 years in the making. The speaker-ship began in the early nineteenth century as a rotating honorary position chiefly concerned with the duties of presiding over debates. Speakers overwhelmingly shared the elitist values of the wealthy slave-owner class. A dominant ideology that promoted a rural economy, white supremacy, governmental favors to the wealthy, and limited participation of the citizenry in daily government prevailed for much of the nineteenth century, limiting the policy options of individual Speakers and rendering them interchangeable.

Republican Reconstruction briefly disturbed this governmental slumber. The state began to take responsibility for Texans without wealth, opening public schools and hospitals, providing mental health care, and promoting the growth of roads, railroads, and shipyards. This activist period proved ephemeral, and unreconstructed Confederates recaptured the state government with a vengeance, gutting the state's first-ever genuine public education system and relying on terror and violence to reduce black Texans to near servitude.

This stultifying political climate changed with the rise of agrarian discontent in the 1870s through the 1890s, culminating in the Populist challenge at century's end. After conservatives used violence and voter fraud again, this time to crush the Populists, dissenters within elite ranks, the Progressives, insisted that the modern economy developing in Texas required the aid of government. Agencies proliferated, and industries like railroads, banking, medicine, and dentistry for the first time faced regulations aimed at ensuring fair business practices and safe consumer products. As the state government's responsibilities and obligations increased, policy disputes increased in number and intensity, and for the first time, Speakers' priorities mattered. The Speaker's areas of responsibility and power were explicitly outlined for the first time, and institutional reforms made the speakership a more prominent office. Still, Speakers often saw the position as a stepping-stone to a statewide office or to Congress.

One of the most conservative men to ever serve as Speaker, Coke Stevenson, increased the prominence of the office in the 1930s. Stevenson dominated state politics of the period. He broke precedent not only by serving two consecutive terms as Speaker, but also by receiving extensive public attention while holding the speakership. Speakers openly became legislative players who had to be dealt with by governors, lieutenant governors, lobbyists, and activists seeking to shape public policy.

The discovery of oil in the early twentieth century and federal spending during the Depression and World War II transformed the state into an industrial, urban colossus. The increasing complexity of the economy, the growing racial, religious, and linguistic diversity, and the increasing international competition engendered by the push for free trade turned the job of state legislator, and Speaker, into a year-long duty. Speakers in the post–World War II era dramatically expanded their staffs as the legislature increased the number of state agencies. With that expansion, Speakers increased their power of appointment. Speakers gained control over the Capitol grounds and became more sophisticated in their guidance of the legislative process. This happened as the House became divided as never before into liberal and conservative, urban and rural, male and female, and white, black, and brown factions.

Critics charged that the Speaker's powers had resembled those of a virtual dictatorship by the time of Mutscher in the early 1970s, but after a brief post-Sharpstown backlash, the speakership continued evolving into the state's most powerful political office. This process reached its apotheosis under Craddick. Mutscher, though a powerful Speaker, could still claim only to share power over the Democratic Party with Ben Barnes and Preston Smith. Craddick, however, stood alone at the top of the Republican Party as the most influential policy maker in state government.

The growth in power and influence enjoyed by the Texas House Speaker in this era at times paralleled changes in the office of U.S. House Speaker. During the twentieth century, the Speakers in Congress inspired reactions ranging from reverence to loathing. They operated in a congressional system governed by seniority and divided along party lines. Whether they were Democratic or Republican, all were forced to deal with entrenched interests. They had to maintain order in the House, consider the interests of their party, coordinate legislation with the Senate, and work with the executive branch on programs.

The Speakers of the Texas House of Representatives, like their counterparts in the rest of the South, faced somewhat different circumstances. One-party politics, fewer demands for public services, smaller budgets, and the part-time nature of the body placed fewer demands on southern House Speakers. But the economic boom of the post–World War II years, coupled with the growing demand for state services, raised expectations for House Speakers in Dixie. Meanwhile, the civil rights movement, growing political participation by women, African Americans, and Mexican Americans, and an increase in the number of special interest groups required modern House Speakers to pay more attention to the economic and social changes under way.

In Texas, Speakers' policy-making roles expanded, and like their counterparts in Washington, the Speakers who respected the office and the members found greater success than those who abused the institution and the process. By expanding the responsibilities of the Speaker's office and its bureaucratic structure, the Speaker acquired influence and stature that equaled, or exceeded, the power of the governor and lieutenant governor. The office no longer served merely as a stepping-stone to other elected positions. After 1975, the multiterm Speaker who presided as any other statewide elected official became the norm. Three of the most recent Speakers, Gib Lewis, Pete Laney, and Tom Craddick, held the position for multiple terms. Of even greater importance, each of these Speakers saw the office as the pinnacle of elective leadership in Texas.

The power of modern Speakers cannot be separated from the increasing influence of the lobbyists who form what is often described as a fourth branch of Texas government. Campaign reforms instated after Sharpstown did not banish the lobby, but did require stealthier and more complex maneuvers on the part of would-be influence peddlers. Lobbyists became even more important as the media outlets available to candidates multiplied. House candidates, for instance, once relied primarily on stump speeches, the occasional radio appearance, and printed pamphlets and buttons. To these old media have been added "tightly targeted direct (bulk) mail," television advertising, the Internet, and extensive polling. All of these forms of media are expensive.[67]

As reporters Sam Kinch, Jr., and Ann Marie Kilday point out, campaign costs have skyrocketed. The modern era of campaign spending in Texas began with the election of Bill Clements as governor in 1978. Clements drew on his own deep pockets, but also carried strong Washington and Texas business connections. Clements convinced the Texas business community, which had previously given extensively only in presidential and senatorial races, that local races were important for shaping policy. These local races became even more important to business lobbyists as they increasingly appreciated the role of congressional redistricting in promoting the national Republican Party and a succession of conservative presidents. Clements initiated a fund-raising arms race between the parties in Texas. The Republicans had the advantage of their anti-union, antiregulation, and antitax policies. In the 1980s, a two-year election cycle that included races for governor and most other executive department offices cost candidates less than $20 million. By contrast, the 1997–1998 campaign cycle cost $121 million. All Republican candidates in 1998 raised $83 million, compared to $38 million for all Democrats.[68]

In 1998, incumbents, who enjoyed a tremendous advantage in fundraising because of their ability to deliver favorable legislation to contributors, received $2.50 in campaign contributions for every $1 received by a challenger. Most of that money went to those seen as effective, entrenched incumbents who had served special interests well. About $55 million of the $121 million contributed to all candidates in 1997–1998, or about 46 percent of the total, came from political action committees, almost all formed by big business and professional organizations seeking friendly legislation from Austin. Almost half of the money raised in that period came from only 629 individuals and PACs, who pumped in an average of $95,000 each to favored candidates. "No person who has any sense about what's right and wrong in this world will believe that kind of money . . . doesn't influence a vote," said former Democratic state representative Mike Martin of Galveston.[69]

The advantages enjoyed by incumbents are enhanced during redistricting, when influential members of the House and Senate are able to, in effect, select their constituents. Designing districts has become a devastating tool of continued power for ruling parties, since most electoral districts in the state, and the nation, are drawn to be "can't lose" zones for Republicans and Democrats.[70] All these trends combined—the increased spending on state campaigns, the greater involvement of business PACs in fundraising, the immense financial advantages enjoyed by incumbents, the use of redistricting to guarantee election results, and the widening funding gap between the Republican and Democratic parties—came together under Tom Craddick and magnified his influence over state politics.

Of course, the Texas Legislative Council computer program that provides suggested legislative-district lines can predict voter behavior, but not guarantee it. Nor can it ensure for a Speaker how elected members of his party will behave once they are in office. Furthermore, state and national issues affect voter decisions in ways that often disrupt traditional voting patterns.

Perhaps Texas politics has matured to the point that both parties are competitive and encompass diverse ideologies requiring the art of compromise. Though in many ways a conventional Republican fiscal conservative, Straus showed little appetite in his early days as Speaker for spending time on divisive social issues like school vouchers, abortion, and immigration restriction, controversies that helped poison relations between Democrats and Republicans under Craddick. This could be a good sign for governance in an era when Democrats and Republicans are more evenly divided. To succeed, Straus and his successors must rule more adroitly and with greater sensitivity, perhaps leading narrower, more fragile coalitions made up of like-minded legislators from both major parties. In this case, the speakership will become more democratic with a little *d*. Such a development might make the office less powerful than the governor and lieutenant governor, but it would force Speakers to preside in a manner that more closely reflects the priorities of most Texans. Polling suggests that these priorities include greater funding for education at the public school and university level; more money to provide health coverage for uninsured children; and support for embryonic stem cell research and other scientific projects. In turn, this style of governance could further enhance the position of the House Speaker as the state official most in tune with the hopes and desires of the people of the state.[71]

Another political trend, however, might frustrate Straus's efforts at bipartisanship and make the Democrats and Republicans in the House more ideological. Journalist John Moritz argues that recent rounds of redistricting have created such heavily Republican or Democratic districts that most legislators must win the votes of the ideologues within their own party, since they dominate the primary electorate. This, he says, has increased the tendency of Democrats to lean further left and Republicans further right. In many regards, this trend reflects the direction of national politics.[72]

A Speaker ruling over a more ideologically driven House is still likely to continue as the most powerful political force in the state. Unless more-effective politicians rise to the position of governor and lieutenant governor, that power is not likely to be shared. Now that the institutional power of the office of the Speaker has evolved in the modern era to rival the resources and influence of the governor and lieutenant governor, future Speakers must rely on their character, leadership, and political expertise to address the myriad problems that the state will undoubtedly continue to face.

Notes

Introduction

1. S. C. Gwynne, "Power: 1. Tom Craddick," *Texas Monthly,* February 2005, 98–103, 186–191.

2. Dolph Briscoe, interview by Don Carleton, Dolph Briscoe Center for American History, Austin, Texas, June 17, 2004.

3. Mark Lisheron, "Frustrated Watchers Say House Ought to Pack It Up," *Austin American-Statesman,* July 28, 2005, http://www.statesman.com/news/content/shared/tx/legislature/stories/07/28LEGE.html; "2006 Could Be Watershed Year for Texas Schools," KWTX.com, http://www.kwtx.com/news/head lines/2109687.html (accessed January 13, 2006).

4. Donna Cassata and Laurie Kellman, "Tenacious Tom DeLay Has Had Wild Ride," Associated Press, January 7, 2006, http://www.aberdeennews.com/mld/aberdeennews/news/13575634.htm (accessed January 12, 2006).

5. Texas Constitution (1876), Article 3, Section 9. Texas has been governed under five constitutions since statehood: charters adopted in 1845, 1861, 1866, 1869, and the current constitution, adopted in 1876.

6. Sam Kinch, Jr., "Speaker's Office Now a Prize Plum," *Dallas Morning News,* September 15, 1980.

7. "A Short History on Ira Ingram," Texas—Legislature—House Speakers vertical file, Dolph Briscoe Center for American History, Austin, Texas.

8. Texas Legislative Council, *Presiding Officers of the Texas Legislature, 1846–2002,* 98–107; Kinch, "Speaker's Office."

9. Texas Legislative Council, *Presiding Officers,* 98–193; William Kent Brunette, "The Role of the Texas Speaker in the Texas House of Representatives: An Historical and Contemporary Analysis" (master's thesis, University of Texas at Austin, 1979), 45–50.

10. The periodization model for this book has been modified from Ronald M. Peters, *The American Speakership,* 5–7.

11. Paul Burka, "The Elephants in the Room," *Texas Monthly,* January 2006, 195; Karen Brooks and Christy Hoppe, "Craddick Quits Speakers Race; Straus Posed To Take Over," *Dallas Morning News,* January 5, 2009; Laylan Copelin,

"Speaker Straus Would Roll Back Some Craddick Policies: The Texas House Will Try to Address Old Fights and Prevent New Ones With Proposed Rules for the 2009 Session Legislative Session," *Austin American-Statesman*, January 27, 2009.

Chapter One

1. Brunette, "Role of the Texas Speaker," 58–59.

2. Ibid, 59–62.

3. Ibid., 65–66; Texas Legislative Council, *Presiding Officers*, 98–137. There have been four Speakers since Brunette's study, all white men: Gibson D. "Gib" Lewis, Pete Laney, Tom Craddick, and Joe Straus. Lewis and Laney are Protestants, Craddick is a Catholic, and Straus is Jewish. Lewis is from the Fort Worth area in north-central Texas, Straus is from San Antonio, and Craddick and Laney are from primarily rural areas in West Texas and East Texas, respectively. Lewis is a businessman, having founded Lewis Label Products, Inc., and serves as a political consultant in Austin. Laney is a cotton farmer. Craddick is owner of Mustang Mud, a firm that sells drilling fluids to oil companies. Straus is a principal in a San Antonio insurance firm. See Texas Legislative Council, *Presiding Officers*, 7–8, 231, and Gwynne, "Power: 1. Tom Craddick," 102–103, 186.

4. Brunette, "Role of the Texas Speaker."

5. For more on party politics during the Texas Republic, see Stanley Siegel, *A Political History of the Texas Republic*. The most important works on Sam Houston include James L. Haley, *Sam Houston;* Randolph B. Campbell, *Sam Houston and the American Southwest;* M. K. Wisehart, *Sam Houston: American Giant;* and Marquis James, *The Raven*.

6. Randolph B. Campbell and Richard G. Lowe, *Wealth and Power in Antebellum Texas*, 115.

7. V. O. Key, Jr., *Southern Politics in State and Nation*, 299–301; Chandler Davidson, *Race and Class in Texas Politics*, 7.

8. R. Campbell, *Gone to Texas*, 271–274.

9. Ibid.

10. *The New Handbook of Texas*, s.v. "Reconstruction."

11. For more on the early Republican Party, see Paul D. Casdorph, *A History of the Republican Party in Texas, 1865–1965;* Carl H. Moneyhon, *Republicanism in Reconstruction Texas;* and Roger M. Olien, *From Token to Triumph*.

12. Barry Crouch, "A Spirit of Lawlessness: White Violence, Texas Blacks, 1865–1868," *Journal of Social History* 18 (Winter 1984), 226.

13. Ibid., 218–219.

14. *The New Handbook of Texas*, s.vv. "Reconstruction," "Constitution of 1869."

15. Betty Jeffus Sandlin, "The Texas Constitutional Convention of 1868–1869" (PhD diss., Texas Tech University, 1970); R. Campbell, *Gone to Texas*, 285–286.

16. Kenneth E. Hendrickson, *The Chief Executives of Texas from Stephen F. Austin to John B. Connally, Jr.,* 37; R. Campbell, *Gone to Texas*, 229.

17. R. Campbell, *Gone to Texas*, 281–285, 306.

18. Texas Legislative Council, *Presiding Officers*, 131; *The New Handbook of Texas*, s.v. "Reconstruction."

19. Charles William Ramsdell, *Reconstruction in Texas,* 308; Texas Legislative Council, *Presiding Officers,* 131. Ramsdell's account stands as a particularly racist interpretation of Reconstruction in Texas. Ramsdell persistently depicts freedmen as incompetent, and Texas Republicans as carpetbaggers. A vastly superior account of this period in Texas history can be found in Randolph B. Campbell, *Grass-Roots Reconstruction in Texas, 1865–1880.*

20. R. Campbell, *Gone to Texas,* 284–285.

21. Texas Legislative Council, *Presiding Officers,* 135; *The New Handbook of Texas,* s.v. "Guy Morrison Bryan."

22. Texas Legislative Council, *Presiding Officers,* 135.

23. Guy Morrison Bryan to Rutherford B. Hayes, February 1, 1874, Bryan-Hayes Correspondence typescript edited by E. W. Winkler, Box 2Q451, Guy Morrison Bryan Collection, Dolph Briscoe Center for American History, Austin, Texas (hereafter referred to as the Bryan Collection).

24. Bryan to Hayes, January 8, 1875, Bryan Collection.

25. Bryan, "Hon. Guy M. Bryan," undated typescript, Guy M. Bryan vertical folder, Dolph Briscoe Center for American History, Austin, Texas.

26. The above discussion on the relative powers of the Speaker is derived from the Texas Politics Web site put up by the Liberal Arts Instructional Technology Service, University of Texas at Austin, August 17, 2005, at http://texaspolitics.laits.utexas.edu.

27. R. Campbell, *Gone to Texas,* 284–285.

28. John E. Bebout, *The Texas Constitution,* 4.

29. Lyle C. Brown, Joyce A. Langenegger, Sonia R. Garcia, and Ted Lewis, *Practicing Texas Politics,* 42.

30. Texas Constitution (1876), Article 8, Section 24; Citizens for Tax Justice, "State and Local Taxes Hit Poor and Middle Class Far Harder than the Wealthy," June 26, 1996, http://www.ctj.org/html/whopays.htm.

31. Citizens Conference on State Legislatures, "The Impact of the Texas Constitution on the State Legislature," 55.

32. Lawrence Goodwyn, *The Populist Moment,* 44–53.

33. Ibid., 149.

34. Hendrickson, *Chief Executives of Texas,* 120–123; Texas Legislative Council, *Presiding Officers,* 149–151.

35. Ibid.

36. Hendrickson, *Chief Executives of Texas,* 126.

37. Goodwyn, *Populist Moment,* 6, 15, 18–19, 122–123, 131–132, 137–138, 210, 280–283.

38. R. Campbell, *Gone to Texas,* 336.

39. John B. Boles, *The South through Time,* 401.

Chapter Two

1. For more on the Progressive movement, see John Whiteclay Chambers II, *The Tyranny of Change;* Steven J. Diner, *A Very Different Age;* Arthur S. Link and Richard L. McCormick, *Progressivism;* and Michael E. McGerr, *A Fierce Discontent.*

2. The best account of Progressives in Texas can be found in Lewis L. Gould, *Progressives and Prohibitionists*.

3. Robert A. Calvert and Arnoldo De León, *The History of Texas*, 272. In 1964, the required number of states ratified the Twenty-fourth Amendment to the U.S. Constitution, which abolished poll taxes. The Texas legislature did not get around to approving the amendment until 2009. See Lee Nichols, "Texas Just Abolished Poll Taxes!" austinchronicle.com, May 22, 2009, http://www.austinchronicle.com/gyrobase/Blogs/News?oid=oid:785067 (accessed June 14, 2009).

4. For more on the Texas "white primary" law and its impact on African Americans, see Darlene Clark Hine, *Black Victory*. Hine does a particularly good job of explaining black disenfranchisement as an elite response to the challenge of Populism and of describing how elites modified franchise restrictions to allow continued voting by the state's significant Mexican American population in South Texas.

5. Texas Legislative Council, *Presiding Officers*, 161.

6. Norman D. Brown, *Hood, Bonnet, and Little Brown Jug*, 13.

7. Quoted in Dorothy Blodgett, Terrell Blodgett, and David Scott, "Legislating: Serving in the Texas House of Representatives, 1899–1905," (printout received at the Dolph Briscoe Center for American History, Austin, Texas, February 11, 2004), 10. As this book was being written, the Blodgetts and Scott were writing a thoughtful, comprehensive biography of Neff. This has subsequently been published as *The Land, the Law, and the Lord: The Life of Pat Neff, Governor of Texas, 1921–1925; President of Baylor University, 1932–1947*. The authors thank these writers for sharing their research on Neff's years as a legislator and Speaker of the House.

8. Ibid, 18.

9. Worth Robert Miller, "Building a Progressive Coalition in Texas: The Populist-Democrat Rapprochement, 1900–1907," *Journal of Southern History* 52, no. 2 (May 1986), 172–174; Blodgett, Blodgett, and Scott, "Legislating," 34; Alwyn Barr, *Black Texans*, 79–80.

10. R. Campbell, *Gone to Texas*, 337.

11. Quoted in Gould, *Progressives and Prohibitionists*, 49.

12. Quoted in Blodgett, Blodgett, and Scott, "Legislating," 41.

13. Ibid., 31.

14. Quoted in ibid., 33

15. Quoted in Gould, *Progressives and Prohibitionists*, 272.

16. Blodgett, Blodgett, and Scott, "Legislating," 41–44.

17. Miller, "Progressive Coalition," 174; Blodgett, Blodgett, and Scott, 44–46.

18. Miller, "Progressive Coalition," 174–175; Jim T. Lindsey, audiotape interview by Michael Phillips, Lindsey home, Redwood Valley, Mendocino, California, April 16, 2004, Speaker collection, Dolph Briscoe Center for American History, Austin, Texas.

19. Blodgett, Blodgett, and Scott, "Legislating," 54.

20. Brown, *Hood, Bonnet, and Little Brown Jug*, 171.

21. Quoted in Gould, *Progressives and Prohibitionists*, 61.

22. D. B. Hardeman and Donald C. Bacon, *Rayburn: A Biography*, 46.

23. Texas Legislative Council, *Presiding Officers*, 167.

24. "History of the Speaker's Apartment"; Texas Legislative Council, *Presiding Officers*, 167, 59; William H. Gardner, "Capitol Quarters Row Recalls Probe," *Houston Post*, April 21, 1957.

25. Gardner, "Capitol Quarters Row Recalls Probe."

26. *The New Handbook of Texas*, s.v. "Samuel Taliaferro Rayburn." The most insightful account on Rayburn's state legislative career can be found in Hardeman and Bacon, *Rayburn*. In addition to the works cited in this chapter, a sketch of Rayburn's service in Congress, written by D. Clayton Brown, can be found in Kenneth E. Hendrickson, Michael L. Collins, and Patrick Cox, eds., *Profiles in Power*, 106–121.

27. Hardeman and Bacon, *Rayburn*, 35.

28. C. Dwight Dorough, *Mr. Sam: A Biography of Samuel T. Rayburn, Speaker of the House*, 72–76.

29. Dorough, *Mr. Sam*, 76; Hardeman and Bacon, *Rayburn*, 36.

30. Hardeman and Bacon, *Rayburn*, 37.

31. Robert A. Caro, *The Years of Lyndon Johnson: The Path to Power*, 308–309.

32. The quotations in this paragraph are from Caro, *Years of Lyndon Johnson*, 312, 313.

33. Texas Legislative Council, *Presiding Officers*, 171; Dorough, *Mr. Sam*, 78, 80.

34. Dorough, *Mr. Sam*, 81.

35. Hardeman and Bacon, *Rayburn*, 51.

36. Dorough, *Mr. Sam*, 81–82.

37. Hardeman and Bacon, *Rayburn*, 51; *Texas Legislative Council, Presiding Officers*, 169.

38. Hardeman and Bacon, *Rayburn*, 52–53; Dorough, *Mr. Sam*, 94.

39. Dorough, *Mr. Sam*, 100.

40. Hardeman and Bacon, *Rayburn*, 53.

41. Quoted in D. G. Dulaney and Edward Hake Phillips, *Speak, Mr. Speaker*, 19.

42. Hardeman and Bacon, *Rayburn*, 107–108.

43. The quotations in this paragraph are from Alfred Steinberg, *Sam Rayburn*, 22, 23.

44. Hardeman and Bacon, *Rayburn*, 54.

45. Texas Legislative Council, *Presiding Officers*, 171.

46. Dorough, *Mr. Sam*, 108.

47. Calvert and De León, *History of Texas*, 277–278.

48. Ibid., 279–280, 283–284.

49. *The New Handbook of Texas*, s.v. "Prohibition"; Calvert and De León, *History of Texas*, 293–294.

50. R. Campbell, *Gone to Texas*, 227. By 1990, Southern Baptists numbered 3,259,395 (19.19 percent of the state population), making Texas the state with the largest Baptist population overall and the tenth highest by percentage. The same year, Catholics surpassed Baptists as the largest religious group in the state. See Adherents.com, "The Largest Southern Baptist Communities," http://www.adherents.com/largecom/com_sbc.html (accessed August 20, 2005); *The New Handbook of Texas*, s.v. "Baptist Church."

51. *The New Handbook of Texas*, s.vv. "Baptist Church," "Methodist Church";

Frank S. Mead, *Handbook of Denominations in the United States,* 197–198; Brunette, "Role of the Texas Speaker," 12; Calvert and De León, *History of Texas,* 302. Of the Speakers from 1846 to 2009 whose religious identities could be determined, nineteen at some point claimed Methodist affiliation, sixteen identified as Baptists, seven as Presbyterians, two as Lutherans, two as Episcopalians, and one each belonged to the Church of Christ, Congregationalist, and Christian denominations. Tom Craddick is to date the only Catholic Speaker in state history, and Joe Straus had been the only Jewish presiding officer.

52. The Speakers from 1890 to 1930 included five Methodists (Love, John Wesley Marshall, Chester H. Terrell, John W. Woods, and Robert Ernest Seagler) and four Baptists (Rayburn, Charles Graham Thomas, Robert Lee Satterwhite, and Wingate Stuart Barron); see Brunette, "Role of the Texas Speaker," 132–152.

53. Gould, *Progressives and Prohibitionists,* 287.

54. Quoted in Calvert and De León, *History of Texas,* 296.

55. Ibid.

56. Ibid.

Chapter Three

1. *The New Handbook of Texas,* s.v. "Spindletop Oilfield."

2. Ibid.

3. Patrick Cox, *The First Texas News Barons,* 41–42.

4. Gould, *Progressives and Prohibitionists,* 249–250.

5. R. Campbell, *Gone to Texas,* 358.

6. Barr, *Black Texans,* 80–85.

7. Calvert and De León, *History of Texas,* 252; Barr, *Black Texans,* 137.

8. Jacquelyn Dowd Hall, *Revolt against Chivalry,* 134–135; Cox, *First Texas News Barons,* 34–38; Calvert and De León, *History of Texas,* 252; Barr, *Black Texans,* 137. See also Patricia Bernstein's excellent account of the Washington lynching, *The First Waco Horror.*

9. Wyn Craig Wade, *The Fiery Cross,* 57–59, 80–111, 119–166; David M. Chalmers, *Hooded Americanism,* 19, 22–38. In addition to Chalmers's and Wade's classic works, Charles C. Alexander authored two important regional studies of the Klan: *Crusade for Conformity: The Ku Klux Klan in Texas, 1920–1930* and *The Ku Klux Klan in the Southwest.* Norman D. Brown, *Hood, Bonnet, and Little Brown Jug,* remains the best study of the impact of the Ku Klux Klan on 1920s Texas politics.

10. Chalmers, *Hooded Americanism,* 31–35, 39, 162–174, 291.

11. Ibid., 44–45; Brown, *Hood, Bonnet, and Little Brown Jug,* 67–72; Calvert and De León, *History of Texas,* 303.

12. Chalmers, *Hooded Americanism,* 41; *The New Handbook of Texas,* s.v. "Ku Klux Klan"; Darwin Payne, *Big D,* 75–77; Patricia Evridge Hill, *Dallas: The Making of a Modern City,* 101.

13. *The New Handbook of Texas,* s.v. "Joseph Weldon Bailey."

14. Gould, *Progressives and Prohibitionists,* 263.

15. Ibid., 266.

16. *The New Handbook of Texas,* s.v. "Robert Ewing Thomason"; Texas Legis-

lative Council, *Presiding Officers*, 179; Gould, *Progressives and Prohibitionists*, 271; Robert Ewing Thomason, *Thomason: The Autobiography of a Federal Judge*, 18–19.

17. Thomason, *Thomason*, 20.

18. *The New Handbook of Texas*, s.v. Pat Morris Neff"; Texas Legislative Council, *Presiding Officers*, 179; Gould, *Progressives and Prohibitionists*, 271; Thomason, *Thomason*, 22–26.

19. Gould, *Progressives and Prohibitionists*, 286.

20. Ibid., 286–287, 289.

21. Ibid., 311.

22. R. Campbell, *Gone to Texas*, 377–378; Calvert and De León, *History of Texas*, 311.

23. Calvert and De León, *History of Texas*, 312.

24. Ibid.

25. R. Campbell, *Gone to Texas*, 378.

26. Rupert N. Richardson, Adrian Anderson, Cary D. Wintz, and Ernest Wallace, *Texas: The Lone Star State*, 384–385; Robert Fairbanks, *For the City as a Whole*, 90; Roger Biles, "The New Deal in Dallas," *Southwestern Historical Quarterly* 95, no. 1 (July 1991), 7–8, 15; Robert Prince, *History of Dallas*, 87–88; Hill, *Dallas*, 129.

27. Calvert and De León, *History of Texas*, 312–313; Texas Legislative Council, *Presiding Officers*, 191.

28. Calvert and De León, *History of Texas*, 313.

29. This process is described in George N. Green, *The Establishment in Texas Politics*.

30. Gould, *Progressives and Prohibitionists*, 282.

31. Ibid., 287.

32. Texas Legislative Council, *Presiding Officers*, 193; Robert Dallek, *Lone Star Rising*, 315.

33. Texas Legislative Council, *Presiding Officers*, 193; Booth Mooney, *Mister Texas: The Story of Coke Stevenson*, 16–17.

34. Frederica Burt Wyatt and Hooper Shelton, *Coke Stevenson . . . A Texas Legend*, 46; Booth Mooney, *Mister Texas*, 17–18.

35. Mooney, *Mister Texas*, 18–20.

36. "Legislative Air Follows Holiday Theme in Austin," *Austin American*, January 3, 1933; "Political Parade of '33 Heads Toward Big Dome," *Austin American*, January 9, 1933; "Speakership Race Holds Interest of Gathering Solons," *Austin American*, January 9, 1933; William M. Thornton, "Rival Seekers of Speakership Busy at Austin," *Dallas Morning News*, January 9, 1933; William M. Thornton, "Stevenson Gets Chair of House, Woodul, Senate: Junction Man Chosen to Fill Speakership by 82 Votes to 68 for A. P. Johnson of Dimmit," *Dallas Morning News*, January 11, 1933.

37. Robert A. Caro, *The Years of Lyndon Johnson: Means of Ascent*, 158–159. Caro is so determined to paint Lyndon Johnson as a villain that he provides a fawning, almost saccharine portrait of Stevenson, who appears in the text as unfailingly humble, unselfish, and dedicated to public service. Caro rationalizes or skips over Stevenson's racism and his social Darwinist politics.

38. Hendrickson, *Chief Executives of Texas,* 204.

39. Green, *Establishment in Texas Politics,* 13–14.

40. "Legislature Ends Longest Session in Texas History: Clocks Stopped and Last Minute Legislation Put Through," *Austin American,* June 2, 1933.

41. Mooney, *Mister Texas,* 21.

42. "Remarks By Speaker Ben Barnes, Bay City," Texas—Legislature—House—Speaker vertical file, Dolph Briscoe Center for American History, Austin, Texas.

43. Hendrickson, *Chief Executives of Texas,* 191–192; *The New Handbook of Texas,* s.v. "Lower Colorado River Authority."

44. Patrick Cox, *Ralph W. Yarborough,* 37.

45. Hendrickson, *Chief Executives of Texas,* 192, 194.

46. Sam Kinch, Jr., "Speaker's Office Now a Prize Plum," *Dallas Morning News,* September 15, 1980.

47. Green, *Establishment in Texas,* 3–8.

48. Robert W. Calvert, *Here Comes the Judge,* 1–2, 4.

49. Calvert, *Here Comes the Judge,* 6–7.

50. Ibid., 8–9.

51. Ibid., 15–16, 26–28, 33–45; Texas Legislative Council, *Presiding Officers,* 195.

52. Calvert, *Here Comes the Judge,* 78. Flotorial districts were created when counties with surplus population (for purposes of representation) were combined with neighboring less-populous counties.

53. Ibid., 81.

54. Ibid.

55. Ibid., 80–82.

56. Ibid, 84.

57. Ibid, 84–87; "Coke Stevenson and Allred Make Peace in Politics," *Austin American,* January 12, 1935.

58. Hendrickson, *Chief Executives of Texas,* 194–195; Charles E. Simons, *The American Way,* 14.

59. Calvert, *Here Comes the Judge,* 89.

60. Texas Legislative Council, *Presiding Officers,* 194.

61. Hendrickson, *Chief Executives of Texas,* 195–198; *The New Handbook of Texas,* s.vv. "Wilbert Lee (Pappy) O'Daniel," "Light Crust Doughboys."

62. Texas Legislative Council, *Presiding Officers,* 201; Hendrickson, *Chief Executives of Texas,* 217–218.

63. Hendrickson, *Chief Executives of Texas,* 199–200.

64. David Rupert Murph, "Price Daniel: The Life of a Public Man, 1910–1956" (PhD diss., Texas Christian University, 1975), 83–84, 96, 99–106.

65. Murph, "Price Daniel," 107–116.

66. "New Speaker at Austin," *Dallas Morning News,* January 16, 1947.

67. "Fists Talked for Future Speaker: W. O. Reed Tough Little Guy Who Made Good," *Dallas Morning News,* November 29, 1946.

68. "Fists Talked"; Texas Legislative Council, *Presiding Officers,* 205.

69. "Fists Talked."

70. Texas Legislative Council, *Presiding Officers,* 205.

71. Vicki J. Audette and J. Tom Graham, *Claud H. Gilmer, Country Lawyer*, 118.

72. Ibid., 120.

73. Texas Legislative Council, *Presiding Officers*, 193, 205.

74. Audette and Graham, *Claud H. Gilmer*, 120.

75. Dallek, *Lone Star Rising*, 315–316.

76. Hendrickson, *Chief Executives of Texas*, 204–205, 207.

Chapter Four

1. Anthony Badger, *The New Deal*, 153; Reuben Senterfitt, audiotape interview by Patrick Cox and Michael Phillips, Senterfitt home, San Saba, Texas, March 8, 2004.

2. Senterfitt interview.

3. Sarah T. Phillips, "Acres Fit and Unfit: Conservation, Rural Development, and the American State, 1925–1950" (PhD diss., Boston University, 2004), Chapter Three, 1, 2, 8.

4. *The New Handbook of Texas*, s.v. "Buchanan Dam, Texas"; S. Phillips, "Acres Fit," Chapter 3, 3–4.

5. *The New Handbook of Texas*, 1996, s.vv. "Buchanan Dam, Texas," "Colorado River;" Cox, *Yarborough*, 39–43.

6. S. Phillips, "Acres Fit," Chapter Three, 26–27.

7. Senterfitt interview.

8. Ibid.; Texas Legislative Council, *Presiding Officers*, 209.

9. R. Campbell, *Gone to Texas*, 404–408.

10. Ibid., 409; Senterfitt interview.

11. R. Campbell, *Gone to Texas*, 410.

12. Richardson, Anderson, Wintz, and Wallace, *Texas: The Lone Star State*, 405–406.

13. Ibid., 412; R. Campbell, *Gone to Texas*, 415; Senterfitt interview.

14. Texas Legislative Council, *Presiding Officers*, 203; Audette and Graham, *Claud H. Gilmer*, 114.

15. Texas Legislative Council, *Presiding Officers*, 203; *The New Handbook of Texas*, s.v. "Gilmer-Aikin Laws"; Richardson, Anderson, Wintz, and Wallace, *Texas: The Lone Star State*, 412; R. Campbell, *Gone to Texas*, 413; Calvert and De León, *History of Texas*, 354; Rae Files Still, *The Gilmer-Aikin Bills*, 6.

16. Still, *Gilmer-Aikin Bills*, 37.

17. Audette and Graham, *Claud H. Gilmer*, 133–134, 140–141, 150.

18. Senterfitt interview; Audette and Graham, *Claud H. Gilmer*, 139.

19. Texas Legislative Council, *Presiding Officers*, 207; "A Law Regulating Labor Unions, Etc." Durwood Manford vertical file, Dolph Briscoe Center for American History, Austin, Texas; Calvert and De León, *History of Texas*, 335.

20. Audette and Graham, *Claud H. Gilmer*, 147.

21. Ibid.

22. Dave Cheaves, "House of Representatives Chooses Durwood Manford House Speaker," *Austin American*, January 12, 1949; Margaret Mayer, "Manford

Releases House Committee Assignments: Speaker Frank in Rewarding His Backers," *Austin American,* February 3, 1949.

23. Margaret Mayer, "Everything Goes Wrong at House Session," *Austin American,* February 3, 1949; "House 'Business' Costs Public but Keeps Solons Entertained," *Austin American,* February 3, 1949, 1.

24. "Everything Goes Wrong"; "House 'Business'"; "House Finally Adjourns after 2-Hour Delay," *Austin American,* February 18, 1949.

25. Jim Lindsey, audiotape interview by Michael Phillips, April 16, 2004, Redwood Valley, Mendocino, California.

26. Jimmy Banks, "In 23-hour Session: House Members Catnap, Catwalk," *Dallas Morning News,* February 26, 1949.

27. Raymond Brooks, "Late Start and Piles of Work Spur Special Session Talk," *Austin American,* February 27, 1949.

28. Jay Vessels, "End of Session about June 10 Expected by Speaker Manford," *Austin American,* May 26, 1949.

29. Audette and Graham, *Claud H. Gilmer,* 151.

30. Still, *Gilmer-Aikin Bills,* 63. A salary of $4,500 in 1949 would be approximately $35,700 today. A salary of $5,376 would equal approximately $42,600 today.

31. Audette and Graham, *Claud H. Gilmer,* 152–153.

32. Ibid., 155–156.

33. Still, *Gilmer-Aikin Bills,* 79–80.

34. Ibid., 85–97; Audette and Graham, *Claud H. Gilmer,* 154–157.

35. Audette and Graham, *Claud H. Gilmer,* 158–161.

36. Still, *Gilmer-Aikin Bills,* 117–154.

37. Dewey W. Grantham, *The South in Modern America,* 204–205.

38. "51st Created More Agencies than Any Other Legislature," *Austin American,* 8 July 8, 1949; Richardson, Anderson, Wintz, and Wallace, *Texas: The Lone Star State,* 412; Audette and Graham, Claud H. Gilmer, 172.

39. Ricky F. Dobbs, *Yellow Dogs and Republicans,* 51.

40. Ibid., 54.

41. J. P. Porter, "The Shame of Texas: State Has No Brag Coming on Mental Hospital Condition," *Austin American-Statesman,* March 20, 1949.

42. Ibid.

43. J. P. Porter, "The Shame of Texas: State Hospital Offers Exhibit 'A' in Misery," *Austin American,* March 23, 1949.

44. J. P. Porter, "The Shame of Texas: Mentally Ill Patients Must Watch Others Get Shock Treatment," *Austin American,* March 22, 1949.

45. Ibid.

46. Porter, "State Hospital Offers Exhibit 'A' in Misery."

47. Hendrickson, *Chief Executives of Texas,* 212; Audette and Graham, Claud H. Gilmer, 173.

48. Sam Kinch and Stuart Long, *Allan Shivers,* 73.

49. Ibid., 75.

50. James A. "Jimmy" Turman, audiotape interview by Michael Phillips, Turman home, Corpus Christi, Texas, March 23, 2004.

51. Hendrickson, *Chief Executives of Texas*, 215–217; Cox, *Yarborough*, 96–110.

52. Dobbs, *Yellow Dogs and Republicans*, 105.

53. Texas Legislative Council, *Presiding Officers*, 211; Lindsey interview.

54. Senterfitt interview.

55. Robert M. Morehead, "San Saba's Senterfitt: Man Who Likes to Listen Will Become House Speaker," *Dallas Morning News*, January 8, 1951.

56. Dawson Duncan, "Legislators Start Job on Somber Note: House Sets Record for Announcement of Committee Posts," *Dallas Morning News*, January 10, 1951; Richard M. Morehead, "Speaker's Speedy Action on Assignments Praised," *Dallas Morning News*, January 10, 1951.

57. *The New Handbook of Texas*, s.v. "Texas Legislature"; Allen Duckworth, "Redistricting Long Overdue: Law Governing Membership of Legislature Unobserved," *Dallas Morning News*, January 7, 1951.

58. *The New Handbook of Texas*, s.v. "Texas Legislature."

59. Richard M. Morehead, "Redistricting Wins in House," *Dallas Morning News*, February 20, 1951; "Legislative Districting Bills Signed," *Dallas Morning News*, March 20, 1951; *The New Handbook of Texas*, s.v. "African Americans and Politics"; R. Campbell, *Gone to Texas*, 421; Kinch and Long, *Allan Shivers*, 127.

60. Senterfitt interview; Dawson Duncan, "New Taxes Foretold by House Speaker," *Dallas Morning News*, February 26, 1951.

61. Senterfitt interview.

62. Duncan, "New Taxes."

63. Lindsey interview.

64. Ibid.

65. Ibid.

66. Texas Legislative Council, *Presiding Officers*, 211.

67. Sam Wood, "Legislator Disagrees with Allan," *Austin American*, October 25, 1956.

68. William Rayford Price, audiotape interview by Michael Phillips, Price home, Austin, Texas, April 22, 2004.

69. Calvert and De León, *History of Texas*, 389; Hendrickson, *Chief Executives of Texas*, 216–217; Robert F. Ford, "A.P. Editors Polled: 1956 Bumper Year for Texas News," *Dallas Morning News*, December 30, 1956. Shivers's sale equals approximately $3.2 million in 2005 dollars.

70. Texas Legislative Council, *Presiding Officers*, 213; Bo Byers, "Representative Drops Out of Race for Speaker of House," *Austin American*, May 15, 1953.

71. David Carr, audiotape interview with Michael Phillips, Carr home, Austin, Texas, August 7, 2004.

72. Texas Legislative Council, *Presiding Officers*, 213.

73. "Carr Sees Progress in Legislature," *Dallas Morning News*, December 7, 1956.

74. Texas Legislative Council, *Presiding Officers*, 213.

75. "Final Drive Opens in Speaker Race," *Dallas Morning News*, January 4, 1959; "Carr-Burkett Battle Expected for Speaker, *Daily Texan*, January 11, 1959; "Speaker Wins 3rd [*sic*] Term, 79–71," *Austin American*, January 14, 1959.

76. Richard M. Morehead, "Waggoner Carr: Legislator," *Dallas Morning News,* December 9, 1956.

77. Richard M. Morehead, "Carr Says Texas Legislature Should Pass Money Bills First," *Dallas Morning News,* January 6, 1957; "55th Session Starts Smooth: To Consider Money First; Segregation, Water Later," *Daily Texan,* January 9, 1957.

Chapter Five

1. Barr, *Black Texans,* 135–136.

2. Ibid., 205–206; *The New Handbook of Texas,* s.v. "Education for African Americans."

3. Mike Boone, "Segregating Spanish-Speaking Students in Texas Schools: 1900–1945," *Journal of Philosophy and History of Education* 49 (1999).

4. *The New Handbook of Texas,* s.vv. "Education for African Americans," "Civil Rights Movement"; Arnoldo De León, *Mexican Americans in Texas,* 101–102, 116; Barr, *Black Texans,* 144–145.

5. De León, *Mexican Americans in Texas,* 116–119; *The New Handbook of Texas,* s.v. "Civil Rights Movement."

6. Barr, *Black Texans,* 206–207.

7. *The New Handbook of Texas,* s.v. "Mansfield School Desegregation Incident." The best and fullest account of the Mansfield desegregation trauma can be found in Robin Duff Ladino, *Desegregating Texas Schools: Eisenhower, Shivers, and the Crisis at Mansfield High.* For Shivers's public stands opposing desegregation, see Dobbs, *Yellow Dogs and Republicans,* and Cox, *Yarborough.*

8. Calvert and De León, *History of Texas,* 388–391. In the early 1830s, South Carolina senator John Calhoun most fully articulated the doctrine of interposition. Calhoun's doctrine rested on two premises. First, that the U.S. Constitution represented a compact between fully "sovereign states" whose membership in the Union was voluntary and conditional. Second, the Constitution's Tenth Amendment, which stated that powers not specifically granted to the federal government were retained by the states, gave state governments the right to "interpose," or block, enforcement of a federal-government mandate if the state deemed a measure unconstitutional. Segregationists resisting pro-civil-rights decisions by the U.S. Supreme Court later used these same arguments. For more on the interrelated ideas of nullification and interposition, consult Garry Wills, *A Necessary Evil,* 123–178.

9. Lindsey interview. Lindsey did not recall a specific date for the bombings.

10. Ibid.

11. Texas Legislative Council, *Presiding Officers,* 225; Price interview.

12. Price interview.

13. Ibid. Robert Johnson, a conservative Democrat, served in the Texas House from 1957 to 1963, representing Irving.

14. Turman interview.

15. Texas Legislative Council, *Presiding Officers,* 215; Turman interview.

16. Turman interview.

17. Allen Duckworth, "Speaker Turman Believes in Avoiding Either Extreme," *Dallas Morning News,* January 22, 1961.

18. Ibid.

19. Charlie Fern, "Jimmy Turman and the Origins of Compassionate Conservatism," a paper presented at the East Texas Historical Association Fall Program, Nacogdoches, Texas, September 16, 2005, 4. In the 1959 session, Turman proposed a bill to ban nudist colonies after such an establishment was discovered in Turman's home county of Fannin. See "Bill in Legislature: Texas Nudists Reject Secret Hearing Offer," *Dallas Morning News,* April 29, 1959.

20. Quoted in Fern, "Jimmy Turman," 4.

21. Turman interview.

22. Texas Legislative Council, *Presiding Officers,* 201; Hendrickson, *Chief Executives of Texas,* 217–218; Murph, "Price Daniel," 83–84, 96.

23. Cox, *Yarborough,* 127–137; Hendrickson, *Chief Executives of Texas,* 218–220.

24. Turman interview.

25. Ibid.

26. Price interview.

27. Ibid.

28. Turman interview.

29. Ibid.

30. Allen Duckworth, "Turman Follows Rayburn's Path," *Dallas Morning News,* January 11, 1961.

31. Price interview.

32. Hoyt Purvis, "New Speaker's Role to Be a Powerful One," *Daily Texan,* January 11, 1961.

33. Turman interview.

34. Ibid.

35. U.S. Bureau of the Census, *The Eighteenth Decennial Census of the United States. Census of the Population: 1960,* vol. 1: *Characteristics of the Population,* part 45, "Texas," 45–674.

36. Calvert and De León, *History of Texas,* 414.

37. Boles, *The South through Time,* 410, 469.

38. Kenneth B. Ragsdale, *The Year America Discovered Texas: Centennial '36,* 304.

39. Duckworth, "Speaker Turman."

40. Ibid.

41. James Lehrer, "Rep. Turman Suggests Tax on Beer, Pop," *Dallas Morning News,* March 4, 1961; Texas Legislative Council, *Presiding Officers,* 215; Hendrickson, *Chief Executives of Texas,* 221–222; Lieutenant Governor Ben Barnes, audiotape interview by Patrick Cox and Michael Phillips, Barnes office, Austin, Texas, September 27, 2004; Turman interview.

42. Price interview.

43. "6 Legislators Criticize Turman on 'Baby Sitter,'" *Houston Post,* May 26, 1962; Turman interview.

44. These factors are best analyzed in Davidson, *Race and Class in Texas Politics.*

45. Jan Tunnell, audiotape interview by Michael Phillips, March 14, 2004.

46. Ibid.

47. Texas Legislative Council, *Presiding Officers*, 217; Tunnell interview; Dave Harmon and Dave McNeely, "Former Texas House Speaker Recalled as Eloquent Orator," *Austin American-Statesman*, March 8, 2000.

48. Tunnell interview; Texas Legislative Council, *Presiding Officers*, 91, 217; Richard M. Morehead, "Tunnell Coasts in as House Speaker," *Dallas Morning News*, January 9, 1963.

49. "Leaders for a Greater Texas: Byron Tunnell," *Texas Parade*, January 1965, 37.

50. Price interview.

51. Barnes interview.

52. Harmon and McNeely, "Former Texas House Speaker Recalled."

53. Texas Legislative Council, *Presiding Officers*, 217; Cox, *Yarborough*, 177–181.

54. *Texas Parade*, "Leaders for a Greater Texas"; *The New Handbook of Texas*, s.v. "Republican Party." For more on the rise of the Republican Party in Texas, see Davidson, *Race and Class in Texas Politics;* Dobbs, *Yellow Dogs and Republicans;* Green, *Establishment in Texas Politics;* James R. Soukup, Clifton McCleskey, and Harry Holloway, *Party and Factional Division in Texas;* and John R. Knaggs, *Two-Party Texas.*

55. The New *Handbook of Texas*, s.v. "Republican Party."

56. Ibid.

57. Quoted in Robert Dallek, *Flawed Giant: Lyndon Johnson and His Times*, 133.

58. *The New Handbook of Texas*, s.v. "Republican Party."

59. "Favorite in Speaker's Race Plans Change," *Houston Chronicle*, December 2, 1962.

60. Sam Kinch, Jr., and Ben Procter, *Texas under a Cloud*, 76.

61. Barnes interview.

62. Kinch and Procter, *Texas under a Cloud*, 77; Barnes interview. Barnes also relates this story in his recent autobiography, cowritten with Lisa Dickey, *Barn Burning/Barn Building*, 27–29.

63. Barnes interview; the story is also told in Barnes and Dickey, *Barn Burning/Barn Building*, 31–37.

64. Texas Legislative Council, *Presiding Officers*, 197; Barnes interview.

65. Kinch and Procter, *Texas under a Cloud*, 75, 81–82.

66. Barnes and Dickey, *Barn Burning/Barn Building*, 186.

67. Barnes interview.

68. Ibid.

69. Hendrickson, *Chief Executives of Texas*, 225–227.

70. Kinch and Procter, *Texas under a Cloud*, 77–79.

71. Barnes interview.

72. Texas Legislative Council, *Presiding Officers*, 197.

73. Barnes interview.

74. Calvert and De León, *History of Texas*, 396.

75. Barnes interview.

76. Calvert and De León, *History of Texas*, 405.

Chapter Six

1. Kinch and Procter, *Texas under a Cloud*, 16–19.
2. Barnes interview.
3. Kinch and Procter, *Texas under a Cloud*, 18–21.
4. Surprisingly, only five books have been written about the Sharpstown scandal. In addition to Kinch and Procter's account, see Charles Deaton, *The Year They Threw the Rascals Out*; Harvey Katz, *Shadow on the Alamo*; and Mickey Herskowitz, *Sharpstown Revisited*. Former Speaker and state attorney general Waggoner Carr gives a personal account of his Sharpstown trial in *Waggoner Carr: Not Guilty!* See also R. Campbell, *Gone to Texas*, 441–443; and Calvert and De León, *History of Texas*, 408–410.
5. R. Campbell, *Gone to Texas*, 441–442; Calvert and De León, *History of Texas*, 409; *The New Handbook of Texas*, s.v. "Sharpstown Stock-Fraud Scandal."
6. *The New Handbook of Texas*, s.v. "Sharpstown Stock-Fraud Scandal"; Kinch and Procter, *Texas under a Cloud*, 26.
7. *The New Handbook of Texas*, s.v. "Sharpstown Stock-Fraud Scandal"; Kinch and Procter, *Texas under a Cloud*, 28, 30.
8. Texas Legislative Council, *Presiding Officers*, 221; Kinch and Procter, *Texas under a Cloud*, 64.
9. Gus Mutscher, audiotape interview by Patrick Cox, Mutscher office, Brenham, Texas, November 9, 2004; Glen Castlebury, "His Title Is 'Mr. Speaker,'" *Austin American-Statesman*, September 24, 1971; Carolyn Bengtson, "Gus Mutscher: The Eligible Bachelor," *Austin American-Statesman*, June 2, 1968; Kinch and Procter, *Texas under a Cloud*, 64–65.
10. Mutscher interview; Bengtson, "Gus Mutscher"; Kinch and Procter, *Texas under a Cloud*, 64–65.
11. Mutscher interview; Kinch and Procter, *Texas under a Cloud*, 65.
12. Mutscher interview; Kinch and Procter, *Texas under a Cloud*, 65–66.
13. Castlebury, "His Title Is 'Mr. Speaker.'"
14. Mutscher interview; Kinch and Procter, *Texas under a Cloud*, 65–66.
15. Kinch and Procter, *Texas under a Cloud*, 96.
16. Texas Legislative Council, *Presiding Officers*, 221; Calvert and De León, *History of Texas*, 408–409.
17. Gould, *Progressives and Prohibitionists*, 291.
18. Mutscher interview.
19. Jon Ford, "Mutscher Faces a House Rules Revolt: But No Danger of Losing Gavel," *San Angelo Standard-Times*, March 9, 1969; Felton West, "Mutscher Kills Conference Curbs," *Houston Post*, March 25, 1969.
20. Ford, "Mutscher Faces a House Rules Revolt"; West, "Mutscher Kills Conference Curbs"; Castlebury, "His Title Is 'Mr. Speaker.'"
21. Bill Bass, audiotape interview by Michael Phillips, Dolph Briscoe Center for American History, Austin, Texas, June 4, 2004.
22. Bass interview. Jumbo Atwell of Wilmer served as representative from Dallas from 1951 to 1975, a large part of his tenure as the at-large representative for Dallas County.
23. Jon Ford, "Tax Hassle Hurts Speaker's Image," *San Angelo Standard-Times*, August 26, 1969.

24. Castlebury, "His Title Is 'Mr. Speaker'"; "Early Summer Wedding: Mutscher Will Marry Former Miss America," *Houston Chronicle,* April 9, 1969; "Miss Donna Axum, Gus Mutscher Are Wed," *Dallas Morning News,* June 8, 1969; Mary Rice Brogan, "A Capitol Pair: Beauty and the Bachelor," *Houston Chronicle,* June 8, 1969.

25. Castlebury, "His Title Is 'Mr. Speaker.'"

26. Francis Dodds, "Price Vows to Challenge Mutscher for Speaker," *Houston Chronicle,* January 26, 1971.

27. *The New Handbook of Texas,* s.v. "The Dirty Thirty."

28. Robert V. Remini, *The House,* 420–425.

29. Deaton, *They Threw the Rascals Out,* 14–15.

30. Tom Craddick, audiotape interview by Patrick Cox, Speaker's residence, Texas Capitol, Austin, Texas, February 2, 2005.

31. Ibid., 15.

32. Deaton, *They Threw the Rascals Out,* 29.

33. Ibid., 18–19; Mary Rice Brogan, "Indictment of Mutscher First of House Speaker," *Houston Chronicle,* September 24, 1971; Jan Jarboe, "Mutscher, 3 Others Indicted; Jury Scolds State Politicians," *Daily Texan,* September 24, 1971; Sam Kinch, Jr., "Mutscher, Osorio, Two Others Indicted," *Dallas Morning News,* September 24, 1971; "Avows Innocence: Mutscher Plans To Stay Speaker," *Dallas Times Herald,* September 30, 1971; "Mutscher's Decision Disservice to State," *San Angelo Standard-Times,* October 1, 1971; Clayton Hickerson, "State Demo Poll Indicates Mutscher Ought to Resign," *Austin American-Statesman,* November 16, 1971.

34. *The New Handbook of Texas,* s.v. "Sharpstown Stock-Fraud Scandal"; Sam Kinch, Jr., "Mutscher Group Guilty of Bribery, Conspiracy," *Dallas Morning News,* March 16, 1972; Gayle McNutt, "House Speaker Says 'Incredible,'" *Houston Chronicle,* March 15, 1972; Gayle McNutt, "Gus Mutscher Gets 5 Years Suspended Sentence: 3 on Probation, All Will Appeal," *Houston Chronicle,* March 16, 1972.

35. Mutscher interview.

36. "Speaker Steps Aside: Mutscher Tells Staff of Innocence," *Austin American-Statesman,* March 22, 1972; Texas Legislative Council, *Presiding Officers,* 223; Kinch and Procter, *Texas under a Cloud,* 71–72.

37. Mutscher interview.

38. Barnes interview.

39. Grantham, *The South in Modern America,* 281–285. Mutscher's and Barnes's contention that the Sharpstown scandal exploded on the scene in part because of machinations by the Nixon White House received validation from the research of Brian McCall, a Plano state representative who recently attempted to unseat Tom Craddick as Texas House Speaker. McCall notes in *The Power of the Texas Governor: Connally to Bush* that Nixon operatives and convicted Watergate felons Bob Haldeman and John Mitchell apologized to Barnes for targeting him in order to destroy his political career (40).

40. Carr, *Waggoner Carr,* 7–8.

41. Ibid.

42. Ibid., 15–24.

43. Mutscher interview.

44. Barnes interview.

45. Ibid.

46. Carr, *Waggoner Carr,* 49–60.

47. Carr interview.

48. Bass interview.

49. Calvert and De León, *History of Texas,* 410; Calvert, *Here Comes the Judge,* 443.

50. Texas Legislative Council, *Presiding Officers,* 225; Price interview.

51. Price interview.

52. Ernest Stromberger, "Price Pushing Speaker's Race," *Dallas Times Herald,* March 1971; Texas Legislative Council, *Presiding Officers,* 225; "New Speaker Price Took Quick, Quiet Way Up," *Houston Chronicle,* March 29, 1972.

53. Stromberger, "Price Pushing Speaker's Race."

54. Price interview.

55. Ibid.

56. Deaton, *They Threw the Rascals Out,* 149.

57. *The New Handbook of Texas,* s.v. "Sharpstown Stock-Fraud Scandal"; Kinch and Procter, *Texas under a Cloud,* 125.

58. Deaton, *They Threw the Rascals Out* 145–146.

59. Price interview.

60. Deaton, *They Threw the Rascals Out* 146; "Price, Head Race Heats up with Handbills, Phone Calls," *Houston Post,* May 28, 1972.

61. Price interview.

62. Deaton, *They Threw the Rascals Out* 144–145.

63. Ibid., 108–109; *The New Handbook of Texas,* s.v. "Sharpstown Stock-Fraud Scandal"; Texas Legislative Council, *Presiding Officers,* 227.

64. Texas Legislative Council, *Presiding Officers,* 201, 227; Dave Montgomery, "Ice Cream Parlor Push: Daniel's Career Took Root outside Smoke-Filled Rooms," *Dallas Times Herald,* January 27, 1974; Martha Dreyer, "Price Daniel, Jr.: Mail Order Bookman," *Houston Chronicle Magazine,* February 5, 1961; "Tragedy Stalked Gifted Politician," *Sherman Democrat,* January 30, 1981.

65. "Price Daniel, Jr. Engaged," *Dallas Morning News,* December 24, 1965; "Miss Wommack Is Wed to Price Daniel, Jr.," *Houston Post,* April 17, 1966; "Daniel to Run for House Seat," *San Antonio Express,* January 25, 1968; "Price Jr. May Go for Speaker," *Houston Post,* March 24, 1971.

66. Bass interview.

67. Ibid.

68. Ibid.; Montgomery, "Ice Cream Parlor Push."

69. Molly Ivins, "Mr. Speaker Daniel," *Texas Observer,* February 2, 1973.

70. Ivins, "Mr. Speaker Daniel"; Bass interview.

71. Ivins, "Mr. Speaker Daniel"; Bo Byers, "Just How Liberal Will Daniel Be?" *Houston Chronicle,* August 9, 1972.

72. Bass interview.

73. Montgomery, "Ice Cream Parlor Push."

74. Bass interview.

75. Scott Carpenter, "Named After Governors; His Pop Seeks Speaker Post," *San Angelo Standard-Times,* April 4, 1971; "Daniel in Speaker's Race, Wants Con-

trol Reforms," *Houston Post,* June 22, 1971; Dave McNeely, "Conference Panel Power Price Daniel, Jr. Target," *Dallas Morning News,* July 1, 1971; Ralph Williams, "Rep. Daniel Pledges to Introduce 4 Reform Bills," *Houston Post,* July 22, 1971.

76. Ernest Stromberger, "Daniel Proposes 1-Term Limit for Speaker's Office," *Dallas Times Herald,* June 22, 1971; Mary Rice Brogan, "Daniel in Speakers Race; Pledges to 'Clean Up House,'" *Houston Chronicle,* June 22, 1971.

77. Bass interview; "Daniel Claims 103 Votes for Speaker," *Dallas Morning News,* June 17, 1972; Henry Holcomb, "Daniel Claims Victory," *Houston Post,* June 17, 1972; Art Wiese, "Daniel Speaker Foe Withdraws," *Houston Post,* August 9, 1972.

78. Mary Rice Brogan, "Daniel Gives Priorities for Legislature," *Houston Chronicle,* December 13, 1972; "Rep Daniel to Propose Law for Shield of News Sources," *Dallas Times Herald,* December 7, 1972; Sam Kinch, Jr., "Daniel Elected Unanimously," *Dallas Morning News,* January 17, 1973; Lee Manross, "Daniel Trims Staff in Economy Move," *Dallas Times-Herald,* January 16, 1973; "Press Group Picks Daniel for Award," *Dallas Times-Herald,* April 1, 1973.

79. Sam Kinch, Jr., "'Kid' Daniel Shows He Has Guts," *Dallas Morning News,* December 16, 1972.

80. Bass interview.

81. Sam Kinch, Jr., "Price Daniel Walks Line Between Dictator, Pushover."

82. Ivins, "Mr. Speaker Daniel."

83. Bill Collier, "Speaker Daniel: His Democracy Is Admired, But Results Are Awaited," *Houston Chronicle,* March 18, 1973.

84. Richard Morehead, "Longest Five Minutes for Daniel," *Houston Chronicle,* May 31, 1973; "Daniel Prefers It Simple: Speaker Tells Views on New Constitution," *Dallas Times Herald,* September 5, 1973.

85. Richardson, Anderson, Wintz, and Wallace, *Texas: The Lone Star State,* 437.

86. Bass interview.

87. Bill Hartman, audiotape interview with Michael Phillips, Doubletree Hotel, Austin, Texas, September 2, 2004.

88. Ibid.

89. Richardson, Anderson, Wintz, and Wallace, *Texas: The Lone Star State,* 437.

90. Hartman interview.

91. Ibid.

92. Richardson, Anderson, Wintz, and Wallace, *Texas: The Lone Star State,* 437; Darrell Hancock, "Warnings Haunting Daniel at Convention," *Houston Post,* July 30, 1974; Saralee Tiede, "Price Daniel Weathers Assault on His Leadership," *Dallas Times Herald,* July 3, 1974.

93. Dave Montgomery, "Daniel Blames Briscoe, Labor Politics for Failure," *Dallas Times Herald,* July 31, 1974.

94. Ibid.

95. Hartman interview.

96. Saralee Tiede, "Daniel's Future: Was Convention Flop a Mortal Political Wound?" *Dallas Times Herald,* August 4, 1974.

97. Richardson, Anderson, Wintz, and Wallace, *Texas: The Lone Star State*, 437.

98. Bill Clayton, audiotape interview by Michael Phillips, Clayton office, Austin, Texas, April 16, 2004.

99. Bass interview.

100. Saralee Tiede, "Daniel's Future"; Texas Legislative Council, *Presiding Officers*, 227; "Tragedy Stalked Gifted Politician." Daniel died after being fatally shot by his second wife in 1981. Details of his tragic death and its legal aftermath can be found in Steve Salerno, *Deadly Blessing*.

Chapter Seven

1. Jimmy Banks, *Gavels, Grit, and Glory*, 1–2.

2. Quoted in Molly Ivins, "Cirque du DeLay," *Texas Observer*, April 1, 2005; "Molly Ivins Quotes," Thinkexist.com, http://en.thinkexist.com/quotation/as_they_say_around_the-texas-legislature-if_you/216480.html (accessed February 23, 2006).

3. Mike Ward, *The Capitol of Texas*, 123, 126.

4. Paul Burka, Emily Yoffe, Kaye Northcott, and Ellen Williams, "The Ten Best and the Ten Worst Legislators," *Texas Monthly*, July 1987.

5. Quoted in Ward, *Capitol of Texas*, 128.

6. Price interview.

7. Banks, *Gavels, Grit, and Glory*, 332–333.

8. Texas Legislative Council, *Presiding Officers*, 229.

9. Quoted in Banks, *Gavels, Grit, and Glory*, 17, 33.

10. Banks, *Gavels, Grit, and Glory*, 42–43.

11. Clayton interview. The Texas A&M Board of Regents, the state legislature, and other institutions fought a long, unsuccessful battle in the first four decades of the twentieth century to outlaw hazing at the university. Reforms instituted by A&M president Earl Rudder in the 1950s and 1960s—such as dropping the requirement that students belong to the Corps of Cadets and making the campus coeducational—changed campus culture, resulting in a decline in the practice of hazing. See Henry C. Dethloff, *A Centennial History of Texas A&M, 1876–1976*, and John A. Adams, Jr., *Keepers of the Spirit: The Corps of Cadets at Texas A&M University, 1876–2001*.

12. Banks, *Gavels, Grit, and Glory*, 48–49; Texas Legislative Council, *Presiding Officers*, 229; Clayton interview.

13. Texas Legislative Council, *Presiding Officers*, 229; Clayton interview.

14. Clayton interview.

15. Ibid.

16. Texas Legislative Council, *Presiding Officers*, 229.

17. Clayton interview.

18. Quoted in Banks, *Gavels, Grit, and Glory*, 74–75.

19. Clayton interview.

20. Quoted in Banks, *Gavels, Grit, and Glory*, 76.

21. Clayton interview.

22. Banks, *Gavels, Grit, and Glory,* 79.

23. Clayton interview; Banks, *Gavels, Grit, and Glory,* 77–81, 85–86.

24. "Texas Politicians: Words to Live By," http://ops.tamu.edu/x075bb/humor/txpolitics.txt (accessed June 27, 2009).

25. Clay Robinson, "Former House Speaker, 'Country Slicker,' Dies; Billy Clayton Served as a Texas Lawmaker for 20 Years," *Houston Chronicle,* January 8, 2007.

26. Quoted in Banks, *Gavels, Grit, and Glory,* 105.

27. *Daily Texan,* n.d.

28. Ibid., 105, 142, 157; Art Wiese, "Rep. Clayton Announces House Speaker Race," *Houston Post,* June 6, 1973; Saralee Tiede, "Meet the New Speaker," *Dallas Morning News,* January 5, 1975; Dave Hendricks, "Knee Deep, but Honest, Neanderthal," *Daily Texan,* January 14, 1975; Derek Howard, "Just the Facts, Larry," *Daily Texan,* September 17, 1974; Saralee Tiede, "Speaker Billy Clayton—Rough on Social Legislation," *Dallas Times Herald,* June 8, 1975.

29. Numan V. Bartley, *The New South, 1945–1980,* 402–405.

30. Texas Legislative Council, *Presiding Officers,* 229.

31. Calvert and De León, *History of Texas,* 389–390, 427.

32. Ibid., 427.

33. Banks, *Gavels, Grit, and Glory,* 131.

34. Calvert and De León, *History of Texas,* 427–428; Banks, *Gavels, Grit, and Glory,* 130–132.

35. Calvert and De León, *History of Texas,* 428.

36. Banks, *Gavels, Grit, and Glory,* 130.

37. Ibid., 144–151, 157.

38. Ibid., 161, 169.

39. "Clayton Pushes for Speaker," *Dallas Morning News,* June 6, 1973; Wiese, "Clayton Announces House Speaker Race"; Dave Montgomery, "Seeks Speakership: Clayton Disclaims Interest Conflict," *Dallas Times Herald,* June 6, 1973; "Clayton to Vie for Speaker," *Summer Texan,* June 7, 1973.

40. Wiese, "Clayton Announces House Speaker Race"; Montgomery, "Clayton Disclaims Conflict."

41. "Clayton Pushes for Speaker"; Banks, *Gavels, Grit, and Glory,* 185.

42. Banks, *Gavels, Grit, and Glory,* 175, 177.

43. Carolyn Barta, "Clayton Says Fair Shake Due," *Dallas Morning News,* December 20, 1974.

44. Banks, *Gavels, Grit, and Glory,* 165, 185, 187; Carolyn Barta, "Clayton Says Fair Shake Due," *Dallas Morning News,* December 20, 1974.

45. Barta, "Clayton Says Fair Shake Due."

46. Barta, "Clayton Says Fair Shake Due"; Sam Kinch, Jr. "A Country-Slicker Speaker," *Dallas Morning News,* September 7, 1974; Dave Hendricks and Scott Tagliarino, "Clayton Wins Speakership: 64th Legislature Opens with Ceremonies," *Daily Texan,* January 15, 1975.

47. Hendricks and Tagliarino, "Clayton Wins Speakership."

48. Bob Bain, "Clayton Grabs Key to Records," *Fort Worth Star-Telegram,* April 13, 1975.

49. Ibid.

50. Ibid.; Bob Bain, "Clayton Limits Access to Representatives' Records," *Fort Worth Star-Telegram;* Banks, *Gavels, Grit, and Glory,* 206–207, 214.

51. Michael L. Collins, "Lloyd Bentsen," in Hendrickson, Collins, and Cox, *Profiles in Power,* 254–262.

52. Davidson, *Race and Class in Texas Politics,* 183–184.

53. Ibid., 188.

54. Ibid., 184–189.

55. Sam Kinch, Jr., "'Unitary' Primary Sought: Clayton Wants to Return Democrats to the Fold," *Dallas Morning News,* June 26, 1976.

56. Monica Reeves, "House Speaker Apparently Backs Off on Plan to Sting 'Bees' on Primary," *Houston Post,* May 24, 1979; George Strong, "George Strong Political Analysis: The Killer Bees, 20 years ago," http://www.georgestrong.com/analysis-arc/0246.html (accessed May 17, 2009); Texas Senate News, "Other Senate News," February 9, 2001, http://www.senate.state.tx.us/75r/Senate/Archives/Arch01/p020901w.htm (accessed February 28, 2006).

57. Strong, "George Strong Political Analysis: The Killer Bees, 20 years ago."

58. R. Campbell, *Gone to Texas,* 448–449.

59. Ibid., 449.

60. *The New Handbook of Texas,* s.v. "Republican Party."

61. Saralee Tiede, "Speaker Billy Clayton—Rough on Social Legislation," *Dallas Times Herald,* June 8, 1975; Fred Bonavita, "Clayton to Seek 2nd House Speaker Term; Claims Votes to Win," *Houston Post,* June 13, 1975; Banks, *Gavels, Grit, and Glory,* 159.

62. Andy Welch, "Clayton Beefing Up State Staff, Expenses," *Denton Record-Chronicle,* June 6, 1976.

63. Texas Legislative Council, *Presiding Officers,* 229.

64. Clayton interview.

65. Texas Legislative Council, *Presiding Officers,* 229.

66. Saralee Tiede, "Speaker's Efficiency Moves Criticized," *Dallas Times Herald,* October 26, 1976.

67. Tiede, "Speaker's Efficiency Moves."

68. Dave Montgomery, "Billy's Boys: The 'In-Crowd' of Texas House," *Dallas Times Herald,* May 16, 1979.

69. Sam Kinch, Jr., "No Room at the Top for Clayton," *Dallas Morning News,* March 19, 1977.

70. Banks, *Gavels, Grit, and Glory,* 276–277.

71. Ibid., 276, 278, 282, 289, 291–293; "FBI Claims Payment Tip of Payoff Iceberg," *Wichita Falls Record News,* February 19, 1980; Dave Montgomery, "House Speaker Confirms Higher Figure Mentioned," *Dallas Times Herald,* February 18, 1980.

72. Clayton interview.

73. Robert Rawitch, "Clayton Implicated in New 'Sting': Insurance Crimes Probed," *Dallas Times Herald,* February 9, 1980.

74. Saralee Tiede, "House Members Consider Future without Clayton," *Dallas Times Herald,* February 14, 1980; George Kuempel, "Clayton Vows He Won't Give

Up His Job," *Dallas Morning News,* February 11, 1980; Patrick Martinets, "Bribe Allegations Weaken Clayton's Grip on Speaker's Job," *Fort Worth Star-Telegram,* February 12, 1980; Tom Baker, "Texas House Group to Review Leadership," *Daily Texan,* February 12, 1980; Saralee Tiede, "Washington Ready to Run for Speaker If Clayton Falls," *Dallas Times Herald,* May 14, 1980; Sam Kinch, Jr., "Washington Will Seek Post If Clayton Falls," *Dallas Morning News,* May 14, 1980.

75. Saralee Tiede, "Lobbyists Decide to 'Hang Loose' on Speaker Race," *Dallas Times Herald,* February 12, 1980.

76. Banks, *Gavels, Grit, and Glory,* 293.

77. Ibid., 291, 293, 297; Don Mason, "Clayton Jurors Gained Insight Prosecutor Didn't Plan to Give," *Dallas Morning News,* October 24, 1980.

78. "Clayton Acquitted in Brilab," *Dallas Morning News,* October 23, 1980; "Brilab Jurors Find Clayton Innocent: Jury Is Divided on Clayton's Political Future," *Fort Worth Star-Telegram,* October 23, 1980; "FBI Used Trap to Snare Trio, Angry Jury Said," *Dallas Morning News,* October 23, 1980; Pete Wittenberg, "Clayton, 2 Others Cleared of All Charges," *Houston Post,* October 23, 1980.

79. Ann Arnold, "Clayton Looking beyond 1981: Texas House Speaker May Try for Unprecedented Fifth Term," *Fort Worth Star-Telegram,* January 9, 1981.

80. "House Tables Proposal to Restrict Clayton's Power," *Daily Texan,* January 15, 1981.

81. "Water-Plan Loss Damages Clayton," *Dallas Morning News,* November 5, 1981; "Clayton Lost Clout in Brilab," *Dallas Morning News,* January 26, 1982.

82. Jay Rosser, "Bill Clayton Announces Bid," *Wichita Falls Record News,* December 4, 1981; "For Land Commissioner: Clayton Privately Saying He'll Run," *Houston Post,* December 4, 1981; Mike Cochran, "Billy Clayton Looks to Future in Texas Politics," *Victoria Advocate,* December 20, 1981; George Kuempel, "Clayton Move No Shock to Friends," *Dallas Morning News,* January 26, 1982. Clayton died in Lubbock at the age of seventy-eight on January 6, 2007. See Clay Robinson, "Former House Speaker," *Houston Chronicle,* January 8, 2007, and "Former Texas House Speaker Clayton Dies," *Abilene Reporter News,* January 8, 2007.

Chapter Eight

1. Texas Legislative Council, *Presiding Officers,* 231; Mike Ritchey, "Coincidence or Not, Lewis Is in the Lead," *Fort Worth Star-Telegram,* May 30, 1980; *The New Handbook of Texas,* s.v. "Mexia."

2. Jack Z. Davis, "Speakership His, Lewis Says," *Fort Worth Star-Telegram,* November 12, 1981; Gibson D. "Gib" Lewis, audiotape interview by Patrick Cox and Michael Phillips, Lewis's office, Austin, Texas, June 8, 2004.

3. Lewis interview.

4. Ibid.

5. Texas Legislative Council, *Presiding Officers,* 231.

6. Mike Cochran, "Gib Lewis Takes Long Look Back: Five-Term Speaker Retires under Cloud," *Victoria Advocate,* February 2, 1992.

7. Lewis interview.

8. Texas Legislative Council, *Presiding Officers,* 231; Lewis interview.

9. Texas Legislative Council, *Presiding Officers,* 231.

10. Quoted in Ritchey, "Coincidence or Not."

11. George Kuempel and Earl Golz, "Lewis Plays Politics as Speaker Hopeful," *Dallas Morning News,* September 16, 1980.

12. Ron Hutcheson, "Gib Lewis Sells Self with a Country Flair," *Fort Worth Star-Telegram,* March 1, 1981. For examples of coverage depicting Lewis as unintelligent, see Ritchey, "Coincidence or Not," and Kuempel and Golz, "Lewis Plays Politics."

13. Sam Attlesey, "Gib's Glib Gibberish: Garbled Grammar, Mangled Metaphors Are Just Lewis' Way of Handling Business," *Dallas Morning News,* July 14, 1991. "Humidity" quote is from "Stupid Quotes," http://www.goodquotes.com/ stupidquotes.htm; "uncertainty" is from "Stupid Quotes," http://www.geocities .com/Heartlands/hills/3678/stupid.htm; and "extinguished yourself," "nutrition," "two-headed sword," and "dead horse" are from R. Preston McAfee, "Gib Lewis: Former Speaker of the House," http://www.mcafee.cc/Bin/jokearchive.txt. All sites accessed June 18, 2009.

14. Lewis interview.

15. Hutcheson, "Lewis Sells with a Country Flair."

16. George Kuempel and Earl Golz, "Lawmakers Ask Gib Lewis to Show Check for Watches," *Dallas Morning News,* August 16, 1980; Carl Freund, "Lewis Says 'Donor' Supporting Rival," *Dallas Morning News,* August 19, 1980; Mark Nelson, "Gib Lewis Says Claims a 'Put-Up Job': Candidate for Speaker Denies Lobbyist Paid for Gifts," *Fort Worth Star-Telegram,* August 28, 1980; George Kuempel and Earl Golz, "Lobbyists Chipped In for Watches, Lewis Says," *Dallas Morning News,* October 4, 1980; Ron Hutcheson, "Lewis Sells with a Country Flair."

17. Davis, "Speakership His, Lewis Says."

18. Jack Z. Smith, "Lewis Nearly Bags Legislator," *Fort Worth Star-Telegram,* November 24, 1981.

19. Ron Hutcheson, "Lewis Raises Almost $100,000," *Fort Worth Star-Telegram,* January 20, 1982; Lee Jones, "Speaker Lewis Hopes to Avoid Raising Taxes," *Fort Worth Star-Telegram,* January 12, 1983; Laylan Copelin, "Ethics and Leadership: Supporters Say Lewis' Past Makes Him Slow to Criticize," *Austin American-Statesman,* November 21, 1989.

20. Richard Fish, "Lewis Puzzled by Charges: House Speaker Says He's Not Grabbing for Power," *Dallas Morning News,* January 30, 1980.

21. Lee Jones, "Lewis, House to Love, Honor, Obey after Honeymoon?" *Fort Worth Star-Telegram,* February 27, 1983; Fred Bonavita, "Lewis Says Holdings Unreported," *Houston Post,* March 3, 1983; Lee Jones, "Speaker Reveals His Business Ties in Liquor Industry," *Fort Worth Star-Telegram,* March 3, 1983; "Lewis Probe Unneeded, Ethics Chairman Says," *Houston Post,* March 4, 1983; Felton West, "Gib Lewis Amends Statement," *Houston Post,* March 8, 1983; Felton West, "Admits Making 'Mistake': Lewis Never Read Disclosure Law," *Houston Post,* March 9, 1983; Richard Fish, "Lewis Update Adds 49 Business Interests," *Dallas Morning News,* March 9, 1983; Lee Jones, "State Ethics Panel to Be Proposed," *Fort Worth Star-Telegram,* March 9, 1983; Richard Fish, "Panel to Question Lewis Omissions," *Dallas Morning News,* March 11, 1983; George Kuempel, "Gib Lewis: A Speaker Prone to Making 'Inadvertent' Mistakes," *Dallas Morning News,* March

11, 1983; Richard Fish, "State Ethics Panel Drops Lewis Probe," *Dallas Morning News*, July 20, 1983; "Gib Lewis Exonerated by Panel," *Houston Post*, July 20, 1983.

22. Lewis interview.

23. Calvert and De León, *History of Texas*, 437–438; R. Campbell, *Gone to Texas*, 452.

24. Calvert and De León, *History of Texas*, 437–438; R. Campbell, *Gone to Texas*, 452; Clay Robison, "Failed Session Prompts Look at One That Worked: In 1984 School Finance System Was Altered, Passed in 30 Days," *Austin Chronicle*, May 19, 2004.

25. Calvert and De León, *History of Texas*, 437–438.

26. Robison, "Failed Session Prompts Look."

27. Ibid.

28. *Frontline*, "The Battle over School Choice. Interviews: Molly Ivins," http://www.pbs.org/wgbh/pages/frontline/shows/vouchers/interviews/ivins .html (accessed March 5, 2006).

29. R. Campbell, *Gone to Texas*, 452; Robison, "Failed Session Prompts Look"; Clay Robison, "Teachers May Be Feeling Nostalgic for Gov. White," *Austin Chronicle*, January 14, 2006.

30. Clay Robinson, "Teachers May Be Feeling Nostalgic"; R. Campbell, *Gone to Texas*, 452.

31. R. Campbell, *Gone to Texas*, 453.

32. Payne, *Big D*, 399–400.

33. *The New Handbook of Texas*, s.v. *"Rodríguez v. San Antonio ISD";* Molly Ivins, "Who Deserves Credit for Texas?" July 27, 2000, Free Press Web site, http://www.freepress.org/columns/display/1/2000/171 (accessed March 6, 2006).

34. Ibid.

35. R. Campbell, *Gone to Texas*, 457–458.

36. Ibid., 458.

37. Calvert and De León, *History of Texas*, 439.

38. Mike Leggett, "Rules Overlooked in Stocking of Lewis' Ranches with Deer," *Austin American-Statesman*, March 9, 1989; Mike Leggett, "Lewis to Give Deer, Elk Back to Department," *Fort Worth Star-Telegram*, March 10, 1989; Debbie Graves, "Speaker Denies Special Treatment by Wildlife Agency," *Austin American-Statesman*, March 22, 1989.

39. Copelin, "Ethics and Leadership"; Laylan Copelin, "Ethics Issue Sweeps State Legislature," *Austin American-Statesman*, January 6, 1991.

40. Mike Ward, "Gib Lewis Ahead in Campaign Fight—Against Himself," *Austin American-Statesman*, October 28, 1990; Debbie Graves, "Lewis Is No Stranger to Controversy," *Austin American-Statesman*, December 9, 1990; Mike Ward, "Gib Lewis Hires Lawyers, Publicists to Help in Inquiry," *Austin American-Statesman*, December 11, 1990; Debbie Graves and Mike Ward, "Lewis Predicts Vindication from Grand Jury Probe," *Austin American-Statesman*, December 18, 1990.

41. Laylan Copelin and Debbie Graves, "House Re-elects Lewis as Speaker on 146–1 Vote," *Austin American-Statesman*, January 9, 1991.

42. "Gib Lewis Is Indicted: Speaker Faces 2 Misdemeanor Counts Involving Law Firm," *Austin American-Statesman*, December 28, 1990; Debbie Graves, "Be-

tween Lobby Parties, Lewis Skewers Critics," *Austin American-Statesman,* April 24, 1991.

43. Chris Damon, "Gib Lewis Jailed: Speaker Fails to Appear for Pretrial Hearing," *Daily Texan,* October 2, 1991; Mike Ward, "Remark by Lewis Fuels Re-election Speculation," *Austin American-Statesman,* October 3, 1991; Dave McNeely, "Latest Mistake Erodes Support for Lewis," *Austin American-Statesman,* October 6, 1991; Bruce Hight, "House Members Circle Stealthily for Speaker Post," *Austin American-Statesman,* October 6, 1991; Debbie Graves, "Lewis Remains Undaunted despite Proposal to Oust Him," *Austin American-Statesman,* January 4, 1992.

44. Laylan Copelin, "Lewis Hangs up Speaker's Gavel: Longest Term Ever as House Leader Will End Next Year," *Austin American-Statesman,* January 9, 1992.

45. Mike Ward, "Lewis Legacy Gets Mixed Reviews," *Austin American-Statesman,* January 9, 1992; Brown, Langenegger, Garcia, and Lewis, *Practicing Texas Politics,* 165.

46. Brown, Langenegger, Garcia, and Lewis, *Practicing Texas Politics,* 166; Texas Legislative Council, *Presiding Officers,* 225, 229; Clayton interview; Davidson, *Race and Class in Texas Politics,* 107.

47. President Reagan's administration supported funding the Contras, anti-communist guerillas seeking to overthrow the leftist Sandinista regime ruling Nicaragua in the 1980s. When Congress denied funding for the Contras, the Reagan administration used funds from illegal arms sales to Iran to funnel money to the Central America guerilla group, which was accused of human right abuses, including the murder of political opponents. The anti-American Iranian regime, which previously held fifty-one American hostages at the American embassy in Tehran for 444 days from 1979 to 1981, and was accused of supporting the terrorist groups that were kidnapping Americans in Lebanon, needed the weapons for its war against Iraq. When the arms sales to Iran were revealed, Congress investigated the scandal, which the press dubbed the Iran-Contra affair.

48. Bass interview.

49. Texas Legislative Council, *Presiding Officers,* 7; James E. "Pete" Laney, audiotape interview with Patrick Cox, Laney's office, Texas State Capitol, Austin, Texas, February 15, 2005.

50. Laney interview.

51. Ibid.

52. Ibid.; Texas Legislative Council, *Presiding Officers,* 7.

53. Texas Legislative Council, *Presiding Officers,* 7.

54. Dave McNeely, "Bringing Pride to the Texas House," *State Legislatures Magazine,* July–August 2002, http://www.ncsl.org/programs/pubs/702laney.htm (accessed March 7, 2006).

55. Texas Legislative Council, *Presiding Officers,* 244.

56. McNeely, "Bringing Pride to the Texas House."

57. Ibid.

58. Tran, Lynn, and Andrew Wheat, "Mortgaged House: Campaign Contributions to Texas Representatives, 1995–1996 (Austin: Texans for Public Justice, 1998), 1; available at http://info.tpj.org/reports/house/index.htm (accessed May 17, 2009).

59. Tran and Wheat, "Mortgaged House," 1, 19; Patrick Kelly Graves, "What They Get—How Moneyed Interests Influence the Texas Legislature," 30.

60. Graves, "What They Get," 52, 53, 54, 56.

61. McNeely, "Bringing Pride to the Texas House."

62. Laney interview.

63. John Moritz, audiotape interview with Michael Phillips, Moritz's residence, Austin, Texas, March 15, 2006.

64. Laney interview.

65. *The New Handbook of Texas,* s.v. "Republican Party."

66. R. Campbell, *Gone to Texas,* 461.

67. *Washington Post,* "The U.S. Congress: Votes Database," http://projects .washingtonpost.com/congress/members/ (accessed June 20, 2008); R. Campbell, *Gone to Texas,* 462–463.

68. Laney interview.

69. R. Campbell, *Gone to Texas,* 462–463.

70. McNeely, "Bringing Pride to the Texas House."

71. Ibid.; Laney interview.

72. Laney interview.

73. Gwynne, "Power: 1. Tom Craddick," 187.

74. McNeely, "Bringing Pride to the Texas House."

75. Jake Bernstein and Dave Mann, "Scandal in the Speaker's Office: A Campaign Scandal Threatens to Swallow Tom Craddick," *Texas Observer,* February 27, 2004, http://www.texasobserver.org/article.php?aid=1575 (accessed May 17, 2009); Texas Legislative Council, *Presiding Officers,* 133.

76. Gwynne, "Power: 1. Tom Craddick," 187.

77. Laney interview.

Chapter Nine

1. The estimate that one million tourists visit the Capitol each year comes from then-governor George W. Bush's foreword to Ward, *Capitol of Texas,* xi.

2. "History of the Speaker's Apartment, Revised June 10, 2003," unpublished manuscript, State Preservation Board Archives, Austin, Texas; Alice Turley and Doug Young, audiotape interview by Michael Phillips, October 7, 2004, State Preservation Board Offices, Austin, Texas.

3. Blodgett, Blodgett, and Scott, "Legislating"; Bonnie Ann Campbell, "Furnishing the Texas State Capitol," *Southwestern Historical Quarterly* 92 (October 1988): 323–360; *General Laws of the State of Texas Passed at the Special Session of the Eighteenth Legislature Convened at the City of Austin January 9, and Adjourned February 6, 1884,* 60–63.

4. Blodgett, Blodgett, and Scott, "Legislating."

5. "The Magnificent Capitol of Texas Put to an Undignified Use," *Austin Daily Statesman,* January 29, 1891.

6. "The Lodgers in the Capitol Building," *Austin Daily Statesman,* March 4, 1895.

7. "No More Lodging: Superintendent Mobley Says Take Up Thy Bed and Walk," *Austin Daily Statesman,* February 24, 1897.

8. "History of the Speaker's Apartment."

9. Pat Neff to Mrs. V. C. Jung, November 14, 1938.

10. Ibid.

11. Blodgett, Blodgett, and Scott, "Legislating"; Mike Fowler and Jack Maguire, *The Capitol Story,* 124; R. Bryan Nichols, "Pat M. Neff: His Boyhood and Early Political Career" (master's thesis, Baylor University, 1951), 72. Other histories of the Texas Capitol include Ben H. Procter, ed., *The Texas State Capitol: Selected Essays from the "Southwestern Historical Quarterly";* Texas Legislative Council, *The Texas Capitol: A History of the Lone Star Statehouse;* and Ward, *Capitol of Texas.*

12. "History of the Speaker's Apartment"; Texas Legislative Council, *Presiding Officers,* 167, 59; William H. Gardner, "Capitol Quarters Row Recalls Probe," *Houston Post,* April 21, 1957.

13. "Texas Capitol—Living Quarters in . . . ," unpublished manuscript, State Preservation Board Archives, Capitol complex, Austin, Texas.

14. "Law Blocks Capitol Renovation," *Dallas Morning News,* September 3, 1970; Wray Weddell, Jr., "Living Quarters, Bills Scored by Taxpayer," *Dallas Morning News,* April 15, 1957; "Official's Quarters: Ex-Senator Wants to Lock Bedrooms in State Capitol," *Dallas Morning News,* April 16, 1957; Wray Weddell, Jr., "By Betts: 'Eviction' of Solons Is Refused," *Dallas Morning News,* April 18, 1957; "Officials Live in Capitol, Judge Rules," *Dallas Morning News,* April 19, 1957; Jimmy Banks, "Hill's Suit to Evict Officials from Apartments Ruled Out," *Dallas Morning News,* April 27, 1957.

15. "Heatly, Price Trade Jabs Over Use of State Funds," *Dallas Morning News,* July 4, 1974; "Residence Opposed," *Dallas Morning News,* February 3, 1974.

16. Ward, *Capitol of Texas,* 130.

17. "Texas Begins Modernization of Speaker's Capitol Rooms," October 24, 1949, *Austin American.*

18. "History of the Speaker's Apartment."

19. "Modernization of Speaker's Capitol Rooms"; Carrie Frnka, "The Speaker's Apartment: House of Representatives," May 1965, report in the State Preservation Board Archives, Capitol complex, Austin, Texas.

20. "History of the Speaker's Apartment"; Rodolfo Resendez, "State Officials Provided Capitol Living Quarters," *Daily Texan,* October 25, 1974; Lois Sager, "Mrs. Manford: Wife Proves Hubby's Best Campaigner," *Dallas Morning News,* February 13, 1949.

21. Carr interview.

22. Lois Hale Galvin, "The House You Live In: Capital Apartment Shows 18th Century Atmosphere," *Austin American,* January 16, 1953.

23. Frnka, "The Speaker's Apartment."

24. Dave McNeely, "Lawmakers Look for a Few Good Capitol Offices," *Austin American-Statesman,* May 1, 1988.

25. Turman interview; Ward, *Capitol of Texas,* 131, 135.

26. Turman interview; Ward, *Capitol of Texas,* 143, 147, 149.

27. Turman interview.

28. Ward, *Capitol of Texas,* 135.

29. Turman interview.

30. Dave McNeely, "Lawmakers Look for Offices."

31. Ibid.

32. Clayton interview.

33. Clayton interview; Patrick Martinets, "'Country Boy' Speaks Loud in House," *Fort Worth Star-Telegram,* October 10, 1976.

34. Texas Legislative Council, *Presiding Officers,* 231.

35. Ward, *Capitol of Texas,* 13–14.

36. Ibid., 20.

37. Texas Legislative Council, *Texas Capitol,* 59; Ward, *Capitol of Texas,* 20.

38. Lewis interview.

39. *The New Handbook of Texas,* s.v. "Capitol."

40. Ibid.; Lewis interview.

41. Lewis interview.

42. Ward, *Capitol of Texas,* 15.

43. Ibid., 15, 19, 21; *The New Handbook of Texas,* s.v. "Capitol."

44. *The New Handbook of Texas,* s.v. "Capitol"; Lewis interview.

45. Lewis interview.

46. Ann Arnold, "Capitol like Fish Bowl," *Dallas Times Herald,* February 9, 1969.

47. Marquita Moss, "Boxes and Blueprints Preceded Ball Gowns," *Dallas Morning News,* January 12, 1969.

48. Waggoner Carr and Byron Varner, *Texas Politics in My Rearview Mirror,* 32–33.

49. Garth Jones, "Something Old, Some Things New Await 61st Legislators," *Austin American,* January 8, 1969.

50. Lindsey interview.

51. Ibid.

52. Nadine Craddick, audiotape interview by Michael Phillips, Speaker's residence, Texas Capitol, Austin, Texas, February 2, 2005.

53. Martha Cole, "Coffee Callers: Two Families Live in State Capitol," *Dallas Morning News,* January 28, 1951.

54. Senterfitt interview.

55. Ann Arnold, "Capitol like Fish Bowl."

56. "'Round the Rotunda," *Houston Chronicle,* March 16, 1969.

57. Moss, "Boxes and Blueprints Preceded Gowns"; "'Round the Rotunda."

58. Carr interview.

59. Ibid.

60. Sanger, "Mrs. Manford"; Lois Hale Galvin, "Mrs. Jim Lindsey: Young Wife of Next House Speaker Looking Forward to Living in Capitol," *Austin American-Statesman,* December 12, 1954; "'Round the Rotunda"; Ann Atterberry, "Nancy Barnes: Campaigner's Dream," September 26, 1971.

61. "A Candidate's Wife: Mrs. James A. Turman," *Houston Post,* April 30, 1962.

62. Moss, "Boxes and Blueprints Preceded Gowns."

63. Atterberry, "Nancy Barnes."

64. Nancy Baker Jones and Ruthe Winegarten, *Capitol Women: Texas Female Legislators, 1923–1999,* 171.

65. Ibid., 11–14.

66. Ibid., 103–104.

67. Ibid., 13–14.

68. Meg McKain Greer, *Grassroots Women: A Memoir of the Texas Republican Party,* 3.

69. Greer, *Grassroots Women,* 9.

70. R. Campbell, *Gone to Texas,* 439–440; Jones and Winegarten, *Capitol Women,* 162.

71. Jones and Winegarten, *Capitol Women,* 153–154.

72. Ibid., 152–154.

73. Ibid., 198–200.

74. *The New Handbook of Texas,* s.v. "Women in Politics."

75. Jones and Winegarten, *Capitol Women,* 171.

Chapter Ten

1. "Texas House of Representatives: Member Tom Craddick," http://www.house.state.tx.us/members/dist82/craddick.php (accessed June 29, 2009); Gwynne, "Power: 1. Tom Craddick," 102; Tom Craddick, audiotape interview by Patrick Cox, Speaker's residence, Texas Capitol, Austin, Texas, February 2, 2005.

2. Gwynne, "Power: 1. Tom Craddick," 103, 186.

3. Tom Craddick interview.

4. Nadine Craddick interview.

5. Tom Craddick interview.

6. Gwynne, "Power: 1. Tom Craddick," 186.

7. Tom Craddick interview.

8. Tom Craddick interview; "Tom Craddick Biography."

9. Gwynne, "Power: 1. Tom Craddick," 186.

10. Ibid.; *The New Handbook of Texas,* s.v. "Sharpstown Stock-Fraud Scandal"; Tom Craddick interview.

11. "Tom Craddick Biography"; Gwynne, "Power: 1. Tom Craddick," 186–187.

12. Wayne Slater and Terrence Stutz, "Bush Re-election a Historic Landslide: Perry Wins Close Lt. Governor's Race," *Dallas Morning News,* November 4, 1998.

13. Ibid.

14. Michael King, "Naked City: Craddick's Record on Race," *Austin Chronicle,* January 3, 2003.

15. Gwynne, "Power: 1. Tom Craddick," 103.

16. R. G. Ratcliffe, "James Leininger: Paymaster of the Radical Republican Religious Right in Texas," *Houston Chronicle,* September 21, 1997; Robert Bryce, "Million Dollar Man," *Austin Chronicle,* January 29, 1999, http://www.austinchronicle.com/issues/vol18/issue22/pols.leiniger.profile.html (accessed January 13, 2006).

17. Paul Burka, "The Elephants in the Room," *Texas Monthly,* January 2006, 195; Debbie Nathan, "Wallet and Spirit: Leininger Contributes to Conservative Causes With Money and Prayer," *Austin Chronicle,* January 29, 1999.

18. Tom Craddick interview.

19. On the factions within the Texas Republican Party, see James W. Lamare,

J. L. Polinard, James Wenzel, and Robert D. Winkle, "Texas: Lone Star (Wars) State," in Charles S. Bullock III and Mark J. Rozell, *The New Politics of the Old South,* 289–291, 296–299; Molly Ivins, *Who Let the Dogs In?* 144–149, 151–152, 188–189; Molly Ivins and Lou DuBose, *Shrub,* 71–83; and Hilary Hylton, "Bush Returns to a Divided Texas Republican Party," *Time,* January 25, 2009, http://www.time.com/time/nation/article/0,8599,1873143,00.html (accessed February 5, 2009).

20. See Thomas Hobbes, *Leviathan,* 67.

21. Thomas Frank, *The Wrecking Crew: How Conservatives Rule,* 128–129.

22. Ian Hill, "State Responses to Budget Crises in 2004: Texas," Report, Urban Institute, February 2004, http://www.urban.org/UploadedPDF/410955_TX_budget_crisis.pdf (accessed January 28, 2006).

23. Christy Hoppe, "No-Tax Pledge Limits GOP Ability to Act: State GOP in a Rut over Schools," *Dallas Morning News,* August 13, 2005.

24. Ian Hill, "State Responses to Budget Crises."

25. Ibid.

26. See http://www.house.state.tx.us/members/dist82/bio/Craddick.htm, accessed June 29, 2009.

27. Ronald Keith Gaddie, "The Texas Redistricting: Measure for Measure," *Extensions,* Fall 2004, http://www.ou.edu/special/albertctr/extensions/fall2004/Gaddie.html (accessed May 17, 2009); Ken Herman, "A New Speaker: Craddick Wins Post as GOP Takes Over," *Austin American-Statesman,* January 15, 2003; Texas Legislative Council, *Presiding Officers,* 133.

28. Gaddie, "Texas Redistricting"; Moritz interview.

29. "Lack of Leadership: Democrats Absence a Telling Example of Craddick's Ineffectiveness," *Austin American-Statesman,* May 13, 2003.

30. Michael King, "The House Adjourns to Oklahoma: In a Session with Little to Celebrate, the Ardmore Texpatriates Deserve at Least Three Cheers," *Austin Chronicle,* May 16, 2003.

31. Gaddie, "Texas Redistricting."

32. Ibid.

33. Ibid.

34. Gaddie, "Texas Redistricting"; Michael King, "On the Lege: Notes from the Permanent Government," *Austin Chronicle,* October 10, 2003, http://www.austinchronicle.com/issues/dispatch/2003-10-10/pols_lege.html (accessed May 17, 2009).

35. See Michel Foucault, *The Essential Works of Michel Foucault, 1954–1984;* "Dictionary for the Study of the Works of Michel Foucault," http://users.sfo.com/~rathbone/foucau10.htm (accessed June 21, 2008); Michel-Foucault.com, http://www.michel-foucault.com/concepts/index.html (accessed June 21, 2008).

36. Calvert and De León, *History of Texas,* 439; "Rita Leaves Some Loath to Share," *Beaumont Enterprise,* January 13, 2006; Burka, "Elephants in the Room," 127, 194.

37. Hoppe, "No-Tax Pledge."

38. Christy Hoppe, "Perry's Big Bet: Schools," *Dallas Morning News,* July 22, 2003; "House Adjourns Special Session in Austin," *Houston Chronicle,* August 19, 2005.

39. Terrence Stutz and Christy Hoppe, "School Finance Bills Unravel in the House: Measures Backed by Republican Leaders Dealt Bipartisan Blow," *Dallas Morning News,* July 26, 2005.

40. Stutz and Hoppe, "School Finance Bills Unravel."

41. Jason Embry, "Craddick Radio Spots Attack Senate School Finance Plan," *Austin American-Statesman,* August 12, 2005.

42. "House Adjourns Special Session."

43. Michael King, "Judge Dietz Finds School Finance System Unconstitutional," *Austin Chronicle,* September 17, 2005.

44. Quoted in Hoppe, "No-Tax Pledge Limits GOP."

45. Bernstein and Mann, "Scandal in the Speaker's Office"; Patricia Kilday Hart, "Speakergate," *Texas Monthly,* May 2004, 78, 95–97; Jay Root and John Moritz, "32 Felony Indictments Returned in DeLay Case," *Fort Worth Star-Telegram,* September 21, 2004; Wendy Benjaminson, "DeLay Faces Viable Republican Challenger," Associated Press, January 12, 2006, http://news.yahoo.com/s/ap_on__re_us/delay_primary_2 (accessed January 12, 2006).

46. Root and Moritz, "32 Felony Indictments"; John Moritz, "Democrats Could Beat DeLay, 2 Polls Show," *Fort Worth Star-Telegram,* January 25, 2006.

47. Jason Embry, "Howard Wins House Race: Democrats Pick Up a Seat in GOP-Controlled House," *Austin American-Statesman,* February 15, 2006; Jason Embry, "Grusendorf Loses House Place: Madla Loses Senate Seat, Dan Patrick Gets GOP Nod," *Austin American-Statesman,* March 8, 2006; Karen Brooks, "Failure to Deal With School Financing Harming Some Incumbents," *Dallas Morning News,* March 8, 2006.

48. Jason Embry, "School Finance Moves One Step Closer to Completion," *Austin American-Statesman,* May 11, 2004.

49. Jason Embry, "Democratic Gains Could Undermine Leadership," *Austin American-Statesman,* November 9, 2006.

50. Robert T. Garrett, "2 Major GOP Donors Show Rift in Party: Supporters Back Efforts to Oust Moderate Members of State House," *Dallas Morning News,* February 3, 2006; Burka, "Elephants in the Room."

51. W. Gardner Selby and Laylan Copelin, "Craddick Prevails," *Austin American-Statesman,* January 10, 2007.

52. "Under the Dome: Craddick Also Gets to Keep His Redecorated Pad," *Dallas Morning News,* January 20, 2007, http://www.dallasnews.com/shared content/dws/news/texassouthwest/legislature/stories/DN-dome_10tex.ART .State.Edition2.36a32f6.html (accessed December 27, 2007); Jay Root and John Moritz, "Rival Drops Out after Bid for Secret Ballot Fails," *Fort Worth Star-Telegram,* January 10, 2007.

53. Charles Kuffner, "Speaker's Race: Two Out, One In," December 28, 2006, http://www.offthekuff.com/mt/archives/008556.html (accessed March 19, 2007).

54. "Craddick Unwavering as House Rebellion Continues," news8austin .com, http://www.news8austin.com/content/legislature_2007/stories/?SecID=561 &ArID=184996 (accessed June 27, 2009).

55. Jay Root and Aman Batheja, "Divided Legislature Inches Toward Rocky Final," *Fort Worth Star-Telegram,* May 27, 2007.

56. Root and Batheja, "Divided Legislature."

57. Karen Brooks, "Craddick Stays in Power: Those Trying to Oust Him Give Up—For Now—But Vow a Challenge Next Session," *Dallas Morning News,* May 28, 2007.

58. Christy Hoppe, "New Texas Speaker to Shift House Dynamic toward Middle," *Dallas Morning News,* January 5, 2009.

59. Rod Dreher, "Poll's Shocking SOS For Texas GOP," *Dallas Morning News,* December 3, 2008.

60. Karen Brooks, "Craddick's Grip on Power as Texas House Speaker to Be Tested Again," *Dallas Morning News,* December 30, 2008.

61. Karen Brooks, "Joe Straus' Trip to Becoming Texas House Speaker Was a Wild Ride," *Dallas Morning News,* January 5, 2009.

62. Texas House of Representatives, Speaker Joe Straus biography, http://www.house.state.tx.us/speaker/bio.htm (accessed February 2, 2009).

63. Brooks, "Joe Straus' Trip"; Laylan Copelin and Jason Embry, "Craddick Out of Speaker Race: 2 in GOP Ready to Do Battle," *Austin American-Statesman,* January 5, 2009.

64. The quotations in this paragraph are from Copelin and Embry, "Craddick Out of Speaker Race."

65. Gromer Jeffers, Jr., "Straight-Ticket Voting on the Rise in Texas," *Dallas Morning News,* November 24, 2008, and "Number Six," "Texas GOP Voter ID Bill Fails," *The Daily Kos,* May 27, 2009, http://www.dailykos .com/story/2009/5/27/736081/-Texas-GOP-voter-ID-bill-fails.

66. Robert T. Garrett, "New Texas Rules Proposed for Texas House Chamber," *Dallas Morning News,* January 26, 2009; Laylan Copelin, "Speaker Straus Would Roll Back Some Craddick Policies," *Austin American-Statesman,* January 27, 2009.

67. Sam Kinch, Jr., *Too Much Money Is Not Enough,* 5–6.

68. Ibid., 5–9, 28–29.

69. Ibid., 5–9, 22.

70. Ibid., 18–19.

71. "Texas Voters Say Improve Public Schools and Reduce Reliance on Property Taxes," Fleishman-Hillard Texas Lone Star Survey, press release, January 12, 2005, http://www.advfn.com/news_Texas-Voters-Say-Improve-Public-Schools-and-Reduce-Reliance-on-Property-Taxes_9945726.html, accessed June 29, 2009; Lauren Reinlie, "A One Man Groundswell," *Texas Observer,* April 29, 2005.

72. Moritz interview.

Bibliography

Archival and Manuscript Sources

Except where otherwise noted, all of the following archival and manuscript materials are kept at the Dolph Briscoe Center for American History (DBCAH), Austin, Texas.

Barnes, Ben. "Remarks by Ben Barnes, Bay City at the dedication of the Ira Ingram Memorial." Texas—Legislature—House—Speakers vertical file, DBCAH.
———. Audiotape interview by Patrick Cox and Michael Phillips, Barnes's office, Austin, Texas, September 27, 2004.
Bass, Bill. Audiotape interview by Michael Phillips, DBCAH, Austin, Texas, June 4, 2004.
Briscoe, Dolph. Interview by Don Carleton, DBCAH, Austin, Texas, June 17, 2004.
Bryan, Guy Morrison. Correspondence with Rutherford B. Hayes. Guy Morrison Bryan Collection, DBCAH.
———. "Hon. Guy M. Bryan." Undated typescript, Guy M. Bryan vertical folder, DBCAH.
Carr, David. Audiotape interview by Michael Phillips, Carr home, Austin, Texas, August 7, 2004. Speaker Collection, DBCAH.
Clayton, Bill. Audiotape interview by Michael Phillips, Clayton's office, Austin, Texas, April 16, 2004. Speaker Collection, DBCAH.
Craddick, Nadine. Audiotape interview by Michael Phillips, Speaker's residence, Texas Capitol, Austin, Texas, February 2, 2005. Speaker Collection, DBCAH.
Craddick, Tom. Audiotape interview by Patrick Cox, Speaker's residence, Texas Capitol, Austin, Texas, February 2, 2005. Speaker Collection, DBCAH.
Frnka, Carrie. Report, "The Speaker's Apartment: House of Representatives," May 1965. State Preservation Board Archives, Capitol complex, Austin, Texas.
Hartman, Bill. Audiotape interview by Michael Phillips, Doubletree Hotel, Austin, Texas, September 2, 2004. Speaker Collection, DBCAH.
"History of the Speaker's Apartment, Revised June 10, 2003." Unpublished manuscript, State Preservation Board Archives, Capitol complex, Austin, Texas.

Laney, James E. "Pete." Audiotape interview by Patrick Cox, Laney's office, Texas State Capitol, Austin, Texas, February 15, 2005. Speaker Collection, DBCAH.

"A Law Regulating Labor Unions, Etc." Houston: Harris County Association for Industrial Peace, n.d. [1943?]. Durwood Manford vertical file, DBCAH.

Lewis, Gibson D. "Gib." Audiotape interview by Patrick Cox and Michael Phillips, Lewis office, Austin, Texas, June 8, 2004. Speaker Collection, DBCAH.

Lindsey, Jim T. Audiotape interview by Michael Phillips, Lindsey's home, Redwood Valley, Mendocino, California, April 16, 2004. Speaker Collection, DBCAH.

Moritz, John. Audiotape interview by Michael Phillips, Moritz's residence, Austin, Texas, March 15, 2006. Speaker Collection, DBCAH.

Mutscher, Gus. Audiotape interview by Patrick Cox, Mutscher's office, Brenham, Texas, November 9, 2004. Speaker Collection, DBCAH.

Neff, Pat. Correspondence with Mrs. V. C. Jung, November 14, 1938. Pat Neff Collection, Baylor University, Waco, Texas.

Price, William Rayford. Audiotape interview by Michael Phillips, Price's home, Austin, Texas, April 22, 2004. Speaker Collection, DBCAH.

Senterfitt, Reuben. Audiotape interview by Patrick Cox and Michael Phillips, Senterfitt's home, Corpus Christi, Texas, March 8, 2004. Speaker Collection, DBCAH.

"A Short History on Ira Ingram." Texas—Legislature—House—Speakers vertical file, DBCAH.

"Texas Capitol—Living Quarters in . . ." Unpublished manuscript, State Preservation Board Archives, Capitol complex, Austin, Texas.

Tunnell, Jan. Audiotape interview by Michael Phillips, March 14, 2004, DBCAH.

Turley, Alice, and Doug Young. Audiotape interview by Michael Phillips, October 7 2004, State Preservation Board Offices, Austin, Texas. Speaker Collection, DBCAH.

Turman, James A. "Jimmy." Audiotape interview by Michael Phillips, Turman's home, Corpus Christi, Texas, March 23, 2004.

Books and Articles

Adams, John A., Jr. *Keepers of the Spirit: The Corps of Cadets at Texas A&M University, 1876–2001.* College Station: Texas A&M Univ. Press, 2001.

Alexander, Charles C. *Crusade for Conformity: The Ku Klux Klan in Texas, 1920–1930.* Houston: Texas Gulf Coast Historical Association, 1962.

———. *The Ku Klux Klan in the Southwest.* Lexington: Univ. of Kentucky Press, 1966.

Audette, Vickie J., and J. Tom Graham, *Claud H. Gilmer, Country Lawyer: Lone Star Lawmaker and Speaker of the House.* Rocksprings, Texas: Carson Gilmer and Norma Jean Babb, 2003.

Axum, Donna. *The Outer You . . . the Inner You.* Waco: Word, 1978.

Badger, Anthony J. *The New Deal: The Depression Years, 1933–1940.* New York: Hill and Wang, 1989.

Banks, Jimmy. *Gavels, Grit, and Glory: The Billy Clayton Story.* Burnet, Texas: Eakin, 1982.

Barnes, Ben. *Barn Burning/Barn Building: Tales of a Political Life from LBJ to George W. Bush and Beyond.* With Lisa Dickey. Albany, Texas: Bright Sky, 2006.

Barr, Alwyn. *Black Texans: A History of African Americans in Texas, 1528–1995.* Norman: Univ. of Oklahoma Press, 1996.

Bartley, Numan V. *The New South, 1945–1980.* Baton Rouge: Louisiana State Univ. Press, 1995.

Bebout, John E. *The Texas Constitution: Problems and Prospects for Revision; Papers Prepared for the Texas Urban Development Commission.* Arlington: Institute of Urban Studies, University of Texas at Arlington, 1971.

Bernstein, Jake, and Dave Mann. "Scandal in the Speaker's Office: A Campaign Scandal Threatens to Swallow Tom Craddick." *Texas Observer,* February 27, 2004. http://www.texasobserver.org/article.php?aid=1575 (accessed May 17, 2009).

Bernstein, Patricia. *The First Waco Horror: The Lynching of Jesse Washington and the Rise of the NAACP.* College Station: Texas A&M Univ. Press, 2005.

Biles, Roger. "The New Deal in Dallas." *Southwestern Historical Quarterly* 95, no. 1 (July 1991): 1–19.

Blodgett, Terrell, Dorothy Blodgett, and David Scott. *The Land, the Law, and the Lord: The Life of Pat Neff, Governor of Texas, 1921–1925; President of Baylor University, 1932–1947.* Austin: Home Place, 2007.

———. "Legislating: Serving in the Texas House of Representatives, 1899–1905." Unpublished manuscript received at the DBCAH, February 11, 2004.

Boles, John. *The South through Time: A History of an American Region.* Englewood Cliffs, N.J.: Prentice Hall, 1995.

Boone, Mike. "Segregating Spanish-Speaking Students in Texas Schools: 1900–1945." *Journal of Philosophy and History of Education* 49 (1999).

Brown, D. Clayton. "Sam Rayburn." In Hendrickson, Collins, and Cox, *Profiles in Power,* 106–120.

Brown, Lyle C., Joyce A. Langenegger, Sonia R. Garcia, and Ted Lewis. *Practicing Texas Politics: A Brief Survey.* 7th ed. New York: Houghton Mifflin, 2002.

Brown, Norman D. *Hood, Bonnet, and Little Brown Jug: Texas Politics, 1921–1928.* College Station: Texas A&M Univ. Press, 1984.

Brunette, William Kent. "The Role of the Texas Speaker in the Texas House of Representatives: An Historical and Contemporary Analysis." Master's thesis, University of Texas at Austin, 1979.

Buenger, Walter L. *The Path to a Modern South: Northeast Texas between Reconstruction and the Great Depression.* Austin: Univ. of Texas Press, 2001.

Burka, Paul. "The Elephants in the Room." *Texas Monthly,* January 2006.

———. "The M Word." *Texas Monthly,* January 2006.

Burka, Paul, Allison Cook, and Kaye Northcott. "The Ten Best and the Ten Worst Legislators." *Texas Monthly,* July 1983.

Burka, Paul, Emily Yoffe, Kaye Northcott, and Ellen Williams. "The Ten Best and the Ten Worst Legislators." *Texas Monthly,* July 1987.

Calvert, Robert A., and Arnoldo De León. *The History of Texas.* Wheeling, Ill.: Harlan Davidson, 1996.

Calvert, Robert W. *Here Comes the Judge: From State Home to State House.* Edited by Joseph M. Ray. Waco: Texas Press, 1977.

Campbell, Bonnie Ann. "Furnishing the Texas State Capitol." *Southwestern Historical Quarterly* 92 (October 1988): 323–360.

Campbell, Randolph B. *Gone to Texas: A History of the Lone Star State.* New York: Oxford Univ. Press, 2003.

———. *Grass-Roots Reconstruction in Texas, 1865–1880.* Baton Rouge: Louisiana State Univ. Press, 1997.

———. *Sam Houston and the American Southwest.* New York: HarperCollins, 1993.

Campbell, Randolph B., and Richard G. Lowe. *Wealth and Power in Antebellum Texas.* College Station: Texas A&M Univ. Press, 1977.

Card, Hank, Kristen Nelson Card, Robert Resnick, and Conrad Deisler. "Stupid Texas Song." *Austin Lounge Lizards: Employee of the Month,* Sugar Hill Records, SHCD-3874.

Caro, Robert A. *The Years of Lyndon Johnson: The Means of Ascent.* New York: Knopf, 1990.

———. *The Years of Lyndon Johnson: The Path to Power.* New York: Knopf, 1982.

Carr, Waggoner. *Waggoner Carr: Not Guilty!* With Jack Keever. Austin: Shoal Creek, 1977.

Carr, Waggoner, and Byron Varner. *Texas Politics in My Rearview Mirror.* Plano, Texas: Republic of Texas Press, 1993.

Carroll, Mark M. *Homesteads Ungovernable: Families, Race, and the Law in Frontier Texas, 1823–1860.* Austin: Univ. of Texas Press, 2001.

Carter, Dan T. *From George Wallace to Newt Gingrich: Race in the Conservative Counterrevolution, 1963–1994.* Baton Rouge: Louisiana State Univ. Press, 1996.

Casdorph, Paul D. *A History of the Republican Party in Texas, 1865–1965.* Austin: Pemberton, 1965.

Chalmers, David M. *Hooded Americanism: The History of the Ku Klux Klan.* Durham, N.C.: Duke Univ. Press, 1987.

Chambers, John Whiteclay, II. *The Tyranny of Change: America in the Progressive Era, 1890–1920.* 2nd ed. New York: St. Martin's, 2000.

Citizens Conference on State Legislatures. "The Impact of the Texas Constitution on the State Legislature." Houston, 1973.

Citizens for Tax Justice. "State and Local Taxes Hit Poor and Middle Class Far Harder than the Wealthy," June 26, 1996. http://www.ctj.org/html/whopays.htm (accessed May 17, 2009).

Collins, Michael L. "Lloyd Bentsen." In Hendrickson, Collins, and Cox, *Profiles in Power,* 254–262.

Cox, Patrick. *The First Texas News Barons.* Austin: Univ. of Texas Press, 2005.

———. *Ralph W. Yarborough: The People's Senator.* Austin: Univ. of Texas Press, 2001.

Crouch, Barry. "A Spirit of Lawlessness: White Violence, Texas Blacks, 1865–1868." *Journal of Social History* 18 (Winter 1984): 217–232.

Dallek, Robert. *Flawed Giant: Lyndon Johnson and His Times, 1961–1973.* New York: Oxford Univ. Press, 1998.

———. *Lone Star Rising: Lyndon Johnson and His Times, 1908–1960.* New York: Oxford Univ. Press, 1991.

Davidson, Chandler. *Race and Class in Texas Politics.* Princeton, N.J.: Princeton Univ. Press, 1990.

Deaton, Charles. *The Year They Threw the Rascals Out.* Austin: Shoal Creek, 1973.

De León, Arnoldo. *Mexican Americans in Texas: A Brief History.* 2nd ed. Wheeling, Ill.: Harlan Davidson, 1999.

Dethloff, Henry C. *A Centennial History of Texas A&M, 1876–1976.* College Station: Texas A&M Univ. Press, 1975.

"Dictionary for the Study of the Works of Michel Foucault." http://users.sfo.com/~rathbone/foucau10.htm (accessed June 21, 2008).

Diner, Steven J. *A Very Different Age: Americans of the Progressive Era.* New York: Hill and Wang, 1998.

Dobbs, Ricky F. *Yellow Dogs and Republicans: Allan Shivers and Texas Two-Party Politics.* College Station: Texas A&M Univ. Press, 2005.

Dorough, C. Dwight. *Mr. Sam: A Biography of Samuel T. Rayburn, Speaker of the House, 1940–1946, 1949–1952, and 1955–1961.* New York: Random House, 1962.

Dulaney, H. G., and Edward Hake Phillips. *Speak, Mr. Speaker.* Bonham, Texas: Sam Rayburn Foundation, 1978.

Fairbanks, Robert. *For the City as a Whole: Planning, Politics, and the Public Interest in Dallas, Texas, 1900–1965.* Columbus: Ohio State Univ. Press, 1998.

Fern, Charlie. "Jimmy Turman and the Origins of Compassionate Conservatism." A paper presented at the East Texas Historical Association Fall Program, Nacogdoches, Texas, September 16, 2005.

Foucault, Michel. *The Essential Works of Michel Foucault, 1954–1984.* New York: New Press, 1997.

Fowler, Mike, and Jack Maguire. *The Capitol Story: The Statehouse in Texas.* Austin: Eakin, 1988.

Frank, Thomas. *The Wrecking Crew: How Conservatives Rule.* New York: Holt, 2008.

Frontline. "The Battle over School Choice. Interviews: Molly Ivins." http://www.pbs.org/wgbh/pages/frontline/shows/vouchers/interviews/ivins.html (accessed March 5, 2006).

———. "The Testing Industry's Big Four." http://www.pbs.org/wgbh/pages/frontline/shows/schools/testing/companies.html (accessed June 22, 2008).

Gaddie, Ronald Keith. "The Texas Redistricting: Measure for Measure." *Extensions,* Fall 2004. http://www.ou.edu/special/albertctr/extensions/fall2004/Gaddie.html (accessed May 17, 2009).

Gammage, Judie. "Quest for Equality: An Historical Overview of Women's Rights Activism in Texas, 1890–1975." PhD diss., North Texas State University, 1982.

General Laws of the State of Texas Passed at the Special Session of the Eighteenth Legislature Convened at the City of Austin January 9, and Adjourned February 6, 1884. Austin: E. W. Swindells, State printer, 1885.

Ginzberg, Ralph. *One Hundred Years of Lynchings.* Baltimore: Black Classics Press, 1962. Reprint, 1988.

Goodwyn, Lawrence. *The Populist Moment: A Short History of the Agrarian Revolt in America.* New York: Oxford Univ. Press, 1978.

Gould, Lewis L. *Progressives and Prohibitionists: Texas Democrats in the Wilson Era.* Austin: Texas State Historical Association, 1992.

Grantham, Dewey W. *The South in Modern America*. New York: HarperCollins, 1994.

Graves, Patrick Kelly. "What They Get—How Moneyed Interests Influence the Texas Legislature." Master's report, University of Texas at Austin, 1997.

Green, George Norris. *The Establishment in Texas Politics: The Primitive Years, 1938–1957*. Norman: Univ. of Oklahoma Press, 1979.

Greer, Meg McKain. *Grassroots Women: A Memoir of the Texas Republican Party*. Boerne, Texas: Wingscape Press, 2001.

Gwynne, S. C. "Power: 1. Tom Craddick." *Texas Monthly*, February 2005.

Hale, Grace Elizabeth. *Making Whiteness: The Culture of Segregation in the South, 1890–1940*. New York: Pantheon, 1998.

Hales, Douglas. *A Southern Family in Black and White: The Cuneys of Texas*. College Station: Texas A&M Univ. Press, 2003.

Haley, James. *Sam Houston*. Norman: Univ. of Oklahoma Press, 2002.

Hall, Jacquelyn Dowd. "'The Mind That Burns in Each Body': Women, Rape, and Racial Violence." *Southern Exposure* 12, no. 6 (1984): 61–71.

———. *Revolt against Chivalry: Jessie Daniel Ames and the Women's Campaign against Lynching*. New York: Columbia Univ. Press, 1993.

Hampton, Henry. *Voices of Freedom: An Oral History of the Civil Rights Movement from the 1950s through the 1980s*. New York: Bantam, 1990.

Hardeman, D. B., and Donald C. Bacon. *Rayburn: A Biography*. Austin: Texas Monthly Press, 1987.

Hart, Patricia Kilday. "Speakergate." *Texas Monthly*, May 2004.

Hendrickson, Kenneth E. *The Chief Executives of Texas from Stephen F. Austin to John B. Connally, Jr.* College Station: Texas A&M Univ. Press, 1995.

Hendrickson, Kenneth E., Michael L. Collins, and Patrick Cox, eds. *Profiles in Power: Twentieth-Century Texans in Washington*. Austin: Univ. of Texas Press, 2004.

Herskowitz, Mickey. *Sharpstown Revisited: Frank Sharp and a Tale of Dirty Politics in Texas*. Austin: Eakin, 1994.

Hill, Ian. "State Responses to Budget Crises in 2004: Texas." Urban Institute, February 2004. http://www.urban.org/UploadedPDF/410955_TX_budget_crisis.pdf (accessed January 28, 2006).

Hill, Patricia Evridge. *Dallas: The Making of a Modern City*. Austin: Univ. of Texas Press, 1996.

Hine, Darlene Clark. *Black Victory: The Rise and Fall of the White Primary in Texas*. Millwood, N.Y.: KTO Press, 1979.

Hobbes, Thomas. *Leviathan*. 1651; Reprint, New York: Dutton, 1973.

Hurst, Jack. *Nathan Bedford Forrest: A Biography*. New York: Knopf, 1993.

Hylton, Hilary. "Bush Returns to a Divided Texas Republican Party." *Time*, January 25, 2009. http://www.time.com/time/nation/article/0,8599,1873143,00.html (accessed May 17, 2009).

Ivins, Molly. *Molly Ivins Can't Say That, Can She?* New York: Vintage, 1991.

———. "Mr. Speaker Daniel." *Texas Observer*, February 2, 1973.

———. "Who Deserves Credit for Texas?" Free Press, July 27, 2000. http://www.freepress.org/columns/display/1/2000/171 (accessed March 6, 2006).

———. *Who Let the Dogs In? Incredible Political Animals I Have Known*. New York: Random House, 2004.

Ivins, Molly, and Lou DuBose. *Shrub: The Short but Happy Political Life of George W. Bush*. New York: Random House, 2000.

Jackson, Emma L. M. "Petticoat Politics: Political Activism among Texas Women in the 1920s." PhD diss., University of Texas at Austin, 1980.

James, Marquis. *The Raven: A Biography of Sam Houston*. Indianapolis: Bobbs-Merrill, 1929.

Jones, Nancy Baker, and Ruthe Winegarten. *Capitol Women: Texas Female Legislators, 1923–1999*. Austin: Univ. of Texas Press, 2000.

Katz, Harvey. *Shadow on the Alamo: New Heroes Fight Old Corruption in Texas Politics*. Garden City, N.Y.: Doubleday, 1972.

Key, V. O. *Southern Politics in State and Nation*. New York: Knopf, 1949.

Kinch, Sam, Jr. *Too Much Money Is Not Enough: Big Money and Political Power in Texas*. With Anne Marie Kilday. Austin: Campaigns for People, 2000.

Kinch, Sam, Jr., and Stuart Long. *Allan Shivers: The Pied Piper of Texas Politics*. Austin: Shoal Creek, 1973.

Kinch, Sam, Jr., and Ben Procter. *Texas under a Cloud: Story of the Texas Stock Fraud Scandal*. Austin: Jenkins, 1972.

Knaggs, John R. *Two-Party Texas: The John Tower Era, 1961–1984*. Austin: Eakin, 1986.

Kuffner, Charles. "Speaker's Race: Two Out, One In." December 28, 2006. http://www.offthekuff.com/mt/archives/008556.html (accessed March 19, 2007).

Ladino, Robin Duff. *Desegregating Texas Schools: Eisenhower, Shivers, and the Crisis at Mansfield High*. Austin: Univ. of Texas Press, 1996.

Lamre, James W., J. L. Polinard, James Wenzel, and Robert D. Winkle. "Texas: Lone Star (Wars) State." In Charles S. Bullock III and Mark J. Rozell, *The New Politics of the Old South*. New York: Rowman and Littlefield, 2007: 67–81.

Lazarou, Kathleen Elizabeth. "Concealed under Petticoats: Married Women's Property and the Law of Texas, 1840–1913." PhD diss., Rice University, 1980.

Liberal Arts Instructional Technology Service, University of Texas at Austin. "Texas Politics" website, http://texaspolitics.laits.utexas.edu, August 17, 2005.

Link, Arthur S., and Richard L. McCormick. *Progressivism*. Wheeling, Ill.: Harlan Davidson, 1983.

López, Ian F. Haney. *White by Law: The Legal Construction of Race*. New York: New York Univ. Press, 1996.

Malone, Ann Patton. *Women on the Texas Frontier: A Cross-Cultural Perspective*. El Paso: Texas Western Press, 1983.

McAfee, R. Preston. "Gib Lewis: Former Speaker of the House." http://www.mcafee.cc/Bin/jokearchive.txt (accessed June 18, 2009).

McArthur, Judith N. *Creating the New Woman: The Rise of Southern Women's Progressive Culture in Texas, 1893–1918*. Chicago: Univ. of Illinois Press, 1998.

McCall, Brian. *The Power of the Texas Governor: Connally to Bush*. Austin: Univ. of Texas Press, 2009.

McCaslin, Richard B. *Tainted Breeze: The Great Hanging at Gainesville, Texas, 1862*. Baton Rouge: Louisiana State Univ. Press, 1994.

McGerr, Michael E. *A Fierce Discontent: The Rise and Fall of the Progressive Movement in America, 1870–1920*. New York: Free Press, 2003.

McNeely, Dave. "Bringing Pride to the Texas House." *State Legislatures Maga-*

zine, July–August 2002. http://www.ncsl.org/programs/pubs/702laney.htm (accessed March 7, 2006).

Mead, Frank S. *Handbook of Denominations in the United States.* 10th ed. Revised by Samuel S. Hill. Nashville: Abingdon, 1995.

Michel-Foucault.com. http://www.michel-foucault.com/concepts/index.html (accessed June 21, 2008).

Miller, Worth Robert. "Building a Progressive Coalition in Texas: The Populist-Democrat Rapprochement, 1900–1907," *Journal of Southern History* 42 (May 1986): 163–182.

"Molly Ivins Quotes," Thinkexist.com, http://en.thinkexist.com/quotation/as_they_say_around_the-texas-legislature-if_you/216480.html, accessed February 23, 2006.

Moneyhon, Carl H. *Republicanism in Reconstruction Texas.* Austin: Univ. of Texas Press, 1980.

Montejano, David. *Anglos and Texans in the Making of Texas, 1836–1986.* Austin: Univ. of Texas Press, 1987.

Mooney, Booth. *Mister Texas: The Story of Coke Stevenson.* Dallas: Texas Printing House, 1947.

Murph, David Rupert. "Price Daniel: The Life of a Public Man, 1910–1956." PhD Diss., Texas Christian University, 1975.

Myers, Lois E. *Letters by Lamplight: A Woman's View of Everyday Life in South Texas, 1873–1883.* Waco, Texas: Baylor Univ. Press, 1991.

Nathan, Debbie. *Women and Other Aliens: Essays from the U.S.-Mexico Border.* El Paso: Cinco Puntos, 1991.

Nichols, R. Bryan. "Pat M. Neff: His Boyhood and Early Political Career." Master's thesis, Baylor University, 1951.

Olien, Roger M. *From Token to Triumph: The Texas Republicans since 1920.* Dallas: Southern Methodist Univ. Press, 1982.

Payne, Darwin. *Big D: Triumphs and Troubles of an American Supercity in the 20th Century.* Rev. ed. Dallas: Three Forks, 2000.

Peters, Ronald M. *The American Speakership: The Office in Historical Perspective.* Baltimore: Johns Hopkins Univ. Press, 1990. Reprint, 1997.

Phillips, Michael. *White Metropolis: Race, Ethnicity, and Religion in Dallas, Texas, 1841–2001.* Austin: Univ. of Texas Press, 2006.

Phillips, Sarah T. "Acres Fit and Unfit: Conservation, Rural Development, and the American State, 1925–1950." PhD diss., Boston University, 2004.

Price, Quanah Quantrill. *Country Editor: A Collection of Excerpts from a Column by the Same Name That Appeared More or Less Regularly in the "Frankston Citizen" of Frankston, Texas, for a Period of Forty-two Years.* Frankston, Texas: Price, 1976.

Prince, Robert. *History of Dallas: From a Different Perspective.* Dallas: Nortex, 1993.

Procter, Ben H., ed. *The Texas State Capitol: Selected Essays from the "Southwestern Historical Quarterly."* Austin: Texas State Historical Association, 1995.

Pyle, Emily. "Te$t Market: High-Stakes Tests Aren't Good for Students, Teachers, or Schools." *Texas Observer,* May 13, 2005. http://www.texasobserver.org/article.php?aid=1947 (accessed June 22, 2008).

Ragsdale, Kenneth B. *The Year America Discovered Texas: Centennial '36.* College Station: Texas A&M Univ. Press, 1987.

Ramsdell, Charles William. *Reconstruction in Texas.* Austin: Univ. of Texas Press, 1910. Reprint, 1970.

Remini, Robert V. *The House: The History of the House of Representatives.* New York: Smithsonian Books, 2006.

Richardson, Rupert N., Adrian Anderson, Cary D. Wintz, and Ernest Wallace. *Texas: The Lone Star State.* Upper Saddle River, N.J.: Prentice Hall, 2001.

Roediger, David R. *The Wages of Whiteness: Race and the Making of the American Working Class.* New York: Verso, 1991.

Salerno, Steve. *Deadly Blessing.* New York: Morrow, 1987.

Sandlin, Betty Jeffus. "The Texas Constitutional Convention of 1868–9." PhD diss., Texas Tech University, 1970.

Saxton, Alexander. *The Rise and Fall of the White Republic: Class Politics and Mass Culture in Nineteenth-Century America.* New York: Verso, 1990.

Siegel, Stanley. *A Political History of the Texas Republic.* Austin: Univ. of Texas Press, 1956.

Simons, Charles E. *The American Way: Coke Stevenson, as Texanic as the Mesquite Tree, Gives Ample Proof That Honesty, Industry, and Frugality Still Are the Seeds of Success.* N.p., n.d. [1941?]. A copy is available at the DBCAH.

Sitkoff, Harvard. *A New Deal for Blacks: The Emergence of Civil Rights as a National Issue; The Depression Decade.* New York: Oxford Univ. Press, 1978.

Soukup, James R., Clifton McCleskey, and Harry Holloway. *Party and Factional Division in Texas.* Austin: Univ. of Texas Press, 1964.

Steinberg, Alfred. *Sam Rayburn: A Biography.* New York: Hawthorn, 1975.

Still, Rae Files. *The Gilmer-Aikin Bills: A Study in the Legislative Process.* Austin: Steck, 1950.

Strong, George. "George Strong Political Analysis: The Killer Bees, 20 years ago." http://www.georgestrong.com/analysis-arc/0246.html (accessed May 17, 2009).

Texas Education Agency. Department of Assessment, Accountability, and Data Quality. Division of Accountability. *College Admissions Testing of Graduating Seniors in Texas High Schools, Class of 2007.* Austin: Texas Education Agency, 2008; http://cistexas.org/research/pdfs/sat-act_2007.pdf.

Texas General Land Office. *Land: A History of the Texas General Land Office.* Austin: Texas General Land Office, 1992.

Texas Government Insider. "Leaders Appoint Members to School Accountability Panel to Address Improving State's System of Standardized Tests." February 1, 2008. http://www.spartnerships.com/newsletter/tgi%202-1-08/tgi.html (accessed June 23, 2008).

Texas Legislative Council. *Presiding Officers of the Texas Legislature, 1846–2002.* Austin: Texas Legislative Council, 2002.

———. *The Texas Capitol: A History of the Lone Star Statehouse.* Austin: Texas Legislative Council, 1998.

Texas Parade. "Leaders for a Greater Texas: Byron Tunnell." January 1965.

Texas Senate News. "Other Senate News." February 9, 2001. http://www.senate.state.tx.us/75r/Senate/Archives/Arch01/p020901w.htm (accessed February 28, 2006).

Thomason, Robert Ewing. *Thomason: The Autobiography of a Federal Judge.* Edited by Joseph M. Ray. El Paso: Texas Western Press, 1971.

Tran, Lynn, and Andrew Wheat. *Mortgaged House: Campaign Contributions to Texas Representatives, 1995–1996.* Austin: Texans for Public Justice, 1998. http://info.tpj.org/reports/house/index.htm (accessed May 17, 2009).

United States Bureau of the Census. *Census of the Population: 1950. Special Reports. States of Birth.* Washington D.C.: United States Government Printing Office, 1953.

———. *The Eighteenth Decennial Census of the United States. Census of the Population: 1960.* Vol. 1: *Characteristics of the Population.* Part 45, Texas. Washington, D.C.: Bureau of the Census, 1961.

Volante, Louis. "Teaching to the Test: What Every Educator and Policy-Maker Should Know." *Canadian Journal of Educational Administration and Policy* 35 (September 25, 2004). http://www.umanitoba.ca/publications/cjeap/articles/volante.html (accessed June 22, 2008).

Wade, Wyn Craig. *The Fiery Cross: The Ku Klux Klan in America.* New York: Simon and Schuster, 1987.

Ward, Mike. *The Capitol of Texas: A Legend Is Reborn.* Atlanta: Longstreet, 1995.

Washington Post. "The U.S. Congress: Votes Database." http://projects.washingtonpost.com/congress/members/ (accessed June 20, 2008).

Wills, Garry. *A Necessary Evil: A History of American Distrust of Government.* New York: Simon and Schuster, 1990.

Winegarten, Ruthe. *Black Texas Women: 150 Years of Trial and Triumph.* Austin: Univ. of Texas Press, 1995.

Wisehart, M. K. *Sam Houston: American Giant.* Washington: Luce, 1962.

Wyatt, Frederica Burt, and Hooper Shelton. *Coke Stevenson . . . A Texas Legend.* Junction, Texas: Shelton, 1976.

Newspapers

Abilene Reporter News
Austin American
Austin American-Statesman
Austin Chronicle
Beaumont Enterprise
Daily Texan
Dallas Morning News
Dallas Times Herald
Denton Record-Chronicle
Fort Worth Star-Telegram

Houston Chronicle
Houston Post
San Angelo Standard-Times
San Antonio Express
Sherman Democrat
Summer Texan
Texas 100 Percent American
Victoria Advocate
Washington Times
Wichita Falls Record News

Index

The abbreviation PS *indicates the unnumbered photo section following page 92.*